GERMAN ROMANTIC
NOVELLAS

The German Library: Volume 34

Volkmar Sander, General Editor

Heinrich von Kleist
and
Jean Paul

GERMAN ROMANTIC NOVELLAS

Edited by Frank G. Ryder and
Robert M. Browning

Foreword by John Simon

CONTINUUM · NEW YORK

1985

The Continuum Publishing Company
370 Lexington Avenue, New York, NY 10017

The German Library
is published in cooperation with Deutsches Haus,
New York University.
This volume has been supported by a grant
from Siemens Capital Corporation.

Library of Congress Cataloging in Publication Data

Main entry under title:
German romantic novellas.

(The German library ; v. 34)
Contents: The Marquise of O ; Michael Kohlhaas ;
The earthquake in Chile ; Betrothal in Santo Domingo /
Heinrich von Kleist — [etc.]
1. Short stories, German—Translations into English.
2. German fiction—18th century—Translations into English.
3. German fiction—19th century—Translations into English.
4. Short stories, English—Translations from German.
5. English fiction—Translations from German.
I. Kleist, Heinrich von, 1777–1811. Selections.
English 1985. II. Jean Paul, 1763–1825. III. Browning,
Robert Marcellus, 1911–   . IV. Ryder, Frank Glessner,
1916–   . V. Series.
PT1327.G38   1985   833′.01′08145   85-5762
ISBN 0-8264-0294-1
ISBN 0-8264-0295-X (pbk.)

Acknowledgments will be found on page 253,
which constitutes an extension of the copyright page.

Contents

Foreword

I t may seem strange at first that Jean Paul Richter and Heinrich von Kleist should be coupled in a volume of Romantic novellas—or anywhere else. Yet Jean Paul may be viewed as the doorway to German Romanticism, and Kleist as its rear exit; between them lies Romanticism proper. And doors, front and back, are essential parts of a house. And what a queer, multiform, almost incongruous edifice Romanticism was, rather like an internecine collaboration between a Gaudi and a Frank Lloyd Wright. Near the beginning of another, somewhat longer, Romantic novella, Friedrich Schlegel's *Lucinde* (1799), the hero evokes one of his states as "a romantic confusion . . . a wondrous mixture of the most diverse memories and longings." And he goes on to describe his "romantic" dream of love: "Wit and rapture now began their alternation and were the shared pulse of our joint life; we embraced with equal wantonness and religiosity." That more or less sums up the self-contradictions of Romanticism and subsumes the disparities of a Jean Paul and a Kleist.

Whereas Kleist's fortunes are in the ascendant in the English-speaking world, those of Jean Paul, once considerable, have sunk out of sight. In 1929, the German scholar Julius Petersen began a lecture to the Jean Paul Society in Bayreuth by reminding his hearers that "the great public library in Boston, on whose facade are engraved the sacred names of world literature, displays at the top of the frieze dedicated to Germany, on the same line, three names: Goethe, Schiller, Richter." The place, Petersen continued, was the city that produced so many translations of Jean Paul; the time, the 1880s, "when no one in the German homeland would have thought of a similar juxtaposition." Jean Paul was indeed popular. In England, Thomas Carlyle translated and championed him—and can there be a more Jean Paulian work than *Sartor Resartus?* De Quincey, who also Englished him, celebrated the "inordinate agility of [his] understanding," and proclaimed him the greatest of German writers along with Schiller. He placed him above Sterne, whom Jean Paul revered, and declared: "John Paul's works are the galaxy of the German literary firmament. I defy a man to lay his hand on that sentence which is not vital and ebullient with wit." In America, in a review of 1843, Edgar Allan Poe could call the very popular William Ellery Channing to task for presuming to imitate Jean Paul. Clearly, to the readers of *Graham's Magazine,* the name of Jean Paul Richter was a household commodity.

Had Richter been an English writer, he could have been grouped among the Preromantics, a vague category, yet barely elastic enough to embrace him. As the great scholar Karl Viëtor put it, "One could call him a classic of *Empfindsamkeit,* did not his humor also evidence sceptical realism." *Empfindsamkeit* (sensibility), was the literary-philosophical reaction to the *Aufklärung* (enlightenment); Jean Paul's works, especially the novels, have a way of slipping into this now badly dated excess of sensibility (the English protagonist of this movement would be Henry Mackenzie, the author of *The Man of Feeling*), but wit and shrewd common sense quickly redress the balance. In an essay in *Die Neue Rundschau* (1923), the poet-essayist Oskar Loerke described Jean Paul's art as one "that reflects everything with superhuman magnificence"; in a book review of 1925, he went even further, calling Richter "an inexplicable marvel without a life story."

And, indeed, the "marvelous" about Jean Paul is what made him one of the three heroes of the earlier German Romantics, along with the Goethe of *Wilhelm Meister* and Shakespeare. For them, Jean Paul stood for what was encapsulated in the very title of one of his best known essays, "The Magic of the Imagination." What endears him to the moderns, however, is his contradictoriness, his rivenness. So the Swiss critic Albert Béguin commented on "that infinite tenderness with which Jean Paul always enveloped the very hallmarks of the intellect *[les choses mêmes de l'intelligence]*." Or, as H. G. Schenck (in *The Mind of the European Romantics*) characterized Jean Paul's novel *Hesperus,* it is the contrasting of "the heart's unquenchable thirst for religion . . . with the intellect's intransigent repudiation of it." Certain images and *topoi* that Jean Paul either invented or perfected could scarcely be more relevant to twentieth-century, Freud-and-Jung-influenced literature. There is the importance of dreams and the escaping into them; there is the split human being or the person and his *doppelgänger* enmeshed in a strange—sometimes hostile, sometimes helpful—relationship; there is the awareness of childhood as the source of the adult personality. In fact, no less a modern genius than Karl Kraus was to declare: "Upon mature consideration, I would, after all, prefer to take the road back to the land of childhood in the company of Jean Paul rather than in that of S. Freud."

"A born voluptuary," Novalis called Richter in a letter to Caroline Schlegel, but it was the revelries of the mind and soul he referred to. For, again in Loerke's words, "Jean Paul's participation in the outer world is mostly symbolic, and only in the inner world wholly real." The fantastic or phantasmagoric aspect so prevalent in his work was what made the two other worthies with whom he is bracketed on the Boston Public Library keep him at arm's length. Schiller considered him "as strange as a man fallen from the moon"; one who was eager "to perceive the things outside himself, only not with the organ with which one sees." Goethe, while conceding that one felt at ease in the presence of this man of goodwill, nevertheless urged that "one be on one's guard with him not to praise him too much or too little." With unpleasant patronization, he referred to this "good, excellent human being, for whom one would have wished an earlier education."

For Jean Paul was, indeed, an autodidact, a man deeply involved in parentheses, digressions, barely relevant asides such as characterize the insecure, self-taught mind either genuinely losing its thread, or trying to cover its flanks with artful sideshows. Even those favorably inclined, such as Friedrich Theodor Vischer (*Aesthetics*, 1846–1857) could pronounce that reading Richter was "work for a horse"; even such an ardent champion as Stefan George had to concede "an often impenetrable underbrush," which, he went on, could be excused as the byproduct of the age, the era of the pigtail *(Zopfstil)*. But queerness was fine with Richter and he would have welcomed Schiller's condescending remark, for he preached: "Tear yourself away from the earth you inhabit, and it will cease to appear muddy to you and will assume in your eyes the radiance it has for a moondweller."

Still, the only ones who have actively condemned Richter in later years were the Marxists, such as Georg Lukács, who, while conceding (in *The Newer German Literature*) that "in the realm of politics, Jean Paul was doubtless personally more radical than Goethe and Schiller," deplores his failure to provide "a more passionate uncovering of the great contradiction of modern life, as in Dickens and the Russian novelists, and [offering] only a petty bourgeois reconciliation with the wretched German reality." Yet, over against this, may it not suffice that, as Hermann Hesse noted in his 1921 essay, Jean Paul shared the genius of modern psychoanalysis, "and knew, cared for, and studied that motley bridge between the conscious and the unconscious, the dream, as hardly another writer did, with the possible exception of Dostoevsky"? And, unlike Lukács, the German writer of the generation following Richter's who was most drawn to what is today called the Left, Ludwig Görres, perceived Jean Paul as "the poet of the lowborn, the bard of the poor."

Even if one does not have an easy time of it with *Vorschule der Ästhetik (Preschool of Aesthetics)*, Jean Paul's long-winded and cloudy, but often amusing and perceptive, treatise on aesthetics and literary theory (which De Quincey pronounced "so surcharged with quicksilver" that he expected it to leap off the table unless weighted down by duller tomes), it is at least an original attempt to assess, among other things, the nature and role of humor and wit in literature. Coleridge paid it the supreme compliment of cribbing much of it (as Margaret R. Hale, its most recent translator, reminds us) for his 1831 lecture on "Wit and Humor," a work of considerable influence. It may be that Goethe was thinking of this work of Richter's when he said, within Schopenhauer's hearing, that whenever he read a few pages of Jean Paul, he was overcome with such nausea that he had to drop the book. This allowed Schopenhauer, in his *Parerga and Paralipomena,* to speculate pertinently on the polarity of the two writers and conclude that "Jean Paul's weak side is that in which Goethe is great, and vice versa."

There, surely, is the rub. Jean Paul was, despite his respect for the sages of Weimar and Jena, a fabulist rather than a novelist, a populist rather than an elitist, a Romantic (or romantic) rather than a Classicist. One need only compare a chapter of *Titan* or *Flegel-jahre* with one of *Wilhelm Meister* to see how, even within the same genre of *Bildungsroman,* Jean Paul and Goethe proceeded in almost diametrically opposite fashion. But the combination of wit and fantasy, bonhomie and satire, pagan fairytale and Christian parable, faith in some sort of salvation, even if not so Christian as Jean Paul's, characterizes the work of a good many twentieth-century writers just as it does his. Günter Grass has avowed his enthusiasm for Richter, and one could probably trace an influence there; more important, however, is the consonance with contemporary writers who may not even have heard of Richter, much less read him—say, Thomas Pynchon or John Barth, or all those Latin American spinners of fantastic tales, even if the greatest among them, Borges, found him "very long-winded and perhaps a passionless writer." But that was when Borges was eighteen; at a later age, he might have responded differently.

Possibly the greatest service this foreword can render Anglo-American readers is to translate a few passages from the tributes to Jean Paul by two of his most distinguished modern German admirers, the poet Stefan George and the poet and *prosateur* Hermann Hesse. In the Hesiodically titled *Tage und Taten (Days and Deeds,* 1903), George wrote, in his typically hieratic style:

> I want to talk to you about a poet, one of the greatest and the most forgotten. . . . It was his sacred striving to find images for the magic of dreams and visions. If others triumphed with the clarity and rightness of words, he scored with their dissolvingly delicate shadings—disclosed their mysterious, invisibly murmuring undercurrents . . . especially as he succeeded—running counter to the example of his contemporaries—to be hearty and yet refined, familiar but not coarse, soft but not blurry. . . . And are they not all a bit of our flesh—his creatures in which we perceive only the warring and reconciling factions of our own souls, who, without being great doers, meditate endlessly and suffer endlessly? . . . If you, august Goethe, with your marble hand and sure footing, bequeathed to our language the noblest architecture, then Jean Paul, the seeker and yearner, surely gave it the most glowing colors and the deepest strains.

And now these excerpts from Hesse's "About Jean Paul" (1921)— a bit excessively Jungian perhaps, but well worth considering:

If I were asked in an examination in what book of more recent times the soul of Germany expressed itself with the greatest force and character, I would name without hesitation Jean Paul's *Flegeljahre*. . . . In Jean Paul, Germany gave birth to one of its most personal, abundant, and muddled spirits, one of the greatest literary talents of all time, whose works constitute a veritable jungle of poetry. . . .

[His was] the journey through life of a true eccentric who wore his heart on his tongue, had no concern for etiquette and suchlike trumpery, offered his fellow man his heart or stepped on his toes, however the moment would have it. . . . It should be taken into account, though, that for the poet let down by the world, for the idealist hostile to reality, it was a quite considerable achievement to counterpose his poor, starving, solitary person to the world, and defiantly persist in his manner and mannerisms, whatever else had to bend or break. And that is how he endured his livelong day. . . .

None of his works would have been written had Jean Paul had the luck to get along more easily with the world and himself. They all arose from this dichotomy; this lack, the void between Here and There, is in all truth the source of his entire creation. . . . This is the secret of the Jean Paulian riches, his superabundance, his lush, tropical fertility: the relationship with the unconscious proceeded for him with playful ease. He had but to pierce a thin membrane in himself to stand on the primeval ground of recollections, where earliest childhood, indeed human and planetary prehistory, is inscribed, the primeval ground that contains all history, from which all religions, all arts sprung up and continue to spring up afresh. . . .

Jean Paul is the prime example of a genius who has not overbred in himself one specialty, but whose ideal is the free play of all powers of the soul, who would say yes to everything, taste everything, love and live everything.

Heinrich von Kleist is quite a different story. If the chief characteristic of Richter's writing is leisureliness, that of Kleist's is onslaught. Kleist's thoughts, feelings, narrative—his very syntax—are a rush, a precipitation the artist tries with desperate, heroic effort to control, contain, prevent from overflowing its banks. If the lower-class Richter revels in digressions, exudes excess with every breath, woos the supernatural and welcomes the divine, the aristocrat Kleist believes only in this world, only in its essentials (though these, even when they pertain to the lowliest people, sharply yet sympathetically observed), only in getting on with it to the tragic or, much more rarely, happy conclusion. People are strange, destinies are strange, strangeness is what the world is made of—behind it all lurks a great lack of design. Even if in his last letters, before his ecstatic double suicide with Henriette Vogel, Kleist spoke of being reunited in the next world with the very few beings he cared about, I wonder how much of that, unless it was sheer euphoria, was mere deference to the faith of the addressees.

When a ghost appears in Kleist, as in "The Beggarwoman of Locarno," it is a curiously matter-of-fact ghost. Though there is humor—or, more often, sardonic wit—in some of Kleist's other works (the novellas have very little humor or joy in them), it is not the jollity of someone who believes in a just Providence. And if Kleist was never so close to starvation as Jean Paul was, he did have an extremely hard time of it, and had only minimal success during his brief life span, whereas Jean Paul saw himself become a celebrity and ended his much longer life free from material worries. To be sure, Jean Paul was attractive and beloved of women as well as a favorite of women readers; Kleist was unattractive, uncompromising, and hopelessly clumsy about almost everything. Few could put up with him, or he with them; it is even possible that he never consummated a relationship with a woman, not even with Henriette. There were serious homosexual stirrings in him, though these too, most likely, remained unfulfilled.

His career—if that is the word for it—was a messy failure in all directions, though the newspaper he briefly published (to say nothing of his drama and fiction) had every right to be a success. His friendships were often just as disastrous as his few stabs at relations with women, though here, too, Kleist was capable of great tenderness as well as of extraordinary inconsiderateness. Most devastating for him, of course, was the lack of recognition for his genius. However much we are all the makers and unmakers of our fortunes, it can be said of poor Kleist that he truly had remarkably bad luck of all sorts, much of it totally divorced from his doings. This extended even to his relations with fellow literati. Wieland, who loved and admired him, was by then too old and out of the mainstream. Goethe, though he tried to help him, ended up treating him shabbily, to which Kleist, wounded in his great pride, responded with a suicidal attack. Arnim and Brentano, who could have helped—and for a while did—fell out with Kleist over a petty matter that was at least as much their fault as his. With Friedrich de La Motte Fouqué Kleist managed to remain on good terms, but geography separated them, and Fouqué was unaware until too late of how needy, how abandoned, Kleist was.

He was not a weakling, not by a long shot. But, for a variety of reasons, unstableness and rootlessness were his lot, and that drivenness that, whether as cause or effect, is the hallmark of his work. It is what gives Kleist his uniqueness as well as his modernity. No one has put indirect discourse to more gripping, more hypnotic use; withal, Kleist knew how to generate speed through hypotaxis stretched to its utmost, rather than through the more customary parataxis. A style based on coordination is dressed, as it were, in shirt and shorts: from such running gear you expect a prose that will give you a fast run for your money. A Kleistian sentence, however, is clad in stately robes and has to tug continually at its skirts to be able to run without tripping. You are aware of the ample contours of such a sentence (at least in the German, whatever may happen in translation) and amazed at the muscular and emotional pull that nevertheless enables it to race ahead.

If Kleist belongs with the Romantics at all, it is only in contradistinction to what the other movements were doing, not in any notable similarities to other writers of the Romantic school. Certainly, there is an exoticism of locale and an intensity of self-assertion along with vehement action. And he was a *poète maudit,* but not one who, like Byron, say, could capitalize on this. His violence, moreover, went well beyond that of even a Hoffmann—a tempestuousness, a tumult matched only, a good quarter century later, by the Büchner of *Woyzeck.* But as to Kleist's only possible antecedents—Lenz, Klinger, and the Storm and Stress—so to the next generation of writers, there is no direct line of connection. It is not till much later that Kleist achieved his position of importance in German, and eventually world, letters. What would this disappointed, dejected man have made of a prophecy foretelling that a mjaor American bestseller would be based in part on *Michael Kohlhaas,* and that this *Ragtime* would go on to become a big Hollywood movie?

Is there a greater injustice in the world than that which allows hacks who will be utterly forgotten after death to lord it over geniuses whose posthumous importance and influence will change the course of literature and our way of perceiving the world? Try as we may, we can do nothing for the poor, heartsick, literarily and humanly rejected Kleist. We can only help ourselves greatly by reading him.

JOHN SIMON

Introduction

Writers who stand apart from trends and movements, who resist being drawn into the black holes of literary classification, may sacrifice instant recognition; but they may also be among the most interesting figures of their time. So it is with Kleist and Jean Paul.

In German literature and elsewhere, the very end of the eighteenth century and the beginning of the nineteenth belonged to the Romantics. They were in actual fact a "movement," united by a conscious rebellion against Weimar Classicism and the Age of Reason. Like the Expressionists a century later, they had their centers, "schools," models, and manifestos. For a decade or more they were the dominant force in letters. Yet three of the greatest writers of the age are not, except in the widest sense, Romanticists—certainly not Classicists either. Each stands, alone and separate, somewhat of an embarrassment to systematic literary history. One, Friedrich Hölderlin, is a seminal figure in modern poetry. The narrative prose of the other two is the concern of this volume.

Heinrich von Kleist, one of Germany's premier dramatists and story writers, was scarcely a great literary success in his own time, but his work is now familiar, even "trendy," in the European and American literary world. Jean Paul Friedrich Richter, known as Jean Paul—he preferred the French pronunciation but accepted the German for *Paul*—was once quite widely read; now he is largely neglected. He left a copious legacy in books of fiction and criticism, of which his countrymen tend to know the titles but not the content, while the rest of the world knows neither—and that is a shame.

Jean Paul divided his fiction into three "schools": the Italian, in which persons of high standing move on a large stage; the Dutch, where persons of lowly rank lead their often comical, occasionally idyllic lives; the German, whose characters are more or less of the same class with their author. (Of the works to be mentioned here, for example, *Titan* and *Hesperus* are Italian, *Siebenkäs* and *Flegeljahre* German, while *Wuz* and *Schmelzle* are Dutch.)

Kleist did not divide his works in any such fashion, nor would it have been like him to do so. But an interesting complementarity obtains between his dramatic works and his stories: Persons of great consequence (gods and princes, for example) appear only in the plays—as prime movers, that is—while the stories come from a middle world of more ordinary persons (horse dealers, planters and blacks, middle-class citizens and soldiers of middle rank, lower nobility, students). This is not to say that the latter class is absent from the plays (cf. *The Broken Pitcher*) or that rulers never figure in the stories—though they do so in less than central roles (cf. the Electors in *Kohlhaas*). This complementary distribution is probably significant: it accounts in part for the modernity and "realism" of his short prose; it warns us, at the least, not to assume that conclusions and observations valid for one genre are automatically transferable to the other. The reader of this volume should not, in other words, fail to read the plays!

As the present selections will attest, Kleist and Jean Paul are radically different in style and substance. They share, however an important concern: the relationship of the individual to reality. If, for Jean Paul, that relationship is ever harmonious it is when (and because) the individual is able to live by himself, in nature or in humble circumstances. Where—as in most cases—it is not harmonious the central fact of the disharmony is apt to be the tension between ordinary existence and higher vision or the ideal.

For Kleist there are no stated or discernible visions, no ideal goals (unless one is inclined to except Kohlhaas's crusade of revenge). Reality, either of human nature in general or of the institutions of society, is capricious, often hostile, and the individual lives in conflict (or unexpected and incomprehensible peace) with this world of threatening uncertainty. If he fails it is because he is incapable of asserting control, not because of the failure of an ideal. The one obvious instance of the triumph of will over circumstance is the Marquise von O's determination to identify her rescuer-seducer.

Heinrich von Kleist was only thirty-four years old when, in 1811, he committed suicide. For all its brevity his is a life full of blank passages and uncertainties—partly of his own devising, as he was given to secrecy. The story is more fully told by Walter Hinderer in his volume of plays (volume 25 in The German Library).

In superficial ways Kleist's career reads like a Byronic adventure: a distinguished military and literary background; service in the army of Prussia, ending in disappointment and the resignation of his commission; reemployment in the service of Prussia, as a civilian; a strange episode of what we should now call industrial espionage; a mysterious trip to Würzburg for an unspecified operation, presumably for some kind of sexual problem, on "the most important day in my life," as he wrote to his fiancée; withdrawal to a Swiss island where he worked on what was meant to be his greatest play, "Robert Guiscard"; flight to Paris, where he burned the play; renewed appointment to the Prussian civil service; arrest by the French on charges of spying (not wholly surprising, given his outspoken dislike for the "maniac" Napoleon); a brief career as publisher and "crusading journalist"; and then his suicide pact with Henriette Vogel.

The basic temper of this errant course through the world is, however, not bravado but frustration, instability, and despair. The despair is not merely existential but also—strikingly—philosophical. Initially convinced of the reality of the world, the reliability of perception, the primacy of ethical concerns and duty, he underwent a kind of negative conversion in which he lost faith in all these things, a loss for which he blamed (or credited) Kant. Using Kant's image, he complained that if all human beings were born with green eyeglasses they would be fated to judge the world green. By extension, all that passes for reality is suspect. "What we call truth," he wrote, may not "truly be the truth." The attempt to attain anything lasting, anything "that will go with us to the grave," is futile. "If the sword's point of this thought does not pierce your heart," he writes to his fiancée, "don't smile at another who feels it as a wound in the depths of his being. . . . I have no goal left in life." It may sound extravagant: a philosophical concept as a spiritual wound. But this is Kleist's formulation of the next epistemological turn in Western thought after Copernicus. To put it roughly, if Copernicus persuaded us that our notion of the earth as center of the universe was a delusion, Kant tells us that *all* perception is contingent, that the locus of "reality" is (at best) in the mind of the perceiver. This *is* a thought with a sword's sharpness.

Whatever the true nature, intensity, and priority of this philosophical crisis—his "Kant-crisis," as it is called—it helps to explain, as cause or as justification, the sudden uprooting of Kleist's existence, his futile attempt to find himself, the attendant and very modern view of life that underlies his narrative prose. This is a fictional world of indeterminacy, where the laws of cause and effect are dissolved or impenetrable, where apparently good actions lead to disaster and transgressions end in happiness—or are perfectly capable of doing so; where the very order of the world is called in question, both its cosmic order and the moral order. Hence the attribute often ascribed to this fictive world: *Bodenlosigkeit,* the total absence of firm ground in reality. For example, in the *Marquise* five soldiers are summarily shot for (presumably) having been about to rape a woman whom an officer of the same force in fact does rape—*after* the intended assault by the soldiers and *before* their consequent execution. The only possible mitigating circumstance; in the former case the woman was still conscious while in the latter she had passed out, a distinction which in itself scarcely accounts for the "happy ending" of the story.

It is small wonder that Kleist appealed greatly to Kafka; a comparison of the two, however, leads to the discovery of differences as well as similarities. In fact the term *Bodenlosigkeit* may be more truly applicable to Kafka. In *his* works, the individual tends to be exposed to an utterly incomprehensible order of things and to be utterly powerless. "Moral" decisions have no firm reference but are, like reality, contingent. What counts is the psychological vulnerability of the victim and the unassailable malevolence or indifference of the person or institution with the upper hand. In Kafka defeat is inevitable. Kleist's characters certainly act as if it weren't. And in his fictional world there remains a tangible precipitate of his own early belief in moral and ethical standards. It is as if there *were* right courses and wrong, but so obscure is the distinction that we can rarely be sure which is which. It is hard to see ethical irrelevance or randomness of consequence in the actions of the Marquise or Don Fernando, of Toni or Lisbeth, who seem for all the world to be doing the right thing, even if they suffer for it. It is equally hard to see Gustav as other than deluded and ethically myopic. Indubitably, Kleist's world is also filled with the opposite: the "irrational" discontinuity of action and consequence. In the *Earthquake*, disaster leads to survival (the coincidence of Jeronimo's inability to take his own life), while ostensible good leads to horrible tragedy (the trip to church, undertaken in the confidence of human decency restored, ending in vicious murder). The shifting stance and contradictory judgments of his narrators add to the indeterminacy.

So we face the unpredictable but not the implausible, the uncertainty of justice but not, I think, an ethical void. Cases of condign reward or punishment—occasional good accruing to those who seem good, ill sometimes befalling those who seem false or evil—stand alongside terrible randomness of circumstance, the blindness of fate and chance. The brilliant apprehension, the shattering portrayal of such an "unsteady state" may be the essence of Kleist's narrative achievement. Perhaps this is what life is really like.

The works of Jean Paul are a study in a different kind of paradox. His novels, stories, and essays are an ironic commentary on what is (or seems to be) versus what might be, ought to be, or would be if we were able to manage it. Sometimes the opposition is general and elevated: the reality of social or political stultification countered by a vision of justice. Sometimes it is narrow and acutely mundane: the impoverishment of small-town existence at odds with the vision (or the pretense) of a life with meaning. Jean Paul clearly preferred the second element of each of these oppositions. But it would be wrong to see him as therefore a revolutionary or a true reformer. The vision of better things is vitiated by its clearly illusory qualities. The prospect of everyday boredom is relieved by its seductive comforts. There is rarely any doubt where the victory lies.

The balance, however, is not cast in terms as simple as victory or defeat. German readers and critics too often make it so, viewing Jean Paul as primarily an *advocate* of the simple, happy life in contented isolation, of the old-shoe comforts of home and garden: *"Reichtum in der Enge," "multum in parvo,"* as a prescription for happiness. The "hero" of our first story, Wuz the little schoolmaster, is taken as a paragon of such contentment. Which is to a limited extent true; but the diagnosis overlooks the subtle and revealing fact not only that he is driven to write compulsively, like his author, in a frustrated search for significance, but also (in an extraordinary twist) that he himself writes the great books of his time, as soon as somebody has told him their titles. He can't afford to buy a book so he writes it! This is very funny, but it is also a mad parable of the need to keep the wider world at arm's length, to *be* something without submitting to comparisons. If Wuz writes—as he does—a *Sorrows of Werther,* he doesn't have to be influenced or constrained by what Goethe wrote. And no one will know the difference, because no one will read Wuz. The joys of narrow horizons are real, though the cost is at least eccentricity, if not a benign case of lunacy. Such ambivalence deprives Jean Paul's satire of any Swiftian sharpness, but it assures a certain timeless validity.

The perils of *not* holding the real world at bay, of actually venturing into it, are amply portrayed in our other story. Schmelzle, an anti-hero if ever there was one, doggedly rationalizes away his own inadequacy, his cowardice, his abject failures. He weaves from the whole cloth of self-delusion an image of courage and importance. This too is funny, but it is also acutely uncomfortable, an extension *ad absurdum* of an all too common human predicament and its all too common human resolution. It would be instructive to compare (or contrast) Wuz and Schmelzle with Walter Mitty.

The split of reality and vision reappears on a larger scale in the larger world of the great novels. *Titan,* with its background of Weimar—Goethe, Schiller, and Herder are all there, incognito—is the work Jean Paul regarded as his greatest. He saw as its purpose a counterattack on inequality of cultural advantage and education (in the broadest sense). But what the hero Albano may accomplish—he is or would be a revolutionary reformer—depends upon his being in fact a prince and upon the sleight of hand of his accession to a throne. And what his "comic" counterpart Schoppe proposes is a sweepingly generous utopia, so unattainable that its only possible upshot is despondency or contempt for the world as it is, a retreat into all-enveloping isolation, caricatured in the wish to return to life at the end of one's own umbilical cord. Inequality and injustice may be seen for what they are, but reform, if realized, is undercut by appearing to depend on intrigue, mistaken identity, and coincidental attainment of power by the right person. Reform as a goal for the future appears an extravagant dream.

In *Hesperus,* a similar disjunction: amelioration of the human condition depends upon the despotic government of an isolated island being replaced, from above, by enlightened rule, under the guidance of a man who turns out to be the lost prince and who, before this happy development, had said that if he *were* a prince he would order his subjects to be happy. It is perhaps worth noting that the full title is *Hesperus or 45 Days of Dogmail;* the underlying sequence of events is revealed to the narrator in installments, swum over to his island by a trained dog.

Walt, the hero of the *Flegeljahre* ("Salad Days") turns reality into dream, into an idyll, somewhat after the manner of Wuz. His brother Vult, a worldly skeptic, guides and maneuvers but never conquers. When they part they have decided to work on a joint novel, of which Walt will do the sentimental part, Vult the satirical. Once again the problematical world is made more safe and tolerable by being split in two, but in this novel the two extremes have at least the hope of reconciliation or peaceful coexistence.

Few of his other novels are free of this curious antinomy. If any of them is really an idyll of everyday life it is *Siebenkäs.*

For Jean Paul as an individual the split was ever present. He was vastly ambitious but his life was for the most part barren and unrewarded. He called his early years an "intellectual Sahara." His escape was to omnivorous (and uneven) reading, to endless writing. Though he was popular he was never really accepted as great. He was always regarded as an outsider, an eccentric, or worse. When he came to Weimar, the literary capital of Germany, Goethe found him a "curious creature"; Schiller said it was like having someone drop in from the moon.

For all his reading and writing he professed to disdain books, "often merely the symptoms of an ailing mind." Poetry he likened to a high fever, sermons to diarrhea, book reviews to jaundice. He said that the title and the motto were what mattered most, and whether they had anything to do with the text was immaterial. (The reader will discover that he felt the same about footnotes.)

Jean Paul was a handsome man, attractive to women but occasionally out of his depth and unable to manage the stronger representatives of the "weaker sex." At his fourth engagement he finally married—a judge's daughter, touchingly devoted to him but so relentlessly domestic that she got on his nerves. There was every reason for the feeling to have been mutual. When the fit of writing was upon him he would leave home with his dog and go to a tavern to work. On longer trips he left written instructions in the form of "commandments": six flies a day for the frogs, four for the spider; and let the birds out for an hour, to fly about.

Perhaps the dominant impression of his work stems from its remarkable style and narrative technique. If the resolution of his plots often depends on the command of a literal sovereign (or the equivalent) the authorial position in the works is no less sovereign. The narrator stands apart, manipulating and commenting. Even Jean Paul's uncompleted autobiography is in the form of a professor's lectures on Jean Paul.

In some respects Jean Paul may seem dated. He has, however, an astonishing affinity with modern writing and criticism. His stance vis-à-vis his own characters, his own text, is complex in the extreme: sometimes playful, sometimes ironic, sometimes sardonic; at times totally involved, at others distanced; often "identifying," often almost mockingly apart. And in the most modern fashion, the text, especially that of *Wuz,* comments on itself, reflects itself, undermines itself.

Given this narrative technique it is perhaps no surprise to find that his language is also self-conscious in the extreme, elaborate, convoluted, eccentric, marked by bizarre associations, whimsical allusions, outrageous metaphors, and compulsive digressions. Jean Paul's language, more than his authorial stance, tends to put off the modern reader, making full credence difficult and depriving events and characters of their chance to be independently memorable. But it is a brilliant deployment of words and images, deserving of serious reading. The author's total accomplishment is both substantial and distinctive; it deserves a higher place in our canon.

F.R.

GERMAN ROMANTIC
NOVELLAS

The Marquise of O—

*(Based on a true incident, the setting of which has been transposed
from the north to the south)*

Heinrich von Kleist

In M—, an important town in northern Italy, the widowed Marquise of O—, a lady of unblemished reputation and the mother
of several well-brought-up children, inserted the following announcement in the newspapers: that she had, without knowledge
of the cause, come to find herself in a certain condition; that she
would like the father of the child she was expecting to disclose his
identity to her; and that she was resolved, out of consideration for
her family, to marry him. The lady who, under the constraint of
unalterable circumstances, had with such boldness taken so strange
a step and thus exposed herself to the derision of society, was the
daughter of Colonel G—, the Commandant of the citadel at M—.
About three years earlier her husband, the Marquis of O—, to
whom she was most deeply and tenderly attached, had lost his life
in the course of a journey to Paris on family business. At the request of her excellent mother she had, after his death, left the
country estate at V— where she had lived hitherto, and had returned with her two children to the house of her father the Commandant. Here she had for the next few years lived a very se-
cluded life, devoted to art and reading, the education of her children
and the care of her parents, until the — War suddenly filled the
neighborhood with the armed forces of almost all the powerful
European states, including those of Russia. Colonel G—, who had
orders to defend the citadel, told his wife and daughter to withdraw either to the latter's country estate or to that of his son, which
was near V—. But before the ladies had even finished balancing
on the scales of feminine reflection the hardships to which they
might be subject in the fortress against the horrors to which they

might be exposed in the open country, the Russian troops were already besieging the citadel and calling upon it to surrender. The Colonel announced to his family that he would now simply act as if they were not present, and answered the Russians with bullets and grenades. The enemy replied by shelling the citadel. They set fire to the magazine, occupied an outwork, and when after a further call to surrender the Commandant still hesitated to do so, an attack was mounted during the night and the fortress taken by storm.

Just as the Russian troops, covered by heavy artillery fire, were forcing their way into the castle, the left wing of the Commandant's residence was set ablaze and the women were forced to leave. The Colonel's wife, hurrying after her daughter who was fleeing downstairs with her children, called out to her that they should all stay together and take refuge in the cellars below; but at that very moment a grenade exploding inside the house threw everything into complete confusion. The Marquise found herself, with her two children, in the outer precincts of the castle where fierce fighting was already in progress and shots flashed through the darkness, driving her back again into the burning building, panic-stricken and with no idea where to turn. Here, just as she was trying to escape through the back door, she had the misfortune to encounter a troop of enemy riflemen, who as soon as they saw her suddenly fell silent, slung their guns over their shoulders and, with obscene gestures, seized her and carried her off. In vain she screamed for help to her terrified women, who went fleeing back through the gate, as the dreadful rabble tugged her hither and thither, fighting among themselves. Dragging her into the innermost courtyard they began to assault her in the most shameful way, and she was just about to sink to the ground when a Russian officer, hearing her piercing screams, appeared on the scene and with furious blows of his sword drove the dogs back from the prey for which they lusted. To the Marquise he seemed an angel sent from heaven. He smashed the hilt of his sword into the face of one of the murderous brutes, who still had his arms round her slender waist, and the man reeled back with blood pouring from his mouth; he then addressed the lady politely in French, offered her his arm and led her into the other wing of the palace which the flames had not yet reached and where, having already been stricken speechless by her ordeal, she now collapsed in a dead faint. Then . . . the officer instructed the Marquise's frightened servants, who presently arrived, to send for a doctor; he assured them that she would soon recover, replaced his hat and returned to the fighting.

In a short time the fortress had been completely taken by the enemy; the Commandant, who had only continued to defend it because he had not been offered amnesty, was withdrawing to the main gate with dwindling strength when the Russian officer, his face very flushed, came out through it and called on him to surrender. The Commandant replied that this demand was all that he had been waiting for, handed over his sword, and asked permission to go into the castle and look for his family. The Russian officer, who to judge by the part he was playing seemed to be one of the leaders of the attack, gave him leave to do so, accompanied by a guard; he then rather hastily took command of a detachment, put an end to the fighting at all points where the issue still seemed to be in doubt, and rapidly garrisoned all the strong points of the citadel. Shortly after this he returned to the scene of action, gave orders for the extinction of the fire which was beginning to spread furiously, and joined in this work himself with heroic exertion when his orders were not carried out with sufficient zeal. At one moment he was climbing about among burning gables with a hose in his hand, directing the jet of water at the flame; the next moment, while his Asiatic compatriots stood appalled, he would be right inside the arsenals rolling out powder kegs and live grenades. Meanwhile the Commandant had entered the house and learned with utter consternation of the misadventure which had befallen his daughter. The Marquise, who without medical assistance had already completely recovered from her fainting fit, as the Russian officer had predicted, was so overjoyed to see all her family alive and well that she stayed in bed only in deference to their excessive solicitude, assuring her father that all she wanted was to be allowed to get up and thank her rescuer. She had already been told that he was Count F—, Lieutenant-Colonel of the — Rifle Corps and Knight of an Order of Merit and of various others. She asked her father to request him most urgently not to leave the citadel without paying them a short call in the residential quarters. The Commandant, approving his daughter's feelings, did indeed return immediately to the fortifications and found the Count hurrying to and fro, busy with a multitude of military tasks; there being no better opportunity to do so, he spoke to him on the ramparts where he was reviewing his injured and disorganized soldiery. Here he conveyed his grateful daughter's message, and Count F— assured him that he was only waiting for a moment's respite from his business to come and pay her his respects. He was in the act of inquiring about the lady's health when several officers came up with reports which snatched him back again into the turmoil of war. At daybreak the general in command of the Russian forces arrived and inspected the citadel. He complimented the Commandant, expressed his regret that the latter's courage had not been better matched by good fortune, and granted him permission, on his word of honor, to go to whatever place he chose. The Commandant thanked him warmly, and declared that the past twenty-four hours had given him much reason to be grateful to the Russians in general and in particular to young Count F—, Lieutenant-Colonel of the — Rifle Corps. The general asked what had happened, and when he was told of the criminal assault on the Commandant's daughter, his indignation knew no bounds. He called Count F— forward by name and, after a brief speech commending him for his gallant behavior, which caused the Count to blush scarlet, he declared that he would have the perpetrators of this shameful outrage shot for disgracing the name of the Tsar, and ordered the Count to identify them. Count F— replied in some confusion that he was not able to report their names, since the faint glimmer of the lamps in the castle courtyard had made it impossible for him to recognize their faces. The general, who had heard that at the time in question the castle had been on fire, expressed surprise at this, remarking that after all persons known to one could be recognized in the darkness by their voices; the Count could only shrug his shoulders in embarrassment, and the general directed him to investigate the affair with the utmost urgency and rigor. At this moment someone pressed forward through the assembled troops and reported that one of the miscreants wounded by Count F— had collapsed in the corridor, and had been dragged by the Commandant's servants to a cell in which he was still being held prisoner. The general immediately had him brought under guard to his presence, where he was summarily interrogated; the prisoner named his accomplices and the whole rabble, five in number, were then shot. Having dealt with this matter, the general ordered the withdrawal of his troops from the citadel, leaving only a small garrison to occupy it; the officers quickly returned to the various units under their command; amid the confusion of the general dispersal the Count approached the Commandant and said how sorry he was that in the circumstances he could do no more than send his respectful compliments to the Marquise; and in less than an hour the whole fortress was again empty of Russian troops.

The family were now considering how they might find a future opportunity of expressing their gratitude to the Count in some way, when they were appalled to learn that on the very day of his departure from the fortress he had lost his life in an encounter with enemy troops. The messenger who brought this news to M— had himself seen him, with a mortal bullet-wound in the chest, being carried to P—, where according to a reliable report he had died just as his bearers were about to set him down. The Commandant, going in person to the post-house to find out further details of what had happened, merely learnt in addition that on the battlefield, at the moment of being hit, he had cried out "Giulietta! This bullet avenges you!" whereupon his lips had been sealed forever. The Marquise was inconsolable at having missed the opportunity of throwing herself at his feet. She reproached herself bitterly that when he had refused, presumably for reasons of modesty, to come and see her in the castle, she had not gone to him herself; she grieved for the unfortunate lady, bearing the same name as herself, whom he had remembered at the very moment of his death, and made vain efforts to discover her whereabouts in order to tell her of this unhappy and moving event; and several months passed before she herself could forget him.

It was now necessary for the Commandant and his family to move out of the citadel and let the Russian commander take up residence there. They first considered settling on the Colonel's estate, of which the Marquise was very fond; but since her father did not like living in the country, the family took a house in the town and furnished it suitably as a permanent home. They now reverted entirely to their former way of life. The Marquise resumed the long-interrupted education of her children, taking up where she had left off, and for her leisure hours she again brought out her easel and her books. But whereas she had previously been the very paragon of good health, she now began to be afflicted by repeated indispositions, which would make her unfit for company for weeks at a time. She suffered from nausea, giddiness and fainting fits, and was at a loss to account for her strange condition. One morning, when the family were sitting at tea and her father had left the room for a moment, the Marquise, emerging from a long reverie, said to her mother: "If any woman were to tell me that she had felt just as I did a moment ago when I picked up this teacup, I should say to myself that she must be with child." The Commandant's wife said she did not understand, and the Marquise repeated her statement, saying that she had just experienced a sensation exactly similar to those she had had a few years ago when she had been expecting her second daughter. Her mother remarked with a laugh that she would no doubt be giving birth to the god of Fantasy. The Marquise replied in an equally jesting tone that at any rate Morpheus, or one of his attendant dreams, must be the father. But the Colonel returned to the room and the conversation was broken off, and since a few days later the Marquise felt quite herself again, the whole subject was forgotten.

Shortly after this, at a time when the Commandant's son, who was a forestry official, also happened to be at home, a footman entered and to the family's absolute consternation announced Count F—. "Count F—!" exclaimed the father and his daughter simultaneously; and amazement made them all speechless. The footman assured them that he had seen and heard aright, and that the Count was already standing waiting in the anteroom. The Commandant himself leapt to his feet to open the door to him, and he entered the room, his face a little pale, but looking as beautiful as a young god. When the initial scene of incomprehension and astonishment was over, with the parents objecting that surely he was dead and the Count assuring them that he was alive, he turned to their daughter with a gaze betokening much emotion, and his first words to her were to ask her how she was. The Marquise assured him that she was very well, and only wished to know how he, for his part, had come to life again. The Count, however, would not be diverted, and answered that she could not be telling him the truth: to judge by her complexion, he said, she seemed strangely fatigued, and unless he was very much mistaken she was unwell, and suffering from some indisposition. The Marquise, touched by the sincerity with which he spoke, answered that as a matter of fact this fatigue could, since he insisted, be interpreted as the aftermath of an ailment from which she had suffered a few weeks ago, but that she had no reason to fear that it would be of any consequence. At this he appeared overjoyed, exclaiming: "Neither have I!"—and then asked her if she would be willing to marry him. The Marquise did not know what to think of this unusual behavior. Blushing deeply, she looked at her mother, and the latter stared in embarrassment at her son and her husband; meanwhile the Count approached the Marquise and, taking her hand as if to kiss it, asked again whether she had understood his question. The Commandant asked him if he would not be seated, and placed a chair for him, courteously but rather solemnly. The Commandant's wife said: "Count, we shall certainly go on thinking you are a ghost, until you have explained to us how you rose again from the grave in which you were laid at P—." The Count, letting go of the young lady's hand, sat down and said that circumstances compelled him to be very brief. He told them that he had been carried to P— mortally wounded in the chest; that there he had despaired of his life for several months; that during this time his every thought had been devoted to the Marquise; that such contemplation had held him in an indescribable embrace of delight and pain; that after his recovery he had finally rejoined the army; that he had there been quite unable to set his mind at rest; that he had several times taken up his pen to relieve the agitation of his heart by writing to the Colonel and the Marquise; that he had been suddenly sent to Naples with dispatches; that he did not know whether from there he might not be ordered to go on to Constantinople; that he would perhaps even have to go to St. Petersburg; that in the meantime there was a compelling need in his soul, a certain matter which he had to settle if he was to go on living; that as he was passing through M— he had been unable to resist the impulse to take a few steps towards the fulfilment of this purpose; in short, that he deeply desired the happiness of the Marquise's hand in marriage, and that he most respectfully, fervently and urgently begged them to be so kind as to give him their answer on this point. The Commandant, after a long pause, replied that he of course felt greatly honored by this proposal, if it was meant seriously, as he had no doubt it was. But on the death of her husband, the Marquis of O—, his daughter had resolved not to embark on any second marriage. Since, however, the Count had not long ago put her under so great an obligation, it was not impossible that her decision might thereby be altered in accordance with his wishes; but that for the present he would beg him on her behalf to allow her some little time in which to think the matter over quietly. The Count assured him that these kind words did indeed satisfy all his hopes; that they would in other circumstances even completely content him; that he was very well aware of the great impropriety of finding them insufficient; but that pressing circumstances, which he was not in a position to particularize further, made it extremely desirable that he should have a more definite reply; that the horses that were to take him to Naples were already harnessed to his carriage; and that if there was anything in this house that spoke in his favor—here he glanced at the Marquise—then he would most earnestly implore them not to let him depart without kindly making some declaration to that effect. The Colonel, rather disconcerted by his behavior, answered that the gratitude the Marquise felt for him certainly justified him in entertaining considerable hopes, but not so great as these; in taking a step on which the happiness of her whole life depended she would not proceed without due circumspection. It was indispensable that his daughter, before committing herself, should have the pleasure of his closer acquaintance. He invited him to return to M— after completing his journey and his business as ordered, and to stay for a time in the family's house as their guest. If his daughter then came to feel that she could hope to find happiness with him—but not until then—he, her father, would be delighted to hear that she had given him a definite answer. The Count, his face reddening, said that during his whole journey here he had predicted to himself that this would be the outcome of his impatient desire; that the distress into which it plunged him was nevertheless extreme; that in view of the unfavorable impression which he knew must be created by the part he was at present being forced to play, closer acquaintance could not fail to be advantageous to him; that he felt he could answer for his reputation, if indeed it was felt necessary to take into account this most dubious of all attributes; that the one ignoble action he had committed in his life was unknown to the world and that he was already taking steps to make amends for it; that, in short, he was a man of honor, and begged them to accept his assurance that this assurance was the truth. The Commandant, smiling slightly, but without irony, replied that he endorsed all these statements. He had, he said, never yet made the acquaintance of any young man who had in so short a time displayed so many admirable qualities of character. He was almost sure that a short period of further consideration would dispel the indecision that still prevailed; but before the matter had been discussed both with his own son and with the Count's family, he could give no other answer than the one he had already given. To this the Count rejoined that his parents were both dead and he was his own master; his uncle was General K——, whose consent to the marriage he was prepared to guarantee. He added that he possessed a substantial fortune, and was prepared to settle in Italy. The Commandant made him a courteous bow, but repeated that his own wishes were as he had just stated, and requested that this subject should now be dropped until after the Count's journey. The latter, after a short pause in which he showed every sign of a great agitation, remarked, turning to the young lady's mother, that he had done his utmost to avoid being sent on this mission; that he had taken the most decisive possible steps to this end, venturing to approach the Commander-in-Chief as well as his uncle General K——; but that they had thought that this journey would dispel a state of melancholy in which his illness had left him, whereas instead it was now plunging him into utter wretchedness. The family were nonplussed by this statement. The Count, wiping his brow, added that if there were any hope that to do so would bring him nearer to the goal of his wishes, he would try postponing his journey for a day or perhaps even for a little longer. So saying he looked in turn at the Commandant, the Marquise, and her mother. The Commandant cast his eyes down in vexation and did not answer him. His wife said: "Go, go, my dear Count, make your journey to Naples; on your way back give us for some time the pleasure of your company, and the rest will see to itself." The Count sat for a moment, seeming to ponder what he should do. Then, rising and setting aside his chair, he said that since the hopes with which he had entered this house had admittedly been over-precipitate and since the family very understandably insisted on closer acquaintance, he would return his dispatches to headquarters at Z—— for delivery by someone else, and accept their kind offer of hospitality in this house for a few weeks. So saying he paused for a moment, standing by the wall with his chair in his hand, and looked at the Commandant. The latter replied that he would be extremely sorry if the Count were to get himself into possibly very serious trouble as a result of the passion which he seemed to have conceived for his daughter; that he himself, however, presumably knew best what his duties were; that he should therefore send off his dispatches and move into the rooms which were at his disposal. The Count was seen to change color on hearing this; he then kissed his hostess's hand respectfully, bowed to the others, and withdrew.

When he had left the room, the family was at a loss to know what to make of this scene. The Marquise's mother said she could hardly believe it possible that having set out for Naples with dispatches he would send them back to Z— merely because on his way through M— he had failed, in a conversation lasting five minutes, to extract a promise of marriage from a lady with whom he was totally unacquainted. Her son pointed out that for such frivolous behavior he would at the very least be arrested and confined to barracks. "And cashiered as well!" added the Commandant. But, he went on, there was in fact no such danger. The Count had merely been firing a warning salvo, and would surely think again before actually sending back the dispatches. His wife, hearing of the danger to which the young man would be exposing himself by sending them off, expressed the liveliest anxiety that he might in fact do so. She thought that his headstrong nature, obstinately bent on one single purpose, would be capable of precisely such an act. She most urgently entreated her son to go after the Count at once and dissuade him from so fatal a step. Her son replied that if he did so it would have exactly the opposite effect, and merely confirm the Count's hopes of winning the day by his intended stratagem. The Marquise was of the same opinion, though she predicted that if her brother did not take this action it was quite certain that the dispatches would be returned, since the Count would prefer to risk the consequences rather than expose his honor to any aspersion. All were agreed that his behavior was extraordinary, and that he seemed to be accustomed to taking ladies' hearts, like fortresses, by storm. At this point the Commandant noticed that the Count's carriage was standing by his front door with the horses harnessed and ready. He called his family to the window to look, and asked one of the servants who now entered whether the Count was still in the house. The servant replied that he was downstairs in the servants' quarters, attended by an adjutant, writing letters and sealing up packages. The Commandant, concealing his dismay, hurried downstairs with his son and, seeing the Count busy at work on a table that did not well befit him, asked whether he would not rather make use of his own apartments, and whether there was not anything else they could do to meet his requirements. The Count, continuing to write with great rapidity, replied that he was deeply obliged, but that he had now finished his business; as he sealed the letter he also asked what time it was; he then handed over the entire portfolio to the adjutant and wished him a safe journey. The Commandant, scarcely believing his eyes, said as the adjutant left the house: "Count, unless your reasons are extremely weighty——" "They are absolutely compelling!" said the Count, interrupting him. He accompanied the adjutant to the carriage and opened the door for him. The Commandant persisted: "In that case I would at least send the dispatches." "Impossible!" answered the Count, helping the adjutant into his seat. "The dispatches would carry no authority in Naples without me. I did think of that too. Drive on!" "And your uncle's letters, sir?" called the adjutant, leaning out of the carriage door. "They will reach me in M—," replied the Count. "Drive on!" said the adjutant, and the carriage sped on its way.

Count F— then turned to the Commandant and asked him if he would be kind enough to have him shown to his room. "It will be an honor for me to show you to it at once," answered the bewildered Colonel. He called to his servants and to the Count's servants, telling them to look after the latter's luggage; he then conducted him to the apartments in his house which were set aside for guests and there rather stiffly took his leave of him. The Count changed his clothes, left the house to report his presence to the military governor, and was not seen in the house for the whole of the rest of that day, only returning just before dinner.

In the meantime the family were in considerable dismay. The Commandant's son described how categorical the Count's replies had been when his father had attempted to reason with him; his action, he thought, was to all appearances deliberate and considered; what on earth, he wondered, could be the motive of this post-haste wooing? The Commandant said that the whole thing was beyond his comprehension, and forbade the family to mention the subject again in his presence. His wife kept on looking out of the window as if she expected the Count to return, express regret for his hasty action, and take steps to reverse it. Eventually, when it grew dark, she joined her daughter who was sitting at a table absorbed in some work and evidently intent on avoiding conversation. As the Commandant paced up and down, she asked her in an undertone whether she had any idea of how this matter would end. The Marquise, with a diffident glance towards the Commandant, replied that if only her father could have prevailed on him to go to Naples, everything would have been all right. "To Naples!" exclaimed her father, who had overheard this remark. "Ought I to have sent for a priest? Or should I have had him arrested, locked up and sent to Naples under guard?" "No," answered his daughter, "but emphatic remonstrances can be effective." And she rather crossly looked down at her work again. Finally, towards nightfall, the Count reappeared. The family fully expected that, after the first exchange of courtesies, discussion of the point in question would be reopened, and they would then join in unanimously imploring him to retract, if it were still possible, the bold step he had taken. But a suitable moment for this exhortation was awaited in vain throughout dinner. Sedulously avoiding anything that might have led on to that particular topic, he conversed with the Commandant about the war and with his son, the forester, about hunting. When he mentioned the engagement at P—in the course of which he had been wounded, the Marquise's mother elicited from him an account of his illness, asking him how he had fared at so tiny a place and whether he had been provided there with all proper comforts. In answer he told them various interesting details relevant to his passion for the Marquise: how during his illness she had been constantly present to him, sitting at his bedside; how in the feverish delirium brought on by his wound he had kept confusing his visions of her with the sight of a swan, which, as a boy, he had watched on his uncle's estate; that he had been particularly moved by one memory, of an occasion on which he had once thrown some mud at this swan, whereupon it had silently dived under the surface and re-emerged, washed clean by the water; that she had always seemed to be swimming about on a fiery surface and that he had called out to her "Tinka!", which had been the swan's name, but that he had not been able to lure her towards him. For she had preferred merely to glide about, arching her neck and thrusting out her breast. Suddenly, blushing scarlet, he declared that he loved her more than he could say; then looked down again at his plate and fell silent. At last it was time to rise from the table; and when the Count, after a further brief conversation with the Marquise's mother, bowed to the company and retired again to his room, they were all once more left standing there not knowing what to think. The Commandant was of the opinion that they must simply let things take their course. The Count, in acting as he did, was no doubt relying on his relatives without whose intervention on his behalf he must certainly face dishonorable discharge. The Marquise's mother asked her what she felt about him, and whether she could not perhaps bring herself to give him some indication or other that might avert an unfortunate outcome. Her daughter replied: "My dear mother, that is impossible! I am sorry that my gratitude is being put to so severe a test. But I did decide not to marry again; I do not like to chance my happiness a second time, and certainly not with such ill-considered haste." Her brother observed that if such was her firm intention, then a declaration to *that* effect could also help the Count, and that it looked rather as if they would have to give him *some* definite answer, one way or the other. The Colonel's wife replied that since the young man had so many outstanding qualities to recommend him, and had declared himself ready to settle in Italy, she thought that his offer deserved some consideration and that the Marquise should reflect carefully before deciding. Her son, sitting down beside his sister, asked her whether she found the Count personally attractive. The Marquise, with some embarrassment, answered that she found him both attractive and unattractive, and that she was willing to be guided by what the others felt. Her mother said: "When he comes back from Naples, and if between now and then we were to make inquiries which did not reveal anything that ran contrary to the general impression you have formed of him, then what answer would you give him if he were to repeat his proposal?" "In that case," replied the Marquise, "I—since his wishes do seem to be so pressing"—she faltered at this point and her eyes shone—"I would consent to them for the sake of the obligation under which he has placed me." Her mother, who had always hoped that her daughter would re-marry, had difficulty in concealing her delight at this declaration, and sat considering to what advantage it might be turned. Her son, getting up again in some uneasiness, said that if the Marquise were even remotely considering a possibility of one day bestowing her hand in marriage on the Count, some step in this direction must now immediately be taken if the consequences of his reckless course of action were to be forestalled. His mother agreed, remarking that after all they could be taking no very great risk, since the young man had displayed so many excellent qualities on the night of the Russian assault on the fortress that there was every reason to assume him to be a person of consistently good character. The Marquise cast down her eyes with an air of considerable agitation. "After all," continued her mother, taking her by the hand, "one could perhaps intimate to him that until he returns from Naples you undertake not to enter into any other engagement." The Marquise said: "Dearest mother, *that* undertaking I can give him; but I fear it will not satisfy him and only compromise us." "Let me take care of that!" replied her mother, much elated; she looked round for her husband and seemed about to rise to her feet. "Lorenzo!" she asked, "What do you think?" The Commandant, who had heard this whole discussion, went on standing by the window, looking down into the street, and said nothing. The Marquise's brother declared that, on the strength of this noncommittal assurance from her, he would now personally guarantee to get the Count out of the house. "Well then, do so! do so! Do so, all of you!" exclaimed his father, turning round. "That makes twice already I must surrender to this Russian!" At this his wife sprang to her feet, kissed him and their daughter, and asked, with an eagerness which made her husband smile, how they were to set about conveying this intimation without delay to the Count. At her son's suggestion it was decided to send a footman to his room requesting him to be so kind, if he were not already undressed, as to rejoin the family for a moment. The Count sent back word that he would at once have the honor to appear, and scarcely had this message been brought when he himself, joy winging his step, followed it into the room and sank to his knees, with deep emotion, at the Marquise's feet. The Commandant was about to speak, but Count F——, standing up, declared that he already knew enough. He kissed the Colonel's hand and that of his wife, embraced the Marquise's brother, and merely asked if they would do him the favor of helping him to find a coach immediately. The Marquise, though visibly touched by this scene, nevertheless managed to say: "I need not fear, Count, that rash hopes will mislead——." "By no means, by no means!" replied the Count. "I will hold you to nothing, if the outcome of such inquiries as you may make about me is in any way adverse to the feeling which has just recalled me to your presence." At this the Commandant heartily embraced him, the Marquise's brother at once offered him his own travelling-carriage, a groom was dispatched in haste to the post-station to order horses at a premium rate, and there was more pleasure at this departure than has ever been shown at a guest's arrival. The Count said that he hoped to overtake his dispatches in B——, whence he now proposed to set out for Naples by a shorter route than the one through M——; in Naples he would do his utmost to get himself released from the further mission to Constantinople; in the last resort he was resolved to report himself as sick, and could therefore assure them that unless prevented by unavoidable circumstances he would without fail be back in M—— within four to six weeks. At this point his groom reported that the carriage was harnessed and everything ready for his departure. The Count picked up his hat, went up to the Marquise and took her hand. "Well, Giulietta," he said, "this sets my mind partly at rest." Laying his hand in hers he added, "Yet it was my dearest wish that before I left we should be married." "Married!" exclaimed the whole family. "Married," repeated the Count, kissing the Marquise's hand, and when she asked him whether he had taken leave of his senses he assured her that a day would come when she would understand what he meant. The family was on the point of losing patience with him, but he at once most warmly took his leave of them all, asked them to take no further notice of his last remark, and departed.

Several weeks passed, during which the family, with very mixed feelings, awaited the outcome of this strange affair. The Commandant received a courteous letter from General K——, the Count's uncle; the Count himself wrote from Naples; inquiries about him were put through and quite favorable reports received; in brief, the engagement was already regarded as virtually definitive—when the Marquise's indispositions recurred, more acutely than ever before. She noticed an incomprehensible change in her figure. She confided with complete frankness in her mother, telling her that she did not know what to make of her condition. Her mother, learning of these strange symptoms, became extremely concerned about her daughter's health and insisted that she should consult a doctor. The Marquise, hoping that her natural good health would reassert itself, resisted this advice; she suffered severely for several more days without following it, until constantly repeated sensations of the most unusual kind threw her into a state of acute anxiety. She sent for a doctor who enjoyed the confidence of her father; at a time when her mother happened to be out of the house she invited him to sit down on the divan, and after an introductory remark or two jestingly told him what condition she believed herself to be in. The doctor gave her a searching look; he then carefully examined her, and after doing so was silent for a little; finally he answered with a very grave expression that the Marquise had judged correctly how things were. When the lady inquired what exactly he meant he explained himself unequivocally, adding with a smile which he could not suppress that she was perfectly well and needed no doctor, whereupon the Marquise rang the bell and with a very severe sidelong glance requested him to leave her. She murmured to herself in an undertone, as if it were beneath her dignity to address him, that she did not feel inclined to joke with him about such matters. The doctor, offended, replied that he could only wish she had always been as little disinclined to levity as she was now; so saying, he picked up his hat and stick and made as if to take his leave. The Marquise assured him that she would inform her father of his insulting remarks. The doctor answered that he would swear to his statement in any court of law; with that he opened the door, bowed, and was about to leave the room. As he paused to pick up a glove he had dropped, the Marquise exclaimed: "But doctor, how is what you say possible?" The doctor replied that she would presumably not expect him to explain the facts of life to her; he then bowed again and withdrew.

The Marquise stood as if thunderstruck. Recovering herself, she was on the point of going straight to her father; but the strangely serious manner of this man by whom she felt so insulted numbed her in every limb. She threw herself down on the divan in the greatest agitation. Mistrustful of herself, she cast her mind back over every moment of the past year, and when she thought of those through which she had just passed it seemed to her that she must be going crazy. At last her mother appeared, and in answer to her shocked inquiry as to why she was so distressed, the Marquise informed her of what the doctor had just said. Her mother declared him to be a shameless and contemptible wretch, and emboldened her in her resolution to report this insult to her father. The Marquise assured her that the doctor had been completely in earnest and seemed quite determined to repeat his insane assertion to her father's face. Did she then, asked her mother in some alarm, believe there was any possibility of her being in such a condition? "I would sooner believe that graves can be made fertile," answered the Marquise, "and that new births can quicken in the womb of the dead!" "Why then, you dear strange girl," said her mother, hugging her warmly, "what can be worrying you? If your conscience clears you, what can a doctor's verdict matter, or indeed the verdict of a whole panel of doctors? This particular one may be mistaken, or he may be malicious, but why need that concern you at all? Nevertheless it is proper that we should tell your father about it." "Oh, God!" said the Marquise, starting convulsively, "how can I set my mind at rest? Do not my own feelings speak against me, those inner sensations I know only too well? If I knew that another woman was feeling as I do, would I not myself come to the conclusion that that was indeed how things stood with her?" "But this is terrible!" exclaimed her mother. "Malicious! mistaken!" continued the Marquise. "What reasons can that man, whom until today we have always respected, what reasons can he have for insulting me so frivolously and basely? Why should he do so, when I have never said anything to offend him? When I received him here with complete trust, fully expecting to be bound to him in gratitude? When he came to me sincerely and honestly intending, as was evident from his very first words, to help me rather than to cause me far worse pain than I was already suffering? And if on the other hand," she went on, while her mother gazed at her steadily, "I were forced to choose between the two possibilities and preferred to suppose that he had made a mistake, is it in the least possible that a doctor, even one of quite mediocre skill, should be mistaken in such a case?" Her mother replied, a little ironically: "And yet, of course, it must necessarily have been one or the other." "Yes, dearest mother!" answered the Marquise, kissing her hand but with an air of offended dignity and blushing scarlet, "it must indeed, although the circumstances are so extraordinary that I may be permitted to doubt it. And since it seems that I must give you an assurance, I swear now that my conscience is as clear as that of my own children's; no less clear, my beloved and respected mother, than your own. Nevertheless, I ask you to have a midwife called in to see me, in order that I may convince myself of what is the case and then, whatever it may be, set my mind at rest." "A midwife!" exclaimed the Commandant's wife indignantly, "a clear conscience, and a midwife!" And speech failed her. "A midwife, my dearest mother," repeated the Marquise, falling on her knees before her, "and let her come at once, if I am not to go out of my mind." "Oh, by all means," replied her mother. "But the confinement, if you please, will not take place in my house." And with these words she rose and would have left the room. Her daughter, following her with outspread arms, fell to the ground and clasped her knees. "If the irreproachable life I have led," she cried, with anguish lending her eloquence, "a life modelled on yours, gives me any claim at all to your respect, if there is in your heart any maternal feeling for me at all, even if only for so long as my guilt is not yet proved and clear as day, then do not abandon me at this terrible moment!" "But what is upsetting you?" asked her mother. "Is it nothing more than the doctor's verdict? Nothing more than your inner sensations?" "Nothing more, dear mother," replied the Marquise, laying her hand on her breast. "Nothing, Giulietta?" continued her mother. "Think carefully. If you have committed a fault, though that would grieve me indescribably, it would be forgivable and in the end I should have to forgive it; but if, in order to avoid censure from your mother, you were to invent a fable about the overturning of the whole order of nature, and dared to reiterate blasphemous vows in order to persuade me of its truth, knowing that my heart is all too eager to believe you, then that would be shameful; I could never feel the same about you again." "May the doors of salvation one day be as open to me as my soul is now open to you!" cried the Marquise. "I have concealed nothing from you, mother." This declaration, uttered with passionate solemnity, moved her mother deeply. "Oh God!" she cried, "my dear, dear child! How touchingly you speak!" And she lifted her up and kissed her and pressed her to her heart. "Then what in the name of all the world are you afraid of? Come, you are quite ill," she added, trying to lead her towards a bed. But the Marquise, weeping copiously, assured her that she was quite well and that there was nothing wrong with her, apart from her extraordinary and incomprehensible condition. "Condition!" exclaimed her mother again, "what condition? If your recollection of the past is so clear, what mad apprehension has possessed you? Can one not be deceived by such internal sensations, when they are still only obscurely stirring?" "No! no!" said the Marquise, "they are not deceiving me! And if you will have the midwife called, then you will hear that this terrible, annihilating thing is true." "Come, my darling," said the Commandant's wife, who was beginning to fear for her daughter's reason. "Come with me; you must go to bed. What was it you thought the doctor said to you? Why, your cheeks are burning hot! You're trembling in every limb! Now, what was it the doctor told you?" And no longer believing that the scene of which she had been told had really happened at all, she took her daughter by the arm and tried to draw her away. Then the Marquise, smiling through her tears, said: "My dear, excellent mother! I am in full possession of my senses. The doctor told me that I am expecting a child. Send for the midwife; and as soon as she tells me that it is not true I shall regain my composure." "Very well, very well!" replied her mother, concealing her apprehension. "She shall come at once; if that is what you want, she shall come and laugh her head off at you and tell you what a silly girl you are to imagine such things." And so saying she rang the bell and immediately sent one of her servants to call the midwife.

When the latter arrived the Marquise was still lying with her mother's arms around her and her breast heaving in agitation. The Commandant's wife told the woman of the strange notion by which her daughter was afflicted: that her ladyship swore her behavior had been entirely virtuous but that nevertheless, deluded by some mysterious sensation or other, she considered it necessary to submit her condition to the scrutiny of a woman with professional knowledge. The midwife, as she carried out her investigation, spoke of warm-blooded youth and the wiles of the world; having finished her task she remarked that she had come across such cases before; young widows who found themselves in her ladyship's situation always believed themselves to have been living on desert islands; but that there was no cause for alarm, and her ladyship could rest assured that the gay corsair who had come ashore in the dark would come to light in due course. On hearing these words, the Marquise fainted. Her mother was still sufficiently moved by natural affection to bring her back to her senses with the midwife's assistance, but as soon as she revived, maternal indignation proved stronger. "Giulietta!" she cried in anguish, "will you confess to me, will you tell me who the father is?" And she still seemed disposed towards a reconciliation. But when the Marquise replied that she would go mad, her mother rose from the couch and said: "Go from my sight, you are contemptible! I curse the day I bore you!" and left the room.

The Marquise, now nearly swooning again, drew the midwife down in front of her and laid her head against her breast, trembling violently. With a faltering voice she asked her what the ways of nature were, and whether such a thing as an unwitting conception was possible. The woman smiled, loosened her kerchief and said that that would, she was sure, not be the case with her ladyship. "No, no," answered the Marquise, "I conceived knowingly, I am merely curious in a general way whether such a phenomenon exists in the realm of nature." The midwife replied that with the exception of the Blessed Virgin it had never yet happened to any woman on earth. The Marquise trembled more violently than ever. She felt as if she might go into labor at any minute, and clung to the midwife in convulsive fear, begging her not to leave her. The woman calmed her apprehension, assuring her that the confinement was still a long way off; she also informed her of the ways and means by which it was possible in such cases to avoid the gossip of the world, and said she was sure everything would turn out nicely. But these consoling remarks merely pierced the unhappy lady to the very heart; composing herself with an effort she declared that she felt better, and requested her attendant to leave her.

The midwife was scarcely out of the room when a footman brought the Marquise a written message from her mother, who expressed herself as follows: "In view of the circumstances which have come to light, Colonel G— desires you to leave his house. He sends you herewith the papers concerning your estate and hopes that God will spare him the unhappiness of ever seeing you again." But the letter was wet with tears, and in one corner, half effaced, stood the word "dictated." Tears of grief started from the Marquise's eyes. Weeping bitterly at the thought of the error into which her excellent parents had fallen and the injustice into which it had misled them, she went to her mother's apartments, but was told that her mother was with the Commandant. Hardly able to walk, she made her way to her father's rooms. Finding the door locked she sank down outside it, and in a heartrending voice called upon all the saints to witness her innocence. She had been lying there for perhaps a few minutes when her brother emerged, his face flushed with anger, and said that as she already knew, the Commandant did not wish to see her. The Marquise, sobbing distractedly, exclaimed: "Dearest brother!", and pushing her way into the room she cried: "My beloved father!" She held out her arms towards the Commandant, but no sooner did he see her than he turned his back on her and hurried into his bedroom. As she tried to follow him he shouted "Begone!" and tried to slam the door; but when she cried out imploringly and prevented him from doing so he suddenly desisted and letting the Marquise into the room, strode across to the far side of it with his back still turned to her. She had just thrown herself at his feet and tremblingly clasped his knees when a pistol which he had seized went off just as he was snatching it down from the wall, and a shot crashed into the ceiling. "Oh, God preserve me!" exclaimed the Marquise, rising from her knees as pale as death, and fled from her father's apartment. Reaching her own, she gave orders that her carriage should be made ready at once, sat down in utter exhaustion, hastily dressed her children, and told the servants to pack her belongings. She was just holding her youngest child between her knees, wrapping one more garment round it, and everything was ready for their departure in the carriage, when her brother entered and demanded, on the Commandant's orders, that she should leave the children behind and hand them over to him. "These children!" she exclaimed, rising to her feet. "Tell your inhuman father that he can come here and shoot me dead, but he shall not take my children from me!" And armed with all the pride of innocence she snatched up her children, carried them with her to the coach, her brother not daring to stop her, and drove off.

This splendid effort of will gave her back her sense of her own identity, and as if with her own hands she raised herself out of the depths into which fate had cast her. The turmoil and anguish of her heart ceased when she found herself on the open road with her beloved prize, the children; she covered them with kisses, reflecting with great satisfaction what a victory she had won over her brother by the sheer force of her clear conscience. Her reason was strong enough to withstand her strange situation without giving way, and she submitted herself wholly to the great, sacred and inexplicable order of the world. She saw that it would be impossible to convince her family of her innocence, realized that she must accept this fact for the sake of her own survival, and only a few days after her arrival at V— her grief had been replaced by a heroic resolve to arm herself with pride and let the world do its worst. She decided to withdraw altogether into her own life, to devote herself zealously and exclusively to the education of her two children, and to care with full maternal love for the third which God had now given her. Since her beautiful country house had fallen rather into disrepair owing to her long absence, she made arrangements for its restoration, to be completed in a few weeks' time, as soon as her confinement was over; she sat in the summer-house knitting little caps and socks for little feet, and thinking about what use she might most conveniently make of various rooms, which of them for instance she would fill with books and in which of them her easel might be most suitably placed. And thus, even before the date of Count F—'s expected return from Naples, she was quite reconciled to a life of perpetual cloistered seclusion. Her porter was ordered to admit no visitors to the house. The only thing she found intolerable was the thought that the little creature she had conceived in the utmost innocence and purity and whose origin, precisely because it was more mysterious, also seemed to her more divine than that of other men, was destined to bear a stigma of disgrace in good society. An unusual expedient for discovering the father had occurred to her: an expedient which, when she first thought of it, so startled her that she let fall her knitting. For whole nights on end, restless and sleepless, she turned it over and over in her mind, trying to get used to an idea the very nature of which offended her innermost feelings. She still felt the greatest repugnance at the thought of entering into any relationship with the person who had tricked her in such a fashion; for she most rightly concluded that he must after all irredeemably belong to the very scum of mankind, and that whatever position of society one might imagine him to occupy, his origin could only be from its lowest, vilest dregs. But with her sense of her own independence growing ever stronger, and reflecting as she did that a precious stone retains its value whatever its setting may be, she took heart one morning, as she felt the stirring of the new life inside her, and gave instructions for the insertion in the M— news-sheets of the extraordinary announcement quoted to the reader at the beginning of this story.

Meanwhile Count F—, detained in Naples by unavoidable duties, had written for the second time to the Marquise urging her to consider that unusual circumstances might arise which would make it desirable for her to abide by the tacit undertaking she had given him. As soon as he had succeeded in declining his further official journey to Constantinople, and as soon as his other business permitted, he at once left Naples and duly arrived in M— only a few days later than the date on which he had said he would do so. The Commandant received him with an air of embarrassment, said that he was about to leave the house on urgent business, and asked his son to entertain the Count in the meantime. The latter took him to his room and, after greeting him briefly, asked him whether he already knew about what had happened in the Commandant's house during his absence. The Count, turning pale for a moment, answered that he did not. The Marquise's brother thereupon informed him of the disgrace which his sister had brought upon the family, and narrated the events with which our readers are already acquainted. The Count struck his forehead with his hand and exclaimed, quite forgetting himself: "Why were so many obstacles put in my way! If the marriage had taken place, we should have been spared all this shame and unhappiness!" The Commandant's son, staring at him wide-eyed, asked him whether he was so crazy as to want to be married to so contemptible a person. The Count replied that she was worth more than the whole of the world which despised her; that he for his part absolutely believed her declaration of innocence; and that he would go that very day to V— and renew his offer to her. So saying he at once picked up his hat and left, after bidding farewell to the Commandant's son, who concluded that he must have taken leave of his senses.

Taking a horse he galloped out to V—. When he had dismounted at the gate and was about to enter the forecourt, the porter told him that her ladyship was not at home to anyone. The Count inquired whether these instructions, issued presumably to keep away strangers, also applied to a friend of the family, to which the man answered that he was not aware of any exceptions to them; and he then almost at once inquired, in a tone of innuendo, whether the gentleman were not perhaps Count F—? The Count, after glancing at him sharply, answered that he was not; then turning to his servant, but speaking loudly enough for the other man to hear, he said that in these circumstances he would lodge at an inn and announce himself to her ladyship in writing. But as soon as he was out of the porter's sight he turned a corner and slipped quietly round the wall of an extensive garden which lay behind the house. By a door which he found unlocked he entered the garden, walked through it along the paths, and was just about to ascend the terrace to the rear of the house when in an arbor at one side of it he caught sight of the Marquise, her figure charmingly and mysteriously altered, sitting busily working at a little table. He approached her in such a manner that she could not notice him until he was standing at the entrance to the arbor, three short steps from her feet. "Count F—!" she exclaimed as she looked up, blushing scarlet with surprise. The Count smiled, and remained standing motionless in the entrance for some moments; then, with such modest importunity as would not alarm her, he sat down at her side, and before she could make up her mind what to do in so strange a situation, he put his arm gently and lovingly around her waist. "But Count, how is this possible, where have you—" began the Marquise, and then shyly cast down her eyes. "From M—," said the Count, pressing her very gently to him. "I found a back door open and came through it into your garden; I felt sure you would forgive me for doing so." "But when you were in M— did they not tell you—?" she asked, still motionless in his arms. "Everything, dearest lady," replied the Count. "But fully convinced of your innocence—" "What!" cried the Marquise, rising to her feet and trying to free herself from him, "and despite that you come here?" "Despite the world," he went on, holding her fast, "and despite your family, and even despite your present enchanting appearance"—at which words he ardently kissed her breast. "Go away!" she exclaimed, but he continued: "—as convinced, Giulietta, as if I were omniscient, as if my own soul were living in your body." The Marquise cried: "Let me go!" "I have come," he concluded, still without releasing her, "to repeat my proposal and to receive, if you will accept it, the bliss of paradise from your hand." "Let me go immediately!" she cried, "I order you to let me go!", and freeing herself forcibly from his embrace she started away from him. "Darling! adorable creature!" he whispered, rising to his feet again and following her. "You heard me!" cried the Marquise, turning and evading him. "One secret, whispered word!" said the Count, hastily snatching at her smooth arm as it slipped from him. "I *do not want to hear* anything," she retorted, violently pushing him back; then she fled up on to the terrace and disappeared.

He was already half-way up to her, determined at all costs to get a hearing, when the door was slammed in his face, and in front of his hurrying steps he heard the bolt rattle as with distraught vehemence she pushed it home. He stood for a moment undecided what to do in this situation, considering whether he should climb in through a side window which was standing open, and pursue his purpose until he had achieved it; but although it was in every sense difficult for him to desist, it did now seem necessary to do so, and bitterly vexed with himself for letting her slip from his arms, he retreated from the terrace, left the garden, and went to find his horse. He felt that his attempt to pour out his heart to her in person had failed forever, and rode slowly back to M——, thinking over the wording of a letter which he now felt condemned to write. That evening, as he was dining in a public place, very much out of humor, he met the Marquise's brother, who at once asked him whether he had successfully made his proposal in V——. The Count answered curtly that he had not, and felt very much inclined to dismiss his interlocutor with some bitter phrase; but for the sake of politeness he presently added that he had decided to write the lady a letter, which would soon clarify the issue. The Commandant's son said he noticed with regret that the Count's passion for his sister was driving him quite out of his mind. He must, however, assure the Count that she was already on her way to making a different choice; so saying he rang for the latest newspapers and gave the Count the sheet in which was inserted his sister's advertisement appealing to the father of her child. The Count flushed suddenly as he read it; conflicting emotions rushed through him. The Marquise's brother asked him if he did not think that she would find the person she was looking for. "Undoubtedly!" answered the Count, with his whole mind intent on the paper, greedily devouring the meaning of the announcement. Then, after folding it up and stepping over to the window for a moment, he said: "Now everything is all right! Now I know what to do!" He then turned round, and after courteously asking the Commandant's son whether they would soon meet again, he took his leave of him and departed, quite reconciled to his lot.

Meanwhile some very animated scenes had taken place at the Commandant's house. His wife was in a state of extreme vexation at her husband's destructive vehemence and at her own weakness in allowing him to overrule her objections to his tyrannical banishment of their daughter. When she heard the pistol shot in his bedroom and saw her daughter rushing out of it she had fainted away; she had, to be sure, soon recovered herself, but all the Commandant did when she came to her senses was to apologize for causing her this unnecessary alarm, and throw the discharged pistol down on to a table. Later, when it was proposed to claim custody of their daughter's children, she timorously ventured to declare that they had no right to take such a step; in a voice still weak from her recent swoon, she touchingly implored him to avoid violent scenes in the house; but the Commandant, not answering her, had merely turned foaming with rage to his son and ordered him: "Go to her! and bring them back here!" When Count F—'s second letter arrived, the Commandant had ordered that it should be sent out to the Marquise at V—; the messenger afterwards reported that she had simply laid it on one side and dismissed him. Her mother, to whom so much in this whole affair was incomprehensible, more particularly her daughter's inclination to get married again and to someone totally indifferent to her, tried vainly to initiate a discussion of this point. Each time she did so the Commandant requested her to be silent, in a manner more like an order than a request; on one such occasion he removed from the wall a portrait of his daughter that was still hanging there, declaring that he wished to expunge her completely from his memory; he no longer, he said, had a daughter. Then the Marquise's strange advertisement was published. The Commandant had handed the paper containing it to his wife, who read it with absolute amazement and went with it to her husband's rooms, where she found him working at a table, and asked him what on earth he thought of it. The Commandant continuing to write, said: "Oh, she is innocent!" "What!" exclaimed his wife, astonished beyond measure, "innocent?" "She did it in her sleep," said the Commandant, without looking up. "In her sleep!" replied his wife. "And you are telling me that such a monstrous occurrence—" "Silly woman!" exclaimed the Commandant, pushing his papers together and leaving the room.

On the next day on which news was published the Commandant's wife, seated with her husband at breakfast, was handed a news-sheet which had just arrived not yet dry from the printers, and in it she read the following answer: "If the Marquise of O— will be present at 11 o'clock on the morning of the 3rd of — in the house of her father Colonel G—, the man whom she wishes to trace will there cast himself at her feet!"

The Colonel's wife became speechless before she had even read halfway through this extraordinary insertion; she glanced at the end, and handed the sheet to the Commandant. The latter read it through three times, as if he could not believe his own eyes. "Now tell me, in heaven's name, Lorenzo," cried his wife, "what do you make of that?" "Why, the infamous woman!" replied the Commandant, rising from the table, "the sanctimonious hypocrite! The shamelessness of a bitch coupled with the cunning of a fox and multiplied tenfold are as nothing to hers! So sweet a face! Such eyes, as innocent as a cherub!" And nothing could calm his distress. "But if it is a trick," asked his wife, "what on earth can be her purpose?" "Her purpose?" retorted the Colonel. "She is determined to force us to accept her contemptible pretence. She and that man have already learnt by heart the cock-and-bull story they will tell us when the two of them appear here on the third at eleven in the morning. And I shall be expected to say: 'My dear little daughter, I did not know that, who could have thought such a thing, forgive me, receive my blessing, and let us be friends again.' But I have a bullet ready for the man who steps across my threshold on the third! Or perhaps it would be more suitable to have him thrown out of the house by the servants." His wife, after a further perusal of the announcement in the paper, said that if she was to believe one of two incomprehensible things, then she found it more credible that some extraordinary quirk of fate had occurred than that a daughter who had always been so virtuous should now behave so basely. But before she had even finished speaking, her husband was already shouting: "Be so good as to hold your tongue! I cannot bear," he added, leaving the room, "even to hear this hateful matter mentioned."

A few days later the Commandant received a letter from the Marquise referring to the second announcement, and most respectfully and touchingly begging him, since she had been deprived of the privilege of setting foot in his house, to be so kind as to send whoever presented himself there on the morning of the third out to her estate at V—. Her mother happened to be present when the Commandant received this letter, and she noticed by the expression on his face that his feelings had become confused; for if the whole thing was indeed a trick, what motive was he to impute to her now, since she seemed to be making no sort of claim to his forgiveness? Emboldened by this, she accordingly proposed a plan which her heart, troubled by doubts as it was, had for some time been harboring. As her husband still stared expressionlessly at the paper, she said that she had an idea. Would he allow her to go for one or two days out to V—? She undertook to devise a situation in which the Marquise, if she really knew the man who had answered her advertisement as if he were a stranger, would undoubtedly betray herself, even if she was the world's most sophisticated deceiver. The Commandant, with sudden violence, tore his daughter's letter to shreds, and replied to his wife that, as she well knew, he wished to have nothing whatever to do with its writer, and absolutely forbade her mother to enter into any communication with her. He sealed up the torn pieces in an envelope, wrote the Marquise's address on it, and returned it to the messenger as his answer. His wife, inwardly exasperated by this headstrong obstinacy which would destroy any possibility they had of clearing the matter up, now decided to carry out her plan against her husband's will. On the very next morning, while the Commandant was still in bed, she took one of his grooms and drove with him out to V——. When she reached the gate of her daughter's country house, the porter told her that his orders were to admit no one to her ladyship's presence. The Commandant's wife replied that she knew of these orders, but that he was nevertheless to go and announce the wife of Colonel G——. To this the man answered that it would be useless to do so, since his mistress was receiving no one, and there were no exceptions. The Commandant's wife answered that she would be received by his mistress, as she was her mother; would he therefore be good enough to do his errand without further delay. But scarcely had the man, still predicting that this mission would be fruitless, entered the house than the Marquise was seen to emerge from it and come in haste to the gate, where she fell on her knees before her mother's carriage. The latter, assisted by her groom, stepped down from it, and in some emotion raised her daughter from the ground. The Marquise, quite overwhelmed by her feelings, bowed low over her mother's hand to kiss it; then, shedding frequent tears, she very respectfully conducted her through the rooms of her house and seated her on a divan. "My dearest mother!" she exclaimed, still standing in front of her and drying her eyes, "to what happy chance do I owe the inexpressible pleasure of your visit?" Her mother, taking her affectionately by the hand, said that she must tell her she had simply come to ask her forgiveness for the hard-hearted way in which she had been expelled from her parents' house. "Forgiveness!" cried the Marquise, and tried to kiss her hand. But her mother, withdrawing her hand, continued: "For not only did the recently published answer to— your advertisement convince myself and your father of your innocence, but I have also to tell you that the man in question, to our great delight and surprise, has already presented himself at our house yesterday." "*Who* has already—?" asked the Marquise, sitting down beside her mother, "*what* man in question has presented himself—?" And her face was tense with expectation. Her mother answered: "The man who wrote that reply, he himself in person, the man to whom your appeal was directed." "Well, then," said the Marquise, with her breast heaving in agitation, "who is he?" And she repeated: "Who is he?" "That," replied her mother, "is what I should like you to guess. For just imagine: yesterday, as we were sitting at tea, and in the act of reading that extraordinary newspaper announcement, a man with whom we are quite intimately acquainted rushed into the room with gestures of despair and threw himself down at your father's feet, and presently at mine as well. We had no idea what to make of this and asked him to explain himself. So he said that his conscience was giving him no peace, it was he who had so shamefully deceived our daughter; he could not but know how his crime was judged, and if retribution was to be exacted from him for it, he had come to submit himself to that retribution." "But who? who? who?" asked the Marquise. "As I told you," continued her mother, "an otherwise well-brought-up young man whom we should never have considered capable of so base an act. But my dear daughter, you must not be alarmed to hear that he is of humble station, and quite lacks all the qualifications that a husband of yours might otherwise be expected to have." "Nevertheless, my most excellent mother," said the Marquise, "he cannot be wholly unworthy, since he came and threw himself at your feet before throwing himself at mine. But who? who? please tell me *who!*" "Well," replied her mother, "it was Leopardo, the groom from Tyrol whom your father recently engaged, and whom as you may have noticed I have already brought with me to present to you as your fiancé." "Leopardo, the groom!" cried the Marquise, pressing her hand to her forehead with an expression of despair. "Why are you startled?" asked her mother. "Have you reasons for doubting it?" "How? where? when?" asked the Marquise in confusion. "That," answered her mother, "is something he wishes to confess only to you. Shame and love, he told us, made it impossible for him to communicate these facts to anyone except yourself. But if you like we will open the anteroom, where he is waiting with a beating heart for the outcome, and then I shall leave you together, and you will see whether you can elicit his secret from him." "Oh, God in heaven!" cried the Marquise: "it did once happen that I had fallen asleep in the mid-day heat, on my divan, and when I woke up I saw him walking away from it!" Her face grew scarlet with shame and she covered it with her little hands. But at this point her mother fell to her knees before her. "Oh, Giulietta!" she exclaimed, throwing her arms round her, "oh, my dear excellent girl! And how contemptible of me!" And she buried her face in her daughter's lap. The Marquise gasped in consternation: "What is the matter, mother?" "For let me tell you now," continued her mother, "that nothing of what I have been saying to you is true; you are purer than an angel, you radiate such innocence that my corrupted soul could not believe in it, and I could not convince myself of it without descending to this shameful trick." "My dearest mother!" cried the Marquise, full of happy emotion, and stooped down to her, trying to raise her to her feet. But her mother said: "No, I shall not move from your feet, you splendid, heavenly creature, until you tell me that you can forgive the baseness of my behavior." "Am *I* to forgive *you!*" exclaimed her daughter. "Please rise, I do implore you—" "You heard me," said the Commandant's wife. "I want to know whether you can still love me, whether you can still respect me as sincerely as ever?" "My adored mother!" cried the Marquise, now kneeling before her as well, "my heart has never lost any of its respect and love for you. Under such extraordinary circumstances, how was it possible for anyone to trust me? How glad I am that you are convinced that I have done nothing wrong!" "Well, my dearest child," said her mother, standing up with her daughter's assistance, "now I shall love and cherish you. You shall have your confinement in my house; and I shall treat you with no less tenderness and respect than if we had reason to expect your baby to be a young prince. I shall never desert you now as long as I live. I defy the whole world; I *want* no greater honor than your shame—if only you will love me again, and forget the hard-hearted way in which I rejected you!" The Marquise tried to comfort her with endless caresses and assurances, but evening fell and midnight struck before she had succeeded. Next day, when the old lady had recovered a little from her emotion, which had made her feverish during the night, the mother, daughter and grandchildren drove back in triumph, as it were, to M—. Their journey was a very happy one, and they joked about the groom Leopardo as he sat in front of them driving the carriage: the Marquise's mother said she noticed how her daughter blushed every time she looked at his broad shoulders, and the Marquise, reacting half with a sigh and half with a smile, answered: "I wonder after all who the man will be who turns up at our house on the morning of the third!" Then, the nearer they got to M—, the more serious their mood became again, in anticipation of the crucial scenes that still awaited them. As soon as they had arrived at the house, the Commandant's wife, concealing her plans, showed her daughter back to her old rooms, and told her to make herself comfortable; then, saying that she would soon be back, she slipped away. An hour later she returned with her face very flushed. "Why, what a doubting Thomas!" she said, though she seemed secretly delighted, "what a doubting Thomas! Didn't I need a whole hour by the clock to convince him! But now he's sitting there weeping." "Who?" asked the Marquise. "He himself," answered her mother. "Who else but the person with the most cause for it! "Surely not my father?" exclaimed the Marquise. "Weeping like a child," replied her mother. "If I had not had to wipe the tears out of my own eyes, I should have burst out laughing as soon as I got outside the door." "And all this on my account?" asked her daughter, rising to her feet, "and you expect me to stay here and—?" "You shall not budge!" said her mother. "Why did he dictate that letter to me! *He* shall come here to *you,* or *I* shall have no more to do with him as long as I live." "My dearest mother—" pleaded the Marquise, but her mother interrupted her. "I'll not give way! Why did he reach for that pistol?" "But I implore you—" "You *shall* not go to him," replied the Commandant's wife, forcing her daughter to sit down again, "and if he does not come by this evening, I shall leave the house with you tomorrow." The Marquise said that this would be a hard and unfair way to act, but her mother answered (for she could already hear sobs approaching from a distance): "You need not worry; here he is already!" "Where?" asked her daughter, and sat listening. "Is there someone there at the door, quite convulsed with—?" "Of course!" replied the Commandant's wife; "he wants us to open it for him." "Let me go!" cried the Marquise, leaping from her chair. But her mother answered: "Giulietta, if you love me, stay where you are!"— and at that very moment the Commandant entered the room, holding his handkerchief to his face. His wife placed herself directly between him and her daughter and turned her back on him. "My dearest father!" cried the Marquise, stretching out her arms towards him. "You shall not budge, I tell you!" said her mother. The Commandant stood there in the room, weeping. "He is to apologize to you," continued his wife. "Why has he such a violent temper, and why is he so obstinate? I love him but I love you too; I respect him, but I respect you too. And if I must choose, then

you are a finer person than he is, and I shall stay with you." The
Commandant was standing bent almost double and weeping so
loudly that the walls re-echoed. "Oh, my God, but—" exclaimed
the Marquise, suddenly giving up the struggle with her mother, and
taking out her handkerchief to let her own tears flow. Her mother
said: "It's just that he can't speak!" and moved a little to one side.
At this the Marquise rose, embraced her father, and begged him
to calm himself. She too was weeping profusely. She asked him if
he would not sit down, and tried to draw him on to a chair; she
pushed one up for him to sit on; but he made no answer, he could
not be induced to move, nor even sit down, but merely stood there
with his face bowed low, and wept. The Marquise, holding him
upright, half turned to her mother and said she thought he would
make himself ill; her mother too seemed on the point of losing her
composure, for he was going almost into convulsions. But when
he had finally seated himself, yielding to the repeated pleas of his
daughter, and the latter, ceaselessly caressing him, had sunk down
at his feet, his wife returned to her point, declared that it served
him right, and that now he would no doubt come to his senses;
whereupon she departed and left the two of them in the room.

As soon as she was outside the door she wiped away her own
tears, wondering whether the violent emotional upheaval she had
caused him might not after all be dangerous, and whether it would
be advisable to have a doctor called. She went to the kitchen and
cooked for his dinner all the most nourishing and comforting dishes
she could devise; she prepared and warmed his bed, intending to
put him into it as soon as, hand in hand with his daughter, he should
reappear. But when the dinner table was already laid and there was
still no sign of him, she crept back to the Marquise's room to find
out what on earth was going on. Putting her ear gently against the
door and listening, she caught the last echo of some softly murmured words, spoken, as it seemed to her, by the Marquise; and
looking through the keyhole she noticed that her daughter was even
sitting on the Commandant's lap, a thing he had never before permitted. And when finally she opened the door she saw a sight that
made her heart leap with joy: her daughter, with her head thrown
back and her eyes tightly shut, was lying quietly in her father's arms,
while the latter, with tears glistening in his wide-open eyes, sat in
the armchair, pressing long, ardent, avid kisses on to her mouth,

just like a lover! His daughter said nothing, he said nothing; he sat with his face bowed over her, as if she were the first girl he had ever loved; he sat there holding her mouth near his and kissing her. Her mother felt quite transported with delight; standing unseen behind his chair, she hesitated to interrupt this blissful scene of reconciliation which had brought such joy back to her house. Finally, she approached her husband, and just as he was again stroking and kissing his daughter's mouth in indescribable ecstasy, she leaned round the side of the chair and looked at him. When the Commandant saw her he at once lowered his eyes again with a cross expression and was about to say something; but she exclaimed: "Oh, what a face to make!" And then she in her turn smoothed it out with kisses, and talked jestingly until the atmosphere of emotion was dispelled. She asked them both to come and have dinner, and as she led the way they walked along like a pair of betrothed lovers; at table the Commandant seemed very happy, though he still sobbed from time to time, ate and spoke little, gazed down at his plate, and caressed his daughter's hand.

The question now was, who in the world would turn up at eleven o'clock on the following morning, for the next day to dawn would be the dreaded third. The Marquise's father and mother, as well as her brother who had arrived to share in the general reconciliation, were decidedly in favor of marriage, if the person should be at least tolerably acceptable; everything within the realm of possibility would be done to ensure her happiness. If, on the other hand, the circumstances of the person in question should turn out to be such that even with the help of her family they would still fall too far short of the Marquise's own, then her parents were opposed to her marrying him; they were resolved in that case to let her live with them as before and to adopt the child as theirs. It seemed, however, to be the Marquise's wish to keep her promise in any case, provided the person were not a complete scoundrel, and thus at all costs to provide the child with a father. That evening her mother raised the question of how the visitor was to be received. The Commandant was of the opinion that the most suitable procedure would be, when eleven o'clock came, to leave the Marquise by herself. The latter however insisted that both her parents, and her brother as well, should be present, since she did not want to share any secrets with the expected person. She also thought that this would be his own wish, which in his answer he had seemed to express by suggesting her father's house as the place for the meeting; and she added that she must confess to having been greatly pleased by this answer for that very reason. Her mother thought that under this arrangement the roles played by her husband and son would be most unseemly; she begged her daughter to consent to the two men being absent, but agreed to meet her wishes to the extent of being present herself when the person arrived. After the Marquise had thought it over for a little this last proposal was finally adopted. The night was then passed in a state of suspense and expectancy, and now the morning of the dreaded third had come. As the clock struck eleven both women were sitting in the reception room, festively attired as for a betrothal; their hearts were beating so hard that one could have heard them if the noises of daytime had ceased. The eleventh stroke of the clock was still reverberating when Leopardo entered, the groom whom the Commandant had hired from Tyrol. At the sight of him the women turned pale. "I am to announce Count F——, my lady," he said, "his carriage is at the door." "Count F——!" they exclaimed simultaneously, thrown from one kind of consternation into another. The Marquise cried: "Shut the doors! We are not at home to him!" She rose at once to lock the door of the room herself, and was in the act of thrusting out the groom as he stood in her way, when the Count entered, in exactly the same uniform, with the same decorations and weapons, as he had worn and carried on the day of the storming of the fortress. The Marquise felt she would sink into the ground from sheer confusion; she snatched up a handkerchief she had left lying on her chair and was about to rush off into a neighboring room, when her mother, seizing her by the hand, exclaimed: "Giulietta——!," and her thoughts seemed to stifle any further words. She stared straight at the Count, and repeated, drawing her daughter towards her: "Why, Giulietta, whom have we been expecting——?" The Marquise, turning suddenly, cried: "Well? You surely cannot mean him——?" She fixed on the Count such a look that it seemed to flash like a thunderbolt, and her face went deathly pale. He had gone down on one knee before her; his right hand was on his heart, his head meekly bowed, and there he remained, blushing scarlet and with downcast eyes, saying nothing. "Who else?" exclaimed her mother, her voice almost failing.

"Who else but him? How stupid we have been—!" The Marquise stood over him, rigidly erect, and said: "Mother, I shall go mad!" "Foolish girl," replied her mother, and she drew her towards her and whispered something into her ear. The Marquise turned away and collapsed on to the sofa with both hands pressed against her face. Her mother cried: "Poor wretched girl! What is the matter with you? What has happened that can have taken you by surprise?" The Count did not move, but knelt on beside the Commandant's wife, and taking the outermost hem of her dress in his hand he kissed it. "Dear, gracious, noble lady!" he whispered, and a tear rolled down his cheek. "Stand up, Count," she answered, "stand up! Comfort my daughter; then we shall all be reconciled, and all will be forgiven and forgotten." The Count rose to his feet, still shedding tears. He again knelt down in front of the Marquise, gently took her hand as if it were made of gold and the touch of his own might tarnish it. But she, standing up, cried: "Go away! go away! go away! I was prepared to meet a depraved man, but not—not a devil!" And so saying she moved away from him as if he were a person infected with the plague, threw open the door of the room and said: "Call my father!" "Giulietta!" cried her mother in astonishment. The Marquise stared at them each in turn with annihilating rage; her breast heaved, her face was aflame; no Fury's gaze could be more terrifying. The Commandant and his son arrived. "Father," said the Marquise, as they were in the act of entering the room, "I cannot marry this man!" And dipping her hand into a vessel of holy water that was fastened to the door, she scattered it lavishly over her father, mother and brother, and fled.

The Commandant, disconcerted by this strange occurrence, asked what had happened, and turned pale when he noticed that at this decisive moment Count F— was in the room. His wife took the Count by the hand and said: "Do not ask; this young man sincerely repents all that has happened; give him your blessing, give it, give it—and all will still turn out for the best." The Count stood there utterly mortified. The Commandant laid his hand on his head; his eyelids twitched, his lips were as white as chalk. "May the curse of heaven be averted from your head!" he exclaimed. "When are you intending to get married?" "Tomorrow," answered the Marquise's mother on the Count's behalf, for the latter was unable to utter a word. "Tomorrow or today, whichever you like; I am sure no time will be too soon for my lord the Count, who has shown such admirable zeal to make amends for his wrongdoing." "Then I shall have the pleasure of seeing you tomorrow at eleven o'clock at the Church of St. Augustine!" said the Commandant; whereupon he bowed to him, asked his wife and son to accompany him to his daughter's room, and left the Count to himself.

The family made vain efforts to discover from the Marquise the reason for her strange behavior; she was lying in an acutely feverish condition, refused absolutely to listen to any talk of getting married, and asked them to leave her alone. When they inquired why she had suddenly changed her mind and what made the Count more repugnant to her than any other suitor, she gave her father a blank wide-eyed stare and made no answer. Her mother asked whether she had forgotten that she was herself a mother; to which she replied that in the present case she was bound to consider her own interests before those of the child, and calling on all the angels and saints as witnesses she reasserted her refusal to marry. Her father, to whom it seemed obvious that she was in a hysterical state of mind, declared that she must keep her word; he then left her, and put in hand all the arrangements for the wedding after an appropriate written exchange with the Count. He submitted to him a marriage contract by which he would renounce all conjugal rights while at the same time binding himself to fulfil any duties that might be imposed upon him. The document came back wet with tears, bearing the Count's signature. When the Commandant handed it the next morning to the Marquise she had somewhat recovered her composure. Still sitting in her bed, she read the paper through several times, folded it up thoughtfully, opened it again and re-read it; then she declared that she would come to the Church of St. Augustine at eleven o'clock. She rose, dressed without saying a word, got into the carriage with her parents and brother when the hour struck, and drove off to the appointed meeting-place.

The Count was not permitted to join the family until they reached the entrance to the church. During the ceremony the Marquise stared rigidly at the painting behind the altar and did not vouchsafe even a fleeting glance at the man with whom she was exchanging rings. When the marriage service ended, the Count offered her his arm; but as soon as they reached the church door again the Countess took her leave of him with a bow; her father inquired whether he would occasionally have the honor of seeing him in his daughter's apartments; whereupon the Count muttered something unintelligible, raising his hat to the company, and disappeared. He moved into a residence in M— and spent several months there without ever once setting foot in the Commandant's house, where the Countess continued to live. It was only owing to his delicate, dignified, and wholly exemplary behavior on all occasions on which he came into any contact at all with the family, that when in due course the Countess was delivered of an infant son he was invited to the christening. The Countess, still confined and sitting in her bed under richly embroidered coverlets, saw him only for an instant when he presented himself and greeted her from a respectful distance. Among the other presents with which the guests had welcomed the newcomer, he threw on to his son's cradle two documents; after his departure one of these turned out to be a deed of gift of 20,000 rubles to the boy, and the other a will making the boy's mother, in the event of the Count's death, heiress to his entire fortune. From that day on the Commandant's wife saw to it that he was frequently invited; the house was open to him and soon not an evening passed without his paying the family a visit. His instinct told him that, in consideration of the imperfection inherent in the order of the world, he had been forgiven by all of them, and he therefore began a second wooing of the Countess, his wife; when a year had passed he won from her a second consent, and they even celebrated a second wedding, happier than the first, after which the whole family moved out to the estate at V—. A whole series of young Russians now followed the first, and during one happy hour the Count asked his wife why, on that terrible third day of the month, when she had seemed willing to receive the most depraved of men she had fled from him as if from a devil. Throwing her arms round his neck, she answered that he would not have seemed a devil then if at their first meeting he had not appeared to her in the likeness of an angel.

Translated by David Luke

Michael Kohlhaas

FROM AN OLD CHRONICLE

Heinrich von Kleist

Toward the middle of the sixteenth century there lived on the banks of the Havel a horse dealer by the name of Michael Kohlhaas, the son of a schoolmaster, one of the most upright and at the same time one of the most terrible men of his day. Until his thirtieth year this extraordinary man would have been thought the very model of a good citizen. In a village that still bears his name, he owned a farm on which he quietly earned a living by his trade; the children with whom his wife presented him were brought up in the fear of God to be industrious and honest; there was not one of his neighbors who had not benefited from his benevolence or his fair-mindedness—the world, in short, would have had every reason to bless his memory, if he had not carried one virtue to excess. But his sense of justice turned him into a brigand and a murderer.

He was riding out of the territory of Brandenburg one day with a string of young horses, all fat and glossy-coated, and was turning over in his mind how he would use the profit he hoped to make on them at the fairs—part of it, like the good manager he was, to get new profits, but part, too, for present enjoyment—when he reached the Elbe, and near an imposing castle standing in Saxon territory he came upon a toll gate that he had never found on that road before. He halted his horses just when a heavy shower of rain was coming down and shouted for the tollkeeper, who after a while showed his surly face at the window. The horse dealer told him to open the gate. "What's been happening here?" he asked, when the tollkeeper, after a long interval, emerged from the house.

"Seignorial privilege," answered the latter as he opened the gate, "bestowed upon the Junker Wenzel von Tronka."

"So," said Kohlhaas; "the Junker's name is Wenzel?" and he gazed at the castle, which overlooked the field with its glittering battlements. "Is the old Junker dead then?"

"Died of a stroke," the tollkeeper said as he raised the toll bar.

"Oh! I'm sorry to hear that," Kohlhaas replied. "He was a decent old gentleman, who liked to see people come and go and helped along trade and traffic whenever he could; he once put down some cobblestones because a mare of mine broke her leg over there where the road goes into the village. Well, what do I owe you?" he asked, and had trouble getting out the groschen demanded by the keeper from beneath his cloak which was flapping in the wind. "All right, old fellow," he added, when the keeper muttered "Quick, quick!" and cursed the weather; "If they had left the tree for that pole standing in the forest it would have been better for both of us." And he gave him the money and started to ride on. He had hardly passed under the toll bar, however, when a new voice rang out from the tower behind him: "Hold up there, horse dealer!" and he saw the castellan slam a window shut and come hurrying down to him. "Now what?" wondered Kohlhaas and halted with his horses. Buttoning one waistcoat after another around his ample middle, the castellan came up to him and, leaning into the wind, asked for his pass.

"Pass?" said Kohlhaas, a little disconcerted. So far as he knew, he had none, was his answer, but if somebody would only tell him what in the name of God the thing was, he might just happen to have one in his pocket. The castellan eyed him obliquely and said that without a permit from the sovereign no dealer could bring horses across the border. The horse dealer assured him that he had already crossed the border seventeen times in his life without such a permit; that he knew every one of the regulations of his trade; that in all likelihood the whole thing would turn out to be a mistake, for which reason he wished to give it some thought; and that he would like it, since he had a long day's ride ahead of him, if he were not needlessly detained any longer. But the castellan answered that he was not going to slip through the eighteenth time, that the ordinance had recently been issued for just that reason, and that he must either get a permit for himself right now or go back to where he had come from. After a moment's reflection, the horse dealer, whom these illegal demands were beginning to exasperate, got down from his horse, handed the reins to a groom, and said that he would speak to the Junker von Tronka himself about the matter. He made straight for the castle, too; the castellan, muttering something about penny-pinching moneygrubbers and what a good thing it was to squeeze them, followed him; and the two men, measuring each other with their glances, entered the hall. The Junker happened to be making merry with friends over wine, and they had all burst into uproarious laughter at a joke just as Kohlhaas approached with his complaint. The Junker asked him what he wanted; the knights, on catching sight of the stranger, fell silent; but no sooner did the latter launch into his request about the horses than the whole company cried out, "Horses! Where are they?" and ran to the window. Seeing the shiny-coated string below, they followed the suggestion of the Junker and trooped down into the courtyard; the rain had stopped; castellan, steward, and grooms gathered around them, and the entire yard looked the horses over. One knight praised the bay with the white blaze on his forehead, another liked the chestnut, a third patted the piebald with the tawny spot; and all thought that the horses were like stags and that no finer ones were raised in the country. Kohlhaas cheerfully replied that the horses were no better than the knights who were going to ride them, and invited them to buy. The Junker, who was very tempted by the big bay stallion, went so far as to ask its price; his steward urged him to buy a pair of blacks that he thought they could use in the fields, since they were short of horses; but when the horse dealer named his price, the knights thought it too dear, and the Junker said that Kohlhaas would have to ride to the Round Table and look for King Arthur if that was the kind of money he wanted for his stock. Kohlhaas, noticing the castellan and the steward whispering together while they shot meaningful looks at the blacks, and moved by a dark presentiment, did everything in his power to sell the horses. He said to the Junker, "Sir, I bought those blacks there six months ago for twenty-five gold gulden; give me thirty and they are yours." Two of the knights standing next to the Junker remarked quite audibly that the horses were probably worth that much; the Junker, however, felt that he might be willing to pay money for the bay but not for the blacks, and he got ready to go back into the castle; whereupon Kohlhaas said that the next time he came that way with his animals they might perhaps strike a bargain, took leave of the Junker, and, gathering up the reins of his horse, started to ride off. But just then the castellan stepped out of the crowd and said it was his understanding that he could not travel without a pass. Kohlhaas turned and asked the Junker if there actually were such a requirement, which would seriously interfere with his whole trade. The Junker, as he walked away, replied with an embarrassed air, "Yes, Kohlhaas, I'm afraid you must have a pass. Speak to the castellan about it and go on your way." Kohlhaas assured him that he had not the least intention of evading whatever regulations there might be for the export of horses; promised that when he went through Dresden he would take out a permit at the privy chancellery; and asked to be allowed to go through just this once since he had known nothing at all about the requirement. "Oh well," said the Junker as the wind began to blow again and whistled between his skinny legs, "let the poor wretch go on. Come!" he said to the knights, turned, and started toward the castle. The castellan, turning to the Junker, said that Kohlhaas at least should leave a pledge behind as security for his taking out the permit. The Junker stopped again inside the castle gate. Kohlhaas asked the amount of security, in money or in articles, that he would have to leave in pledge for the blacks. The steward muttered in his beard that he might just as well leave the blacks themselves. "Of course," said the castellan. "That's just the thing; as soon as he has the pass he can come and fetch his horses whenever he pleases." Taken aback by such a shameless demand, Kohlhaas told the Junker, who was wrapping the skirts of his doublet about his shivering body, that what he wanted to do was to sell the blacks; but just then a gust of wind blew a splatter of rain and hail through the gate and the Junker, to put an end to the business, called out, "If he won't give up the horses, just throw him back over the toll bar," and he went in. The horse dealer, seeing that he had no choice but to yield, decided to give in to the demand, unhitched the blacks and led them into a stable that the castellan pointed out to him. He left a groom behind with them, gave him some money, and warned him to take good care of the horses until his return; and, uncertain in his own mind whether such a law might not after all have been passed in Saxony to protect the infant occupation of horse breeding, Kohlhaas continued his journey to Leipzig, where he intended to visit the fair, with the rest of the string.

Arriving in Dresden, in one of whose suburbs he owned a house and stables that served him as headquarters for the business he did at the smaller fairs around the country, he went immediately to the chancellery, where he learned from the councilors, some of whom he knew personally, that, just as he had first suspected, the story about the pass was a fable. Kohlhaas, whom the displeased councilors provided with the written certificate he asked of them, testifying to the fact that there was no such regulation, smiled to himself at the skinny Junker's joke, although he could not for the life of him see what the point of it was; and a few weeks later, having satisfactorily disposed of his horses, he returned to Tronka Castle with no more bitterness in his heart than was inspired by the ordinary distress of the world.

The castellan made no comment on the certificate when Kohlhaas showed it to him and told the horse dealer, who asked him if he could now have his horses back, that he only needed to go down to the stables and get them. But Kohlhaas learned with dismay, even while crossing the yard, that his groom had been thrashed for his insolence, as it was called, a few days after being left behind at the castle and had been driven away. He asked the boy who gave him this news what the groom had done, and who had taken care of the horses in the meantime, but the boy said he did not know and, turning from the horse dealer, whose heart was already swollen with misgivings, he opened the stable door. The horse dealer was indescribably shocked when instead of his two sleek, well-fed blacks he saw a pair of scrawny, worn-out nags: ribs like rails on which objects could have been hung, manes and coats matted from lack of care and attention—the very image of misery in the animal kingdom! Kohlhaas, at whose sight the beasts whinnied and stirred feebly, was beside himself, and demanded to know what had happened to his animals. The boy answered that they had not suffered any harm and that they had had proper feed, too, but since it had been harvest time and there was a shortage of draft animals, they had been used a bit in the fields. Kohlhaas cursed the shameful, deliberate outrage, but, feeling how helpless he was, he stifled his fury and was getting ready to leave the robbers' nest with his horses again—for there was nothing else he could do—when the castellan, attracted by the sound of voices, appeared and asked him what the matter was.

"What's the matter!" Kohlhaas shot out. "Who gave the Junker von Tronka and his people permission to put the blacks I left here to work in the fields?" He asked if that was a decent thing to do, tried to rouse the exhausted beasts with a flick of his whip, and showed him that they did not move. The castellan, after looking at him contemptuously for a while, retorted, "Look at the brute! Shouldn't the clown thank God just to find his nags are still alive?" He asked who was expected to take care of them after the groom had run away, and if it was not right for the horses to pay for their feed by working in the fields. He ended by saying that Kohlhaas had better not try to start anything or he would call the dogs and restore order in the yard that way.

The horse dealer's heart thumped against his doublet. He wanted to pitch the good-for-nothing tub of guts into the mud and grind his heel into his copper-colored face. But his sense of justice, which was as delicate as a gold balance, still wavered; he could not be sure, before the bar of his own conscience, whether the man was really guilty of a crime; and so, swallowing his curses, he went over to the horses and silently weighed all the circumstances while unknotting their manes, then asked in a subdued voice: what was the reason for the groom's having been turned out of the castle? The castellan replied, "Because the rascal was insolent in the stable yard! Because he tried to stand in the way of a change we needed to make in the stabling and wanted us to put the mounts of two young gentlemen who came to the castle out on the high road overnight for the sake of his own two nags!" Kohlhaas would have given as much as the horses were worth to have had the groom right there so as to compare his account of things with that of the loud-mouthed castellan. He was still standing there, combing the tangles out of the blacks' manes with his fingers and wondering what to do next, when the scene suddenly changed and the Junker Wenzel von Tronka, coming home from coursing hares, galloped into the castle yard at the head of a troop of knights, grooms, and dogs. The castellan, when the Junker asked him what had happened, started right in, with the dogs' howling murderously from one side on their catching sight of the stranger and the knights' shouting them down from the other, to give the Junker a viciously distorted account of the uproar the horse dealer was making just because his pair of blacks had been exercised a bit. With a scornful laugh he said that the horse dealer even refused to recognize the horses as his own. Kohlhaas cried out, "Those are not my horses, your worship! Those are not the horses which were worth thirty gold gulden! I want my well fed and healthy horses back!"

The Junker, whose face paled for a moment, dismounted and said, "If the son of a bitch won't take his horses back, he can let things stay just as they are. Come, Günther!" he cried, "Hans, come!" while he beat the dust from his breeches with his hand; as he passed under the gate with the knights, he shouted, "Fetch some wine!" and entered the castle. Kohlhaas said he would rather call the knacker and have his horses thrown into the carrion pit than bring them back the way they were to his stables at Kohlhaasenbrück. Turning his back on the animals and leaving them where they were, he mounted his bay and, swearing he would know how to get justice for himself, rode away.

He was already galloping full tilt down the road to Dresden when the thought of the groom and what they had accused him of at the castle slowed him to a walk and, before he had gone a thousand paces, he turned his horse around and headed for Kohlhaasenbrück, intending, as seemed right and prudent to him, to hear the groom's side of the story first. For in spite of the humiliations he had suffered, a correct feeling, based on what he already knew about the imperfect state of the world, made him inclined, in case the groom were at all guilty, as the castellan claimed, to put up with the loss of his horses as being after all a just consequence. But this was disputed by an equally commendable feeling, which took deeper and deeper root the farther he rode and the more he heard at every stop about the injustices perpetrated daily against travelers at Tronka Castle, that, if the whole incident proved to have been premeditated, as seemed probable, it was his duty to the world to do everything in his power to get satisfaction for himself for the wrong done him, and a guarantee against future ones for his fellow citizens.

No sooner had he arrived at Kohlhaasenbrück, embraced his faithful wife Lisbeth, and kissed his children who were shouting with glee around his knees, than he asked after Herse the head groom: had anything been heard from him? "Oh yes, Michael dear," Lisbeth answered, "that Herse! Just imagine, the poor man turned up here about a fortnight ago, terribly beaten and bruised; so beaten, in fact, that he can't even draw a full breath. We put him to bed, where he kept coughing up blood, and after we asked him over and over again what had happened he told us a story that nobody understands. How you left him behind at Tronka Castle in charge of some horses they wouldn't let pass through there; how they had mistreated him shamefully and forced him to leave the castle; and how it had been impossible for him to bring the horses with him."

"I see," said Kohlhaas, taking off his cloak. "I suppose he is all recovered now?"

"Pretty well, except for his coughing blood. I wanted to send a groom to Tronka Castle right away to look after the horses until you got back there. Since Herse has always been an honest servant to us—in fact, more loyal than anybody else—I felt I had no right to doubt his story, especially when he had so many bruises to confirm it, and to suspect him of losing the horses in some other way. But he pleaded with me not to expect anybody to venture into that den of thieves, and to give the animals up if I didn't want to sacrifice a man's life for them."

"Is he still in bed?" asked Kohlhaas, taking off his neckerchief.

"He has been walking around the yard again," she said, "these last few days. But you will see for yourself," she went on, "that it's all quite true, and that it is another one of those outrages against strangers they have been allowing themselves lately up at Tronka Castle."

"Well, I'll have to investigate the business first," Kohlhaas replied. "Would you call him in here, Lisbeth, if he is up and around?" With these words he lowered himself into an armchair while his wife, who was delighted to see him taking things so calmly, went to fetch the groom.

"What have you been doing at Tronka Castle?" asked Kohlhaas when Herse followed Lisbeth into the room. "I can't say that I am too pleased with your conduct."

The groom's pale face showed spots of red at these words, and he was silent for a moment. Then he said, "You are quite right, sir. When I heard a child crying inside the castle, I threw a sulphur match into the Elbe that Providence had put in my pocket to burn down that robbers' nest I was chased out of, and I thought to my-self· Let God lay it in ashes with one of his lightning bolts, I won't!"

Kohlhaas was taken aback. "But how did you manage to get yourself chased out of the castle?" he asked.

"They played me a nasty trick, sir," Herse replied, wiping the sweat from his forehead. "But what's done is done and can't be undone. I wouldn't let them work the horses to death in the fields, so I said they were still young and had never really been in har-ness."

Kohlhaas, trying to hide his confusion, replied that Herse had not told the exact truth, since the horses had been in harness for a little while at the beginning of the past spring. "As you were a sort of guest at the castle," he continued, "you really might have obliged them once or twice when they needed help to bring the harvest in faster."

"But I did do that, sir," Herse said. "I thought that, as long as they were giving me such nasty looks, it wouldn't, after all, lose me the blacks, and so on the third morning I hitched them up and brought in three wagonloads of grain."

Kohlhaas, whose heart began to swell, looked down at the ground and said, "They didn't say a word about that, Herse!"

Herse swore it was so. "How was I rude?—I didn't want to yoke the horses up again when they had hardly finished their midday feeding; and when the castellan and the steward offered me free fodder if I would do it, so I could put the money you had given me for feed in my own pocket, I told them I would do something they hadn't bargained for: I turned around and walked off."

"But surely you weren't driven away from the castle for that?" said Kohlhaas.

"Mercy, no," cried the groom. "For a very wicked crime in-deed! That evening the mounts of two knights who came to Tronka Castle were led into the stable and my horses were tied to the sta-ble door. When I took the blacks from the castellan, who was tak-ing care of the quartering himself, and asked him where my ani-mals were to go now, he pointed to a pigsty knocked together out of laths and boards that was leaning against the castle wall."

"You mean," interrupted Kohlhaas, "that it was such a sorry shelter for horses that it was more like a pigsty than a stable?"

"It was a pigsty, sir," Herse replied, "really and truly a pigsty, with pigs running in and out; I couldn't stand up straight in it."

"Perhaps there was no other shelter for the blacks," Kohlhaas said. "In a way, the knights' horses had first call."

"There wasn't much room," the groom answered, letting his voice sink. "All told, there were seven knights at the castle. If it had been you, you would have had the horses moved a little closer together. I said I would look for a stable to rent in the village; but the castellan replied that he had to keep the horses under his own eyes and that I wasn't to dare take them out of the yard."

"Hm!" said Kohlhaas. "What did you say to that?"

"Since the steward said the two visitors would only be staying overnight and would be riding on the next morning, I put the horses into the pigsty. But the next day came and went without their making a move; and on the third day I heard that the gentlemen were going to stay some weeks longer at the castle."

"Well, after all, Herse," said Kohlhaas, "it wasn't as bad in the pigsty as it seemed to you when you first poked your nose into it."

"That's true," the groom answered. "After I had swept the place out a little, it wasn't so bad. I gave the girl a groschen to put her pigs somewhere else. And by taking the roof boards off at dawn and laying them on again at night, I arranged it so that the horses could stand upright during the day. So there they stood, their heads poking out of the roof like geese in a coop, and looked around for Kohlhaasenbrück or wherever life was better."

"Well then," Kohlhaas said, "why in the world did they drive you away?"

"Sir, I'll tell you," the groom replied. "Because they wanted to get rid of me. Because, as long as I was there, they couldn't work the horses to death. In the yard, in the servants' hall, everywhere, they made ugly faces at me; and because I thought to myself, 'You can pull your jaws down till you dislocate them, for all I care,' they picked a quarrel and threw me out."

"But the pretext!" cried Kohlhaas. "They must have had some pretext!"

"Oh of course," answered Herse, "the best imaginable! The second day after we had moved into the pigsty, that evening I took the horses, which had got mucky in spite of everything, and started to ride them over to the horse pond. Just as I was passing through the castle gate and began to turn off, I heard the castellan and the steward clattering after me out of the servants' hall with men, dogs, and sticks, shouting, 'Stop thief! Catch the rogue!' as if they were possessed. The gatekeeper blocked my way; and when I asked him and the wild mob running after me, 'What the devil's the matter?'—'What's the matter!' answered the castellan, and he caught my two blacks by the bridle. 'Where do you think you are going with those horses?' he asked, grabbing me by the front of my shirt. 'Where am I going?' I said. 'Thunder and lightning! I'm riding over to the horse pond. Did you think I——?'—'To the horse pond!' the castellan shouted. 'I'll teach you, you rogue, to go swimming along the high road to Kohlhaasenbrück!' And with a vicious jerk he and the steward, who had caught me by the leg, flung me down from the horse so that I measured my full length in the mud. 'Murder!' I cried. 'There are harness and blankets and a bundle of laundry belonging to me in the stable!' But while the steward led the horses away, he and the grooms jumped on me with feet and whips and clubs, leaving me half dead on the ground outside the castle gate. When I cried, 'The robbers! Where are they going with my horses?' and got to my feet, the castellan screamed, 'Out of the castle yard, you! Sick him, Caesar! Sick him, Hunter! Sick him, Spitz!' And a pack of more than twelve dogs rushed at me. Then I tore something from the fence, a picket maybe, I can't remember, and stretched out three dogs dead on the ground at my feet; but just when I had to fall back because of the terrible bites I had gotten, there was a shrill whistle: 'Whee—oo!' the dogs scurried back to the yard, the gate slammed shut, the bolt shot home, and I fell down unconscious on the road.''

Kohlhaas, white in the face, said with forced shrewdness, "Didn't you really want to escape, Herse?" And when the latter, with a deep blush, stared at the ground, the horse dealer said, "Confess it! You didn't like it one bit in the pigsty; you thought to yourself how much better it was, after all, in the stable at Kohlhaasenbrück."

"Thunder!" cried Herse. "Harness and blankets I left behind in the pigsty, and a bundle of laundry, I tell you! Wouldn't I have taken along the three gulden I wrapped in a red silk neck cloth and hid behind the manger? Blazes, hell, and the devil! When you talk like that, I feel again like lighting that sulphur match I threw away!"

"All right, never mind," said the horse dealer. "No harm meant. Look, I believe every word you've told me; and if the matter ever comes up, I am ready to take holy communion myself on the truth of what you say. I am sorry things haven't gone better for you in my service. Go back to bed now, Herse, won't you, let them bring you a bottle of wine, and console yourself: justice shall be done you!" And he stood up, jotted down a list of the things the head groom had left behind in the pigsty, noted the value of each, also asked him what he estimated the cost of his doctoring at, and, after shaking hands with him once more, dismissed him.

Then he told Lisbeth, his wife, the full story of what had happened, explained its meaning, said his mind was made up to seek justice at the law, and had the satisfaction of seeing that she supported his purpose heart and soul. For she said that many other travelers, perhaps less patient ones than himself, would pass by that castle; that it was doing God's work to put a stop to such disorders; and that she would manage to get together the money he needed to pay the expenses of the lawsuit. Kohlhaas called her his brave wife, spent that day and the next very happily with her and the children and, as soon as his business permitted, set out for Dresden to lay his complaint before the court.

There, with the help of a lawyer he knew, he drew up a list of charges which described in detail the outrage the Junker Wenzel von Tronka had committed against him and his groom Herse, and which petitioned the court to punish the knight according to the law, to restore his, Kohlhaas', horses to him in their original condition, and to have him and his groom compensated for the damages they had sustained. His case seemed an open-and-shut one. The fact that his horses had been illegally detained pretty well decided everything else; and even if one supposed that they had taken sick by sheer accident, the horse dealer's demand that they should be returned to him in sound condition would still have been a just one. Nor did Kohlhaas, as he looked about the capital, lack for friends who promised to give his case their active support; the large trade he did in horses had made him acquainted with the most important men of the country, and his honest dealing had won him their good will. He dined cheerfully a number of times with his lawyer, who was himself a man of consequence; left a sum of money with him to defray the legal costs; and, fully reassured by the latter as to the outcome of the suit, returned, in a few weeks' time, to his wife Lisbeth in Kohlhaasenbrück. Yet months passed and the year was nearing its close before he even received an official notice from Saxony about the suit he had instituted there, let alone any final decision. After he had petitioned the court several more times, he sent a confidential letter to his lawyer asking what was responsible for the excessive delay, and learned that the Dresden court, upon the intervention of an influential person, had dismissed his suit out of hand.

When the horse dealer wrote back in astonishment, asking what the explanation for this was, the lawyer reported that the Junker Wenzel von Tronka was related to two young noblemen, Hinz and Kunz von Tronka, one of whom was Cupbearer to the sovereign's person, and the other actually Chamberlain. He advised Kohlhaas to waste no more time with court proceedings, but to go to Tronka Castle where the horses still were and try to get them back himself; gave him to understand that the Junker, who was just then stopping in the capital, had apparently left orders with his people to turn them over to him; and closed with a request to be excused from acting any further in the matter in case Kohlhaas was still not satisfied.

The horse dealer happened to be in Brandenburg at this time, where the Governor of the city, Heinrich von Geusau, within whose jurisdiction Kohlhaasenbrück lay, was just then occupied in setting up a number of charitable institutions for the sick and the poor, out of a considerable fund that had come to the city. He was especially concerned with roofing over and enclosing a mineral spring for the use of invalids, which was located in one of the nearby villages and which was thought to have greater healing powers than it subsequently proved to possess; and as Kohlhaas had transacted a good deal of business with him during his stay at court and therefore was acquainted with him, the Governor allowed Herse, who ever since those unhappy days at Tronka Castle had suffered from pains in the chest when breathing, to try the curative effects of the little spring. It so happened that the Governor was present at the edge of the basin in which Kohlhaas had placed Herse, giving certain directions, just when a messenger from Lisbeth put into the horse dealer's hands the discouraging letter from his lawyer in Dresden. The Governor, while he was talking to the doctor, noticed Kohlhaas drop a tear on the letter he had received and read; he walked over to Kohlhaas with friendly sympathy and asked him what the bad news was; and when the horse dealer said nothing but handed him the letter, the worthy gentleman clapped him on the shoulder, for he knew the outrageous wrong done Kohlhaas at Tronka Castle as a result of which Herse lay sick right there, perhaps for the rest of his life, and told him not to be discouraged, he would help him to get satisfaction! That evening, when the horse dealer waited upon him in his castle as he had been bidden, he advised him that all he had to do was to draw up a petition to the Elector of Brandenburg briefly describing the incident, enclose the lawyer's letter, and solicit, on account of the violence done him on Saxon territory, the protection of the sovereign. He promised to include the petition in another packet that he was just sending to the Elector, who, if circumstances at all permitted, would unfailingly intervene on his behalf with the Elector of Saxony; and nothing more than this was needed to obtain justice for Kohlhaas from the Dresden court, in spite of all the tricks of the Junker and his henchmen. Overjoyed, Kohlhaas thanked the Governor earnestly for this fresh proof of his good will; said he was only sorry he had not begun proceedings in Berlin right off, without bothering with Dresden; and after duly drawing up the complaint at the chancellery of the municipal court and delivering it to the Governor, he returned to Kohlhaasenbrück feeling more confident than ever before about the outcome of his case. But only a few weeks later he was troubled to learn, from a magistrate who was going to Potsdam on business for the City Governor, that the Elector of Brandenburg had turned the petition over to his Chancellor, Count Kallheim, and the latter, instead of directly requesting the Dresden court to investigate the outrage and punish the culprits, as would have seemed the appropriate course, had first, as a preliminary step, applied to the Junker von Tronka for further information. The magistrate, who stopped in his carriage outside Kohlhaas' house, had apparently been instructed to deliver this message to the horse dealer, but he could not satisfactorily answer the latter's anxious question as to why such a procedure was being followed. He added only that the Governor sent Kohlhaas word to be patient; he seemed in a hurry to be on his way; and not until the very end of the short interview did the horse dealer gather from some remarks he let fall that Count Kallheim was connected by marriage with the house of Tronka.

Kohlhaas, who could no longer take any pleasure either in his horse breeding or his house and farm, hardly even in his wife and children, waited with gloomy forebodings for the new month; and, just as he had expected, Herse came back from Brandenburg at the end of this time, his health a little better for the baths, bringing a rather lengthy resolution accompanied by a letter from the City Governor that said: he was sorry he could do nothing about his case for him; he was sending along a resolution of the Chancery of State that was meant for Kohlhaas; and his advice to him was to go and fetch the horses he had left at Tronka Castle and forget about everything else. The resolution read as follows: that according to the Dresden court report, he was an idle, quarrelsome fellow; the Junker with whom he had left his horses was not keeping them from him in any way; let him send to the castle and take them away, or at least inform the Junker where to send them to him; in any case, he was not to trouble the Chancery of State with such petty quarrels. Kohlhaas, who cared nothing about the horses themselves—his pain would have been just as great if it had been a question of a pair of dogs—was consumed with rage when he received this letter. Every time he heard a noise in the yard, he looked toward the gate, with the unpleasantest feelings of anticipation that had ever stirred in his breast, to see whether the Junker's men had come to give him back, perhaps even with an apology, his starved and worn-out horses—the only instance in which his soul, well-disciplined though it was by the world, was utterly unprepared for something it fully expected to happen. A short time after, however, he learned from an acquaintance, who had traveled the highroad, that his animals were still being worked in the fields at Tronka Castle, now as before, just like the Junker's other horses; and through the pain he felt at seeing the world in such a state of monstrous disorder flashed a thrill of inward satisfaction at knowing that henceforth he would be at peace with himself.

He invited a bailiff, who was his neighbor and who for a long time had had the plan of enlarging his estate by buying property adjoining it, to come and see him and asked him, after the visitor was seated, how much he would give him for all the property Kohlhaas owned in Brandenburg and Saxony, house and farm, immovable or otherwise, the whole lot of it together. His wife, Lisbeth, turned pale at these words. Turning around and picking up her youngest child who was playing on the floor behind her, she shot a deathly glance past the red cheeks of the little boy, who was tugging at her neckerchief, at the horse dealer and the sheet of paper in his hand. The bailiff stared at him in surprise and asked what had put such a strange notion into his head all of a sudden; to which the horse dealer replied, with as much cheerfulness as he could muster: that the idea of selling his farm on the banks of the Havel was not, after all, an entirely new one; the two of them had often discussed the matter together in the past; his house in the outskirts of Dresden was, in comparison with it, just something thrown in that they could forget about; in short, if the bailiff would do as he wished him to and take over both pieces of property, he was ready to close the contract with him. He added, with rather forced humor, that Kohlhaasenbrück was, after all, not the world; there might be purposes in life compared to which that of being a good father to his family was an inferior and unworthy one; in short, he must tell him that his soul aimed at great things, about which he would perhaps be hearing shortly. The bailiff, reassured by these words, said jokingly to Kohlhaas' wife, who was kissing her child over and over again, "Surely he won't insist on being paid right away!" laid his hat and stick which he had been holding between his knees on the table, and took the sheet of paper from the horse dealer's hand to read it over. Kohlhaas, moving his chair closer to him, explained that it was a contingent bill of sale that he had drawn up himself, with a four-weeks' right of cancellation; showed him how nothing was lacking but their signatures and the insertion of the actual purchase price, as well as the amount of forfeit Kohlhaas would agree to pay in case he withdrew from the contract within the four weeks' period; and again urged the bailiff good-humoredly to make an offer, assuring him that he would be reasonable as to the amount and easy as to the terms. His wife marched up and down the room, her bosom heaving with such violence that the kerchief at which the boy had been tugging threatened to come off her shoulders. The bailiff observed that he really had no way of judging how much the Dresden property was worth; whereupon Kohlhaas pushed some letters over to him that he had exchanged with the seller at the time of purchase, and answered that he put it at one hundred gold gulden, though the letters would show that it had cost him almost half as much again. The bailiff reread the bill of sale and found that it gave him the usual right, as buyer, to withdraw from the contract, too, and he said, with his mind already half made up, that of course he would not have any use for the stud horses in his stables; when Kohlhaas replied that he had no intention of parting with the horses, nor with some weapons hanging in the armory, the bailiff hemmed and hawed and at last he repeated an offer—a paltry one indeed, considering the value of the property—that he had made him once before, half in jest and half in earnest, when they were out walking together. Kohlhaas pushed pen and ink over for him to sign. The bailiff, who could not believe his senses, again asked him if he were serious; when the horse dealer answered, a little testily: did he think he was only joking with him, the former, with a very serious face, finally took up the pen and signed; however, he crossed out the clause concerning the forfeit payable by the seller if he should withdraw from the bargain; promised to lend Kohlhaas one hundred gold gulden against a mortgage on the Dresden property, which he absolutely refused to buy from him; and said that Kohlhaas was perfectly free to change his mind at any time within the next two months. The horse dealer, touched by his behavior, warmly shook his hand; and after they had agreed to a main stipulation, which was that a fourth part of the purchase price should be paid immediately in cash and the balance into the Hamburg bank in three months' time, Kohlhaas called for wine in order to celebrate the happy conclusion of their bargain. When the maidservant entered with the wine bottles, he asked her to tell Sternbald, the groom, to saddle his chestnut horse; he meant, he announced, to ride to the capital, where he had some business to attend to; and he let it be understood that in a short time, after he had returned, he would be able to talk more frankly about what, for the present, he must keep to himself. Then, pouring out the wine, he asked about the Poles and the Turks who were just then at war; engaged the bailiff in all sorts of political conjectures on the subject; drank once more to the success of their business; and showed the bailiff to the door.

When the bailiff had left the room, Lisbeth fell on her knees in front of her husband. "If you have any affection for me," she cried, "for me and for the children I have borne you, if you haven't already cast us out of your heart, for what reason I don't know, then tell me what the meaning of all this is!"

"Nothing, my dear wife," said Kohlhaas, "that you need to get upset about, as matters stand at present. I have received a resolution in which I am told that my complaint against the Junker Wenzel von Tronka is mere quarrelsomeness and mischief-making. And as there must be some misunderstanding here, I have decided to present my complaint again, in person, to the sovereign himself."

"But why do you want to sell your house?" she cried, rising with a gesture of despair.

The horse dealer took her gently in his arms and said, "Because, dearest Lisbeth, I will not go on living in a country where they won't protect me in my rights. I'd rather be a dog, if people are going to kick me, than a man! I am sure my wife thinks about this just as I do."

"How do you know," she asked frantically, "that they won't protect you in your rights? If you go to the Elector humbly with your petition, as it is proper that you should, how do you know that it will be tossed aside or that his answer will be to refuse you a hearing?"

"Very well," Kohlhaas said, "if my fears are groundless, neither has my house been sold yet. The Elector himself, I know, is a just man; and if I can only slip past those around him and speak to his own person, I don't doubt that I shall get justice for myself and come happily home again to you and my old trade before the week is out. And then I should only want to stay with you," he added, kissing her, "till the end of my life! However," he continued, "it is best for me to be prepared for everything; and therefore I should like you, if possible, to go away for a while with the children and visit your aunt in Schwerin, whom you have been wanting to visit for some time anyhow."

"What!" exclaimed his wife. "I'm to go to Schwerin? Across the border with the children to my aunt in Schwerin?" And terror made the words stick in her throat.

"Certainly," Kohlhaas said. "And, if possible, right away, since I don't want to be worrying about other things while I am busy with the steps I mean to take in my case."

"Oh, now I understand you!" she exclaimed. "All you want now are arms and horses, whoever wants the rest can have it!" And she turned away from him, threw herself into a chair, and burst into tears.

"Dearest Lisbeth," Kohlhaas said in surprise, "what are you saying? I have been blessed by God with wife and children and worldly goods; am I to wish it were otherwise for the first time today?" He sat down next to her when she flushed at these words, and she threw her arms around his neck. "Tell me," he said, smoothing the hair away from her forehead, "what shall I do? Shall I give up my suit? Shall I go over to Tronka Castle, beg the knight to give me back my horses, and mount and ride them home to you?"

Lisbeth did not dare to say, "Yes! Yes! Yes!"—weeping, she shook her head, hugged him fiercely to her, and covered his breast with fervent kisses.

"Well then," Kohlhaas cried, "if you feel that justice must be done me if I am to continue in my trade, then don't deny me the freedom I need to get it!" And, standing up, he ordered the groom, who had come to report that the chestnut was saddled and ready, to see to it that the bays were harnessed the next day to take his wife to Schwerin. Lisbeth said she had just thought of something. Rising and wiping the tears from her eyes, she asked her husband, who had sat down at his desk, if he would entrust the petition to her and let her go to Berlin in his stead and hand it to the Elector. Kohlhaas, moved by this change in her for more reasons than one, drew her down on his lap and said, "My darling wife, that is hardly possible. The sovereign is surrounded by a great many people, anybody coming near him is exposed to all sorts of annoyances."

Lisbeth replied that in nine cases out of ten it was easier for a woman to approach him than a man. "Give me the petition," she repeated, "and if all you want is an assurance that it will reach his hands, I guarantee he'll receive it!" Kohlhaas, who had had many proofs of her courage as well as her intelligence, asked her how she proposed to go about it; whereupon, looking shamefacedly at the ground, she answered that the castellan of the Elector's palace had courted her in earlier days, when he had served in Schwerin; that it was true he was married now and the father of several children, but that she was still not entirely forgotten—in short, let him leave it to her to make use of this as well as many other circumstances, which it would take too long to describe. Kohlhaas kissed her happily, said that her proposal was accepted, advised her that all she needed to do to speak to the sovereign inside the palace itself was to lodge with the wife of the castellan, gave her the petition, ordered the bays harnessed up, and, bundling her into the wagon, sent her off with his faithful groom, Sternbald.

But of all the unsuccessful steps that he had taken in his case, this journey was the most unfortunate. For only a few days later Sternbald entered the courtyard again, leading the wagon at a walk, inside of which the horse dealer's wife lay prostrate with a dangerous contusion of the chest. Kohlhaas, white-faced, came running over, but could get no coherent account of the cause of the accident. The castellan, according to the groom, had not been at home, so they had had to put up at an inn near the palace; Lisbeth had left the inn the next morning, ordering the groom to remain with the horses; and she had not returned until evening, in her present condition. Apparently she had pressed forward too boldly toward the sovereign's person and, through no fault of his, only because of the brutal zeal of a bodyguard, she had received a blow on the chest from a lance butt. At least that was what the people had said who brought her back unconscious to the inn toward evening; for she herself could hardly speak because of the blood flowing from her mouth. Afterwards a knight came to get the petition from her. Sternbald said he had wanted to jump on a horse and gallop home immediately with the news of the accident; but in spite of all the remonstrances of the surgeon called in to attend her, she had insisted on being carried back to her husband at Kohlhaasenbrück without sending word ahead. Kohlhaas found her more dead than alive from the trip, and put her to bed where, gasping painfully for breath, she lived a few days longer. They tried in vain to bring her back to consciousness so as to get some light on what had happened; she lay in bed staring straight in front of her, her eyes already dim, and would not answer. Only just before her death did she recover consciousness. For when a minister of the Lutheran faith (which, following the example of her husband, she had embraced in what was then its infancy) was standing beside her bed, reading, in a loud voice which mixed pathos and solemnity, a chapter of the Bible, she suddenly looked darkly up at him, took the Bible from his hand as if there were no need to read to her from it, turned page after page, apparently looking for a passage; then her forefinger pointed out this verse to Kohlhaas, who was sitting at her bedside: "Forgive your enemies; do good to them that hate you." As she did so, she squeezed his hand with a look full of tender feeling, and died.

Kohlhaas thought: "May God never forgive me the way I forgive the Junker!" kissed her with the tears streaming down his cheeks, closed her eyes, and left the room. Taking the hundred gold gulden that the bailiff had already sent him for the stables in Dresden, he ordered such a funeral as became a princess better than a horse dealer's wife: an oak coffin with heavy brass mountings, cushions of silk with gold and silver tassels, and a grave eight ells deep, walled with fieldstone and mortar. He himself stood beside the tomb with his youngest child in his arms and looked on at the work. On the day of the funeral the corpse, white as snow, was laid out in a room that he had had hung with black cloth. The minister had just finished speaking with great feeling at the bier, when the sovereign's answer to the petition presented him by the dead woman was delivered to Kohlhaas: he was commanded to fetch the horses home from Tronka Castle and let the matter drop, on pain of imprisonment. Kohlhaas stuffed the letter in his pocket and had the coffin carried out to the wagon. As soon as the grave mound was raised, a cross planted on it, and the funeral guests gone, he flung himself down once more before his wife's now empty bed, then set about the business of his revenge. He sat down and drew up a decree that, by virtue of the authority inborn in him, sentenced the Junker von Tronka, within three days of its receipt, to bring back to Kohlhaasenbrück the pair of blacks he had taken from him and ruined with hard work in the fields, and to fatten them with his own hands in Kohlhaas's stables. He sent the decree to the Junker by mounted messenger, instructing the man to turn around and come right back to Kohlhaasenbrück as soon as he had delivered it. When the three days passed without the horses being returned, Kohlhaas called over Herse; told him about his ordering the nobleman to fatten the blacks; and asked him two things: would he ride with him to Tronka Castle and fetch the Junker out; and would he be willing, after they had brought him to Kohlhaasenbrück, to apply the whip to him in the stables in case he should be slow about carrying out the terms of the decree? When Herse, as soon as he understood what was meant, shouted exultantly: "Sir, this very day!" and, throwing his hat in the air, promised that he would plait a thong with ten knots to teach the Junker how to currycomb, Kohlhaas sold the house and sent the children over the border in a wagon; when darkness fell, he called the other grooms together, seven in number, every one of them as true as gold; gave them arms and horses, and set out for Tronka Castle.

With this handful of men, at nightfall of the third day, he attacked the castle, riding down the tollkeeper and gateman as they stood in conversation in the gateway, and while Herse, amid the sudden bursting into flames of all the barracks in the castle yard, raced up the winding stairs of the castle keep and with thrusts and blows fell upon the castellan and the steward, who were sitting half undressed over a game, Kohlhaas dashed into the castle in search of the Junker Wenzel. In such fashion does the angel of judgment descend from heaven. The Junker, who was in the middle of reading aloud the decree sent him by the horse dealer, amid uproarious laughter, to a crowd of young friends staying with him, had no sooner heard the latter's voice in the castle yard than he turned pale as a corpse, cried out, "Brothers, save yourselves!" and vanished. Kohlhaas, entering the hall, grabbed hold of a Junker Hans von Tronka as the latter came at him and flung him into a corner of the room with such force that his brains splattered over the stone floor, and asked, as the other knights, who had drawn their swords, were being routed and overpowered by his men: where was the Junker Wenzel von Tronka? But, seeing that the stunned men knew nothing, he kicked open the doors of the two rooms leading into the castle wings, searched up and down the rambling structure and, finding no one, went down, cursing, into the castle yard to post guards at the exits. In the meantime, dense clouds of smoke were billowing skywards from the castle and its wings, which had caught fire from the barracks, and, while Sternbald and three other men were busy heaping up everything that was not nailed down tight and heaving it out among the horses for plunder, the corpses of the castellan and the steward, with those of their wives and children, came hurtling out of the open windows of the castle keep accompanied by Herse's exultant shouts. Kohlhaas, as he descended the castle stairs, was met by the Junker's gouty old housekeeper who threw herself at his feet; stopping on the stair, he asked her where the Junker Wenzel von Tronka was; and when she answered, in a faint and trembling voice, that she thought he had taken refuge in the chapel, he called over two men with torches, had the door broken down with crowbars and axes (since the keys had vanished), turned altars and benches upside down, and found again, to his furious disappointment, no trace of the Junker. As Kohlhaas emerged from the chapel, he happened to meet a stable boy, one of the castle's servants, running to bring the Junker's chargers out of a large stone stable that was menaced by the flames. Kohlhaas, who that very instant spied his two blacks in a little thatched shed, asked the boy why he did not save them; and when the latter, sticking the key in the stable door, said the shed was already in flames, Kohlhaas snatched the key out of the lock, flung it over the wall, and, raining blows thick as hail on the boy with the flat of his sword, chased him into the burning shed, amid the terrible laughter of the men around him, and forced him to save the horses. But when the fellow reappeared, pale with fright, leading the horses in his hand a few moments before the shed collapsed behind him, he found that Kohlhaas had left; and when he went over to the grooms in the castle square and asked the horse dealer, who kept turning his back on him, what he should do with the animals now, Kohlhaas suddenly drew his foot back so menacingly that if he had delivered the kick it would have meant his end; mounted his bay without answering him, stationed himself in the castle gate, and in silence waited for daybreak while his men went on with what they were doing. Morning found everything except the walls of the castle burned to the ground, and not a soul left in it but Kohlhaas and his seven men. He dismounted from his horse and in the bright sunlight that bathed every nook and cranny of the castle yard he searched the place once more, and when he had to admit, hard as it was for him, that his attempt on the castle had failed, with a heart full of pain and grief he sent out Herse and some grooms to learn in which direction the Junker had fled. He was especially anxious about a rich nunnery called Erlabrunn that stood on the banks of the Mulde and whose Abbess, Antonia von Tronka, was known in the neighborhood for a pious, charitable, and saintly woman; for it seemed only too probable to the unhappy Kohlhaas that the Junker, lacking every necessity as he did, had taken refuge there, since the Abbess was his own aunt and had been his instructress in his early years. Kohlhaas, after informing himself about this circumstance, mounted the stairs of the castle keep, inside of which a habitable room still remained, and drew up a so-called "Kohlhaas Manifesto," in which he called upon the country to give no aid or comfort to the Junker Wenzel von Tronka, against whom he was waging righteous war, but instead required every inhabitant, including relatives and friends, to hand him over forthwith, on pain of death and the certain destruction by fire of everything they called their own. He had this manifesto scattered throughout the countryside by travelers and strangers; he even gave a copy of it to his groom Waldmann, with exact orders about delivering it into Lady Antonia's hands at Erlabrunn. Then he had a talk with some of the Tronka Castle menials who were dissatisfied with the Junker's service and, drawn by the prospect of plunder, wished to enter his; armed them like foot soldiers with crossbows and daggers and taught them how to ride behind the mounted grooms; and, after turning all the spoils his men had collected into money and dividing it among them, he rested from his sorry labors for an hour or two inside the castle gate.

Toward midday Herse returned and confirmed what Kohlhaas' heart, always ready to expect the worst, had already told him: namely, that the Junker was to be found at the convent of Erlabrunn with the old Lady Antonia von Tronka, his aunt. Apparently he had escaped through a door in the castle's back wall and down a narrow, low-roofed stone stairway that led to some boats on the Elbe. At all events, reported Herse, he had turned up at midnight, in a skiff without rudder or oars, in a village on the Elbe—to the astonishment of the inhabitants, whom the burning of Tronka Castle had brought together out of their houses—and had gone on from there to Erlabrunn in a village cart.

Kohlhaas heaved a deep sigh on hearing this; he asked whether the horses had been fed and, on being told yes, he commanded his troop to mount and in three hours' time stood before Erlabrunn. As he entered the cloister yard with his band, amid the mutterings of a distant storm along the horizon, holding aloft torches he had had lighted outside the place, and his groom Waldmann came up to report that the manifesto had been duly delivered, Kohlhaas saw the Abbess and the Cloister Warden, in agitated conversation, come out under the portal of the convent; and while the latter, the Warden, a little old man with snow-white hair, shot fierce glances at Kohlhaas as his armor was being strapped on and called out bravely to the servants around him to ring the alarm bell, the former, the Canoness, white as a sheet and holding a silver image of the crucified Christ in her hand, came down the slope and prostrated herself with all her nuns before Kohlhaas' horse. Kohlhaas, as Herse and Sternbald overpowered the Warden, who had no sword, and were leading him off a prisoner among the horses, asked her where the Junker Wenzel von Tronka was, and, when she unfastened a great ring of keys from her girdle and said, "In Wittenberg, good Kohlhaas!" adding in a quavering voice, "Fear God and do no evil!"—the horse dealer, pitched back into the hell of his unslaked thirst for revenge, wheeled his horse and was about to cry, "Set the place on fire!" when a huge lightning bolt struck close beside him. Turning his horse back, Kohlhaas asked her if she had received his manifesto; the lady replied in a faint, barely audible voice, "Just a moment ago!"—"When?"—"Two hours after my nephew, the Junker, departed, so help me God!"—And when Waldmann, the groom, to whom Kohlhaas turned with a lowering glance, stuttered out a confirmation of this, saying that the Mulde's waters, swollen by the rains, had prevented his arriving until a few moments ago, Kohlhaas collected himself; a sudden fierce downpour of rain, sweeping across the pavement of the yard and extinguishing the torches, loosened the knot of anguish in his unhappy breast; lifting his hat curtly to the Abbess, he wheeled his horse about, dug his spurs in, and crying, "Follow me, brothers, the Junker is in Wittenberg!" he galloped out of the cloister.

When night fell, he halted at an inn on the highroad, where he had to stop a day to rest his weary horses, and as it was clear to him that with a troop of ten—for that was his strength now—he could not challenge so large a place as Wittenberg, he composed a second manifesto, in which he briefly recounted what had happened to him and summoned "all good Christians," as he put it, to whom he "solemnly promised bounty money and other emoluments of war, to take sides with him against the Junker von Tronka as the common enemy of all Christians." In another manifesto, issued shortly after, he called himself "a free lord of the Empire and the world, owing allegiance to none but God"—a species of morbid and misdirected fanaticism, for which the clink of his money and the prospect of plunder nevertheless procured him a crowd of recruits from among the rabble whom the peace with Poland had turned out of service: and, in fact, he had some thirty-odd men behind him when he crossed back to the right side of the Elbe with the intention of burning Wittenberg to the ground. Horses and men camped under the roof of a tumble-down brick kiln, in the solitude of a dark woods then surrounding the place, and no sooner had he learned from Sternbald, whom Kohlhaas sent into the city in disguise with the manifesto, that it was already known to the people there, than he rode out with his band on the eve of Whitsuntide and set the city afire at different spots simultaneously while the townspeople lay fast asleep. While his men were plundering the suburbs, Kohlhaas stuck a notice up on the door post of the church saying that he, Kohlhaas, had set the city afire, and, if the Junker were not surrendered to him, he would raze the place so thoroughly that, as he put it, he would not have to hunt behind any walls to find him.

The terror of the inhabitants at this unheard-of outrage was indescribable; and no sooner had the fire, which luckily on that rather still summer night burned down no more than nineteen buildings (among them, however, one church) been partly extinguished toward morning, than the elderly Sheriff, Otto von Gorgas, dispatched a company of fifty men to capture the raging maniac. But the captain in command, whose name was Gerstenberg, managed things so badly that the whole expedition, instead of crushing Kohlhaas, only helped him to acquire a formidable military reputation: for when the captain split his force into squads, thinking to draw a ring around Kohlhaas and crush him, the latter, keeping his troop together, attacked his opponent at separate points and defeated him piecemeal, and by the evening of the following day not a man of the whole force on which the hopes of the country had been set stood against him in the field. Kohlhaas, who had lost a number of men in this encounter, again set fire to the city the next morning, his murderous efforts working so well this time that a great many houses and almost all the barns in Wittenberg's outskirts were burned to the ground. Posting his familiar manifesto again, this time on the corner walls of the City Hall itself, he appended to it an account of the utter defeat of Captain von Gerstenberg, whom the Sheriff had sent against him. The Sheriff was enraged by this display of defiance and placed himself with several knights at the head of a troop of one hundred and fifty men. At the Junker Wenzel von Tronka's written request, he gave the latter a guard to protect him against the violence of the people, who absolutely insisted on his being sent out of the city; and after he had posted sentinels in all the neighboring villages as well as on the city walls, to guard against a surprise attack, he sallied out himself on St. Jervis' Day to capture the dragon that was devastating the land. The horse dealer was sharp enough to give this force the slip; and after clever marching on his part, had drawn the Sheriff five leagues away from the city, where by various maneuvers Kohlhaas fooled him into thinking that he meant to withdraw into Brandenburg because of his opponent's superior force, he suddenly wheeled about at nightfall of the third day and made a forced march back to Wittenberg and set fire to the town a third time. Herse, who slipped into the city in disguise, was the one who carried out this terrible feat; and, because of the brisk north wind blowing, the fire spread so rapidly that in less than three hours' time forty-two houses, two churches, several convents and schools, and the Sheriff's own building were heaps of ashes.

The Sheriff, who at daybreak believed that his adversary was in Brandenburg, marched back as fast as he could when he learned what had happened, to find the city in a general uproar; people by the thousands were besieging the Junker's house, which had been barricaded with heavy timbers and posts, and were shrieking at the top of their voices, demanding that he be sent away. Two burgomasters named Jenkens and Otto, present in their official robes at the head of the assembled Town Council, tried in vain to persuade the crowd that they must wait for the return of a courier who had been dispatched to the President of the Chancery of State to seek permission for the Junker's removal to Dresden, where the knight himself had many reasons for wishing to go; but the unreasoning mob, armed with pikes and staves, paid no attention to their words and, after roughly handling some councilors who were demanding that vigorous measures should be taken, were on the point of storming the house and leveling it to the ground when the Sheriff, Otto von Gorgas, rode into the city at the head of his troop of horse. This worthy old knight, who was accustomed to inspiring the people to respectful obedience by his mere presence, had succeeded, by way of making up for the failure of the expedition from which he was returning, in taking prisoner, right in front of the city gates, three stray members of the incendiary's band; and while the fellows were put in chains before the eyes of the crowd, he made the Town Council a shrewd speech, assuring them that he was on Kohlhaas' track and that he thought he would soon be able to bring in the incendiary himself in chains: thanks to all these reassurances, he was able to dispel to some extent the fears of the crowd and get them to accept the Junker's presence until the return of the courier from Dresden. He dismounted from his horse and, after having the posts and palisades cleared away, he entered the house, accompanied by some knights, where he found the Junker falling from one fainting fit into another while two attending physicians tried to bring him around with aromatics and stimulants; and since Sir Otto felt that this was no time to bandy words with him about the conduct he had been guilty of, he merely told the Junker, with a look of quiet contempt, that he should get dressed and follow him, for his own safety, to the knights' prison. When he appeared in the street wearing a doublet and a helmet they had put on him, with his chest half exposed on account of the difficulty he had in breathing, leaning on the arm of the Sheriff and his brother-in-law the Count von Gerschau, a shower of terrible curses fell on him. The people, whom the lansquenets had great difficulty in restraining, called him a bloodsucker, a miserable public pest, and a tormentor of men, the curse of Wittenberg and the ruin of Saxony; and, after a sorry march through the devastated streets, during which the Junker's helmet fell off several times without his missing it and was clapped back on his head by the knight walking behind him, they reached the prison at last; protected by a strong guard, he disappeared into a tower dungeon. Meanwhile the return of the courier with the Elector's resolution aroused fresh alarm in the city. For the Saxon government, to whom the citizens of Dresden had appealed directly in an urgent petition, refused to hear of the Junker's staying in the capital before the incendiary had been captured; instead, it called on the Sheriff, with all the forces at his command, to protect the Junker where he was, since he had to be somewhere; at the same time, so as to quiet their fears, it told the good city of Wittenberg that a force of five hundred men under Prince Friedrich of Meissen was already on its way to guard them from any further molestation by Kohlhaas. The Sheriff saw clearly that such a decree would never pacify the people: for not only had several small victories, which the horse dealer won outside the city, given rise to extremely disquieting rumors about the size his band had grown to, but his way of waging war in the black of night, with ruffians in disguise and with pitch, straw, and sulphur, unheard of and quite unprecedented as it was, would have baffled an even larger force than the one advancing under the Prince of Meissen. After a moment's reflection, Sir Otto decided to suppress completely the decree he had received. He merely posted a letter from the Prince of Meissen at all the street corners, announcing the latter's coming; at daybreak a covered wagon rumbled out of the courtyard of the knights' prison and took the road to Leipzig, accompanied by four heavily armed troopers who let it be known, though not in so many words, that they were bound for the Pleissenburg; and the people having thus been satisfied concerning the disaster-breeding Junker, whose whole existence seemed involved with fire and sword, the Sheriff set out with three hundred men to join forces with the Prince of Meissen.

Meanwhile Kohlhaas' force, thanks to the strange position the horse dealer had won for himself in the world, had grown to one hundred and nine men; and since he had also managed to lay hands on a store of weapons in Jessen, with which he armed his band to the teeth, he decided, on learning about the two armies bearing down on him, to march against them with the speed of the wind before they could join forces to overwhelm him. Accordingly he attacked the Prince of Meissen the very next night, surprising him near Mühlberg; however, in this battle, to his great grief, he lost Herse, who was struck down at his side by the first volley; but, furious at this loss, he gave such a drubbing to the Prince, who was unable to form his men up in the town, that the several severe wounds the latter got in the three hours' battle and the utter disorder into which his troops were thrown forced him to retreat to Dresden. Foolhardy from his victory, Kohlhaas turned back to attack the Sheriff before he learned about it, fell upon him at midday in the open country near the village of Damerow, and fought him till nightfall, suffering murderous losses, to be sure, but winning corresponding success. The next morning he would certainly have renewed the battle with the remnant of his band if the Sheriff, who had taken up a position in the Damerow churchyard, had not learned from scouts the news of the Prince's defeat at Mühlberg and therefore deemed it wiser to retreat, too, to Wittenberg, to await a more favorable opportunity. Five days after routing these two forces, Kohlhaas stood before the gates of Leipzig and set fire to the city on three sides.

In the manifesto which he scattered abroad on this occasion, he called himself "a viceroy of the Archangel Michael, come to punish with fire and sword, for the wickedness into which the whole world was sunk, all those who should take the side of the Junker in this quarrel." And from the castle at Lützen, which he had taken by surprise and in which he had established himself, he summoned the people to join with him to build a better order of things. With a kind of madness, the manifesto was signed: "Done at the Seat of Our Provisional World Government, the Arch-Castle at Lützen." It was the good luck of the Leipzigers that a steady rain falling from the skies kept the fire from spreading, and, thanks to the speedy work of the fire stations, only a few small shops around the Pleissenburg went up in flames. Nevertheless, the presence of the desperate incendiary, with his delusion that the Junker was in Leipzig, gave rise to unspeakable dismay in the city, and when a troop of one hundred and eighty horse that had been sent against him came fleeing back in rout, nothing remained for the City Council, which did not wish to jeopardize the wealth of Leipzig, but to bar the gates completely and set the citizens to standing watch day and night outside the walls. It was useless for the Council to post notices in the villages roundabout swearing the Junker was not in the Pleissenburg; the horse dealer posted his own notices insisting that he was, and if he was not in the Pleissenburg he, Kohlhaas, would anyhow act as if he were until he was told where he was. The Elector, notified by courier of Leipzig's peril, announced that he was assembling a force of two thousand men, which he would lead himself to capture Kohlhaas. He sternly rebuked Otto von Gorgas for the ambiguous and thoughtless stratagem he had used to divert the incendiary from the neighborhood of Wittenberg. But it is impossible to describe the confusion that seized all Saxony, and especially its capital, when it was learned there that a notice addressed to Kohlhaas had been posted in all the villages around Leipzig, no one knew by whom, saying: "Wenzel the Junker is with his cousins Hinz and Kunz in Dresden."

It was in these circumstances that Doctor Martin Luther, relying on the authority that his position in the world gave him, tried to get Kohlhaas, by dint of reassurances, to return within the confines of the social order; building upon an element of good in the incendiary's breast, he had a notice posted in all the cities and market towns of the Electorate which read as follows:

> Kohlhaas, you who say you are sent to wield the sword of justice, what are you doing, presumptuous man, in the madness of your blind fury, you who are yourself filled with injustice from head to foot? Because the sovereign to whom you owe obedience has denied you your rights, rights in a quarrel over a miserable possession, you rise up, God-forsaken wretch, with fire and sword and, like a wolf of the desert, descend on the peaceful community he protects. You who lead men astray with this declaration full of untruthfulness and cunning: sinner, do you think it will avail you anything before God on that day whose light shall beam into the recesses of every heart? How can you say your rights have been denied you, whose savage breast, lusting for a base private revenge, gave up all attempts to find justice after your first thoughtless efforts came to nothing? Is a bench of constables and beadles who suppress a petition that has been presented to them or withhold a judgment it is their duty to deliver—is this your supreme authority? And need I tell you, impious man, that your sovereign knows nothing about your case: what am I saying?—the sovereign you are rebelling against does not even know your name, so that one day when you come before the throne of God thinking to accuse him, he will be able to say with a serene face, "I have done this man no wrong, Lord, for my soul is a stranger to his existence." The sword you bear, I tell you, is the sword of brigandage and bloodthirstiness, you are a rebel and no soldier of the just God, and your goal on earth is the wheel and the gallows, and in the hereafter the doom that is decreed for crime and godlessness.
>
> MARTIN LUTHER
>
> Wittenberg, etc.

At the castle in Lützen, Kohlhaas was just turning over in his distraught mind a new plan for burning Leipzig—for he gave no credence to the notices posted in the villages saying that the Junker was in Dresden, since they were not signed by anybody, let alone the City Council, as he had demanded—when Sternbald and Waldmann were unpleasantly surprised to notice Luther's placard, which had been posted on the castle gate during the night. For several days the two men hoped in vain that Kohlhaas would catch sight of it himself, since they did not want to have to tell him about it; but though he came out in the evening, it was only to give a few brief commands, he was too gloomy and preoccupied to notice anything, until finally on a morning when two of his men were to hang for violating orders against looting in the neighborhood, they decided to draw it to his attention. He was just returning from the place of execution, with the pomp that he had adopted since the proclamation of his latest manifesto—a large archangelic sword was borne before him on a red leather cushion ornamented with gold tassels, while twelve men with burning torches followed after— and the people were timidly making way for him on either side, when Sternbald and Waldmann, with their swords tucked under their arms, began to march demonstratively around the pillar with the placard on it, in a way that could not fail to excite his wonder. With his hands clasped behind his back, lost in his own thoughts, Kohlhaas had reached the portal when he looked up and stopped short; perceiving the two men respectfully drawing back, he strode rapidly to the pillar with his eyes still fixed absent-mindedly on them. But who can describe what went on in his soul when he saw there the paper that accused him of injustice: signed by the dearest and most revered name he knew, the name of Martin Luther! A dark flush spread across his face. Taking off his helmet, he read the notice twice over from beginning to end; turned back among his men with an uncertain look as if he were about to say something, yet said nothing; took down the sheet from the pillar; read it through again; cried, "Waldmann, saddle my horse!" then, "Sternbald, follow me into the castle!" and disappeared inside. It needed no more than these few words to disarm him instantly, amid all the death and destruction in which he stood. He disguised himself as a Thuringian farmer; told Sternbald that very important business made it necessary for him to go to Wittenberg; turned over the command of the band in Lützen to him in the presence of the leading men; and, with a promise to be back within three days, during which time there was no fear of an attack, rode off.

In Wittenberg he put up at an inn under an assumed name, and at nightfall, wrapped in his cloak and armed with a brace of pistols picked up in the sack of Tronka Castle, he entered Luther's room. Luther, who was sitting at his desk surrounded by books and manuscripts, when he saw the stranger open the door and bolt it behind him, asked him who he was and what he wanted; and no sooner had the man, who held his hat respectfully in his hand, replied with diffident anticipation of the dread his name would arouse, that he was Michael Kohlhaas, the horse dealer, when Luther cried, "Get thee hence!" and, rising from the desk and hurrying toward a bell, he added, "Your breath is pestilence, your presence ruination!" Without stirring from the spot, Kohlhaas drew his pistol and said, "Your Reverence, if you touch that bell this pistol will stretch me lifeless at your feet! Sit down and hear what I have to say; you are safer with me than you are among the angels whose psalms you are inscribing." Luther sat down and said, "What do you want?"

"To show you you are wrong to think I am an unjust man! In your notice you told me that my sovereign knows nothing about my case: very well, get me a safe-conduct and I will go to Dresden and lay it before him."

"Impious and terrible man!" cried Luther, puzzled and at the same time reassured by these words. "Who gives you the right to attack the Junker von Tronka on the authority of your own decree and, when you cannot find him in his castle, to punish with fire and sword the entire community that shelters him?"

Kohlhaas replied, "Your Reverence, nobody from now on! A report I got from Dresden deceived me, misled me! The war I am waging against society is a crime only as long as I have not been cast out of it, as you now assure me I have not been."

"Cast out of society!" exclaimed Luther, staring at him. "What kind of crazy ideas have got hold of you? How could anyone cast you out of the community of the state in which you live? Where, indeed, as long as states have existed has there ever been a case of anybody, no matter who, being cast out of society?"

"I call that man an outcast," Kohlhaas said, clenching his fist, "who is denied the protection of the laws! For I need this protection if my peaceful calling is to prosper; yes, it is for the protection that its laws afford me and mine that I seek shelter in the community; and whoever denies me it thrusts me out among the beasts of the wilderness; he is the one—how can you deny it?—who puts into my hand the club that I defend myself with."

"Who has denied you the protection of the laws?" cried Luther.

"Didn't I write you that the sovereign to whom you addressed your complaint knows nothing about it? If state servants behind his back suppress lawsuits or otherwise make a mockery of his sacred name without his knowledge, who else but God has the right to call him to account for choosing such servants? Do you think, accursed and dreadful man, that you are entitled to judge him for it?"

"Very well," Kohlhaas replied, "if the sovereign has not cast me out of the community under his protection, I will return to it. Get me, I repeat, a safe-conduct to Dresden and I will disperse the band I have collected in the castle at Lützen and again lay my rejected complaint before the courts of the land." Luther, looking annoyed, shuffled the papers that were lying on his desk and made no reply. He was irritated by the defiant attitude this singular man took toward the state; and after thinking about the sentence Kohlhaas had passed on the Junker from Kohlhaasenbrück, he asked him what he wanted from the Dresden court. Kohlhaas answered, "Punishment of the Junker according to the law; restoration of my horses to their previous condition; and compensation for the damages that I as well as my man Herse, who fell at Mühlberg, suffered from the violence done us."

"Compensation for damages!" Luther cried. "You have borrowed by the thousands, from Jews and Christians, on notes and securities, to meet the expenses of your private revenge. Shall all that be counted in the final reckoning, too?"

"God forbid!" said Kohlhaas. "I don't ask back my house and farm and wealth, any more than the cost of my wife's funeral! Herse's old mother will present a bill for her son's medical costs, as well as a list of those things which he lost at Tronka Castle; and the government can have an expert estimate the loss I suffered by not selling the black horses."

Luther said, "Mad, incomprehensible, and terrible fellow!" and looked at him. "Now that your sword has taken the most ferocious revenge imaginable upon the Junker, what makes you insist on a judgment which, if it is finally pronounced, will weigh so lightly on him?"

Kohlhaas answered, as a tear rolled down his cheek, "Your Reverence, that judgment has cost me my wife; Kohlhaas means to show the world that she perished in no unrighteous quarrel. You yield to me in this point and let the court pronounce its judgment, and I will yield to you in all the other disputed points that come up."

Luther said, "Look here, what you are asking is only right, unless the circumstances are different from what the common report says they are; and if you had only managed to have your suit decided by the sovereign before you took your revenge in your own hands, I don't doubt that every one of your demands would have been granted. But all things considered, wouldn't you have done better to have pardoned the Junker for your Redeemer's sake, taken back the pair of blacks, thin and worn out as they were, and mounted and ridden to Kohlhaasenbrück to fatten them in your own stable?"

"Perhaps so," Kohlhaas said, walking over to the window, "perhaps not, either! If I had known that it would need my dear wife's blood to put the horses back on their feet again, I might perhaps have done as your Reverence says and not have made a fuss over a bushel of oats. But since they have cost me so dear now, let the thing run its course, say I; let judgment be pronounced as is my due, and let the Junker fatten my pair of blacks."

Luther took up his papers again, amid all sorts of thoughts, and said he would negotiate for Kohlhaas with the Elector. Meanwhile he would like him to stay quietly in the castle at Lützen; if the sovereign consented to grant him safe-conduct, he would be informed of it by the posting of a public notice. "Of course," he continued, as Kohlhaas bent to kiss his hand, "I don't know whether the Elector will choose mercy over justice, for I understand that he has got an army together and means to capture you in the castle at Lützen; but meanwhile, as I have already told you, there shan't be any lack of effort on my part." And he got up from the chair to dismiss him. Kohlhaas said that the fact that he was interceding for him put his mind completely at rest on that score; whereupon Luther waved him goodbye, but Kohlhaas, abruptly falling on one knee before him, said he had still another favor to ask. The fact was that at Pentecost, when it was his custom to receive Holy Communion, he had failed to go to church because of the military operations he was engaged in; would Luther have the goodness to hear his confession, without further preparation, and grant him in exchange the blessing of the Holy Sacrament? Luther, after a moment's thought in which he looked sharply at him, said, "All right,

Kohlhaas, I'll do it. But the Lord Whose body you hunger to have forgave His enemy. Will you likewise," he said as the other looked at him in surprise, "forgive the Junker who has offended you? Will you go to Tronka Castle, mount your pair of blacks, and ride them back to Kohlhaasenbrück to fatten them there?"

"Your Reverence—" Kohlhaas said, flushing, and seized his hand.

"Well?"

"—even the Lord did not forgive all his enemies. I am ready to forgive my two lords the Electors, the castellan and the steward, the lords Hinz and Kunz, and whoever else has done me wrong in this affair: but, if at all possible, let me have the Junker fatten my two blacks for me."

At these words Luther turned his back on him with a displeased look and rang the bell. Kohlhaas, wiping his eyes, rose from his knees in confusion as a famulus entered the anteroom with a light, in response to the summons; and as the latter vainly rattled the bolted door, Luther meanwhile having sat down to his papers again, Kohlhaas drew the bolt and let the man in. Luther looked sideways for an instant at the stranger and said to the famulus, "Light him out," upon which the latter, surprised to see a visitor, took down the key to the house door from the wall and, returning to the half-opened door, waited for the stranger to leave. Kohlhaas, taking his hat nervously in both hands, said, "And so, your Reverence, I cannot have the comfort of the reconciliation I asked you for?"

Luther answered curtly, "With your Savior, no; with the sovereign—that depends on the effort I promised to make for you." And he motioned to his famulus to perform the service he had called him in for without further ado. Kohlhaas pressed both hands to his breast with an expression of painful emotion, followed the man who lighted him down the stair, and vanished.

The next morning Luther sent a message to the Elector of Saxony in which, after bitterly alluding to the lords Hinz and Kunz von Tronka, Chamberlain and Cupbearer to His Highness, who, as everybody knew, were the ones who had suppressed Kohlhaas' petition, he told him with characteristic candor that under these difficult circumstances there was nothing for it but to accept the horse dealer's proposal and grant him an amnesty so that he might be able to renew his suit. Public opinion, Luther remarked, was on his side to a very dangerous extent, so much so that even in Wittenberg, which had been set on fire three times by him, it was still possible to hear voices raised in his favor; and since Kohlhaas would undoubtedly let the people know about it if his proposal were refused, as well as make his own malicious commentary on the matter, the populace might easily be so far misled that the state would find itself powerless to act against him. He concluded that, in such an extraordinary case, any scruples about entering into negotiations with a subject who had taken up arms against the state must be set aside; that, as a matter of fact, the wrong done Kohlhaas had in a certain sense placed him outside the social union; and in short, so as to put an end to the matter, he should be regarded rather as a foreign power that had attacked the country (and since he was not a Saxon subject, he really might in a way be regarded as such) than as a rebel in revolt against the throne.

When the Elector received this letter, there were present in the palace Prince Christiern of Meissen, Commander-in-Chief of the Realm, uncle of the Prince Friedrich of Meissen who had been defeated at Mühlberg and was still laid up with his wounds; the Lord High Chancellor Count Wrede; Count Kallheim, President of the Chancery of State; and the two lords Hinz and Kunz von Tronka, Cupbearer and Chamberlain, both intimate friends of the sovereign from his youth. The Chamberlain, Sir Kunz, who in his capacity of privy councilor attended to the private correspondence of his master and was authorized to use his name and seal, was the first to speak, and after again explaining in detail that he would never on his own authority have suppressed the complaint lodged with the Tribunal by the horse dealer against his cousin the Junker if it had not been for the fact that he had been misled by false statements into thinking it an unfounded and idle piece of mischief-making, he went on to consider the present state of affairs. He observed that neither divine nor human laws justified the horse dealer in taking such terrible vengeance as he had allowed himself for this mistake; dwelt on the renown that would fall on his accursed head if they treated with him as with a recognized military power; and the ignominy thus reflected upon the sacred person of the Elector seemed so intolerable to him that, carried away by his own eloquence, he said he would rather see the worst happen, which was for the mad rebel's sentence to be carried out and his cousin the Junker marched off to Kohlhaasenbrück to fatten his horses, than for Dr. Luther's proposal to be accepted.

The Lord Chancellor, Count Wrede, half turning toward Sir Kunz, expressed regret that his conduct at the start of this unquestionably awkward business had not been inspired with the same tender solicitude for the reputation of the sovereign as he now displayed in his proposal to settle it. He explained to the Elector the hesitation he felt about using the power of the state to enforce a manifest injustice; remarked, with a significant allusion to the increasing support the horse dealer was gaining in the country, that the thread of the crime threatened to be spun out indefinitely, and declared that the only way to sever it and extricate the government from an ugly situation was to deal honestly with the man and make good, directly and without respect of person, the mistake they had been guilty of.

Prince Christiern of Meissen, when asked by the Elector to give his opinion, turned deferentially to the Lord Chancellor and said that the latter's reasoning naturally inspired him with the greatest respect; but in wishing to help Kohlhaas get justice for himself, the Chancellor overlooked the injury he did to the claims of Wittenberg, Leipzig, and all the country that the horse dealer had scourged in attempting to enforce his own rightful claim to compensation or at least punishment. The order of the state, as regards this man, was so disturbed that it needed more than an axiom borrowed from the science of jurisprudence to set it right. Therefore he agreed with the Chamberlain in favoring the use of the means appointed for such cases: they should get together a force large enough to capture or crush the horse dealer at Lützen.

The Chamberlain, bringing over two chairs from the wall and deferentially setting them down in the room for the Elector and the Prince, said that he was delighted to find a man of such integrity and acumen agreeing with him about the way to settle this puzzling business. The Prince took hold of the chair without sitting down and, looking him right in the face, assured him he had little reason to rejoice, since the first step such a course of action required was to issue a warrant for his, Sir Kunz's, arrest, followed by his trial on charges of misusing the sovereign's name. For though it was necessary to veil from the eyes of justice a series of crimes that led endlessly on to further crimes, for all of which there was not room enough before the throne of judgment, this was not the case with the original offense from which everything had sprung; and the very first thing the state must do was to try the Chamberlain for his life, if it was to own the authority to crush the horse dealer, whose grievance, as they well knew, was exceedingly just and into whose hands they themselves had put the sword he now wielded.

The Elector, toward whom the discomfited Chamberlain looked at these words, turned away, his whole face reddening, and went to the window. Count Kallheim, after an embarrassed silence on everyone's part, said that this was not the way to extricate themselves from the magic circle in which they were caught. With equal justice they might put his nephew Prince Friedrich on trial; for in the strange expedition that he had led against Kohlhaas he had overstepped his instructions in all sorts of ways, and if one were to draw up the long list of those responsible for the embarrassment in which they now found themselves, his name too would figure in it and he would have to be called to account by the sovereign for the events at Mühlberg.

As the Elector, with a perplexed look, walked over to his desk, the Cupbearer, Sir Hinz von Tronka, began to speak in his turn: he could not understand how the right course for the state to follow in this matter had escaped men as wise as those assembled here. The horse dealer, as he understood it, had promised to disband the company with which he had attacked the country, in return for a simple safe-conduct to Dresden and the renewal of the inquiry into his case. But it did not follow from this that he must be granted an amnesty for criminally taking his revenge into his own hands: these were two entirely separate legal concepts, which Dr. Luther as well as the Council of State seemed to have confounded. "After," he continued, laying his finger alongside of his nose, "the Dresden court has pronounced judgment, whatever it may be, in the matter of the black horses, nothing prevents us from arresting Kohlhaas for his incendiarism and brigandage: a politic solution that unites the advantages of both statesmen's views and is certain to win the approbation of the world and of posterity." As the only reply both the Prince and the Lord Chancellor gave to the Cupbearer Sir Hinz's speech was a contemptuous look, and the discussion seemed at an end, the Elector said he would weigh in his mind, between now and the next sitting of the Council, the different opinions he had received.

Apparently the preliminary step contemplated by the Prince had killed all desire in the Elector, who was highly sensitive wherever friendship was concerned, to go ahead with the campaign against Kohlhaas, for which all the preparations were made. At any rate he detained the Lord Chancellor Count Wrede, whose opinion seemed to him the likeliest one, and let the others go; and when the latter showed him letters indicating that the horse dealer's strength had actually grown to some four hundred men—indeed, considering the general discontent in the country owing to the highhanded actions of the Chamberlain, he might count on doubling or tripling that number in a short time—he decided without further ado to accept Dr. Luther's advice. The entire management of the Kohlhaas affair was therefore handed over to Count Wrede; and only a few days later a notice was posted, the gist of which we give as follows:

> We, etc., etc., Elector of Saxony, in especially gracious consideration of the intercession made to us by Dr. Martin Luther, do grant to Michael Kohlhaas, horse dealer of Brandenburg, safe-conduct to Dresden for the purpose of a renewed inquiry into his case, on condition that within three days after sight of this he lay down the arms which he has taken up; but it is understood that in the event that his complaint concerning the black horses is rejected by the court at Dresden, which is hardly likely, he shall be prosecuted with all the severity of the law for seeking to take justice into his own hands; in the contrary event, however, tempering our justice with mercy, we will grant him and all his band full amnesty for the acts of violence committed by him in Saxony.

Kohlhaas had no sooner received from Dr. Luther a copy of this notice which had been posted in every public square in the land, than he went ahead, in spite of its qualified language, and disbanded his following, whom he sent away with gifts, expressions of his gratitude, and suitable admonitions. Whatever he had captured in the way of money, weapons, and military stores he deposited with the courts at Lützen as the property of the Elector; and after sending Waldmann and Sternbald off, the one to the bailiff at Kohlhaasenbrück with letters proposing to repurchase his farm, if that were possible, and the other to Schwerin to fetch his children whom he wished to have by his side again, he left the castle at Lützen and, carrying the remnant of his little property on his person in the form of notes, he made his way unrecognized to Dresden.

Day was just breaking and the whole city still lay asleep as he knocked at the door of the little dwelling in the suburb of Pirna which, thanks to the honesty of the bailiff, still belonged to him, and told his old servant Thomas, who looked after the place, when he opened the door and stared dumbfounded at him, to go to the Government House and report to the Prince of Meissen that Kohlhaas the horse dealer had arrived. The Prince of Meissen, who on hearing this thought it expedient to go at once and see how matters stood between them and this man, found an immense throng of people already gathered in the streets leading to Kohlhaas' house when he appeared soon after with a retinue of knights and men. The news of the presence of the avenging angel who chastised the oppressors of the people with fire and sword had aroused all of Dresden, city and suburbs; the door had to be bolted against the pressure of the curious crowd, and boys clambered up to the windows to catch a glimpse of the incendiary at his breakfast.

As soon as the Prince had made his way into the house with the help of a bodyguard that cleared a path for him and had entered Kohlhaas' room, he asked the horse dealer, whom he found standing half undressed at a table, whether he was Kohlhaas the horse dealer; whereupon the latter drew from his belt a wallet with papers dealing with his affairs, and, respectfully handing it to the Prince, he said yes, adding that after disbanding his company he had come to Dresden, under protection of the safe-conduct granted him by the sovereign, to press his suit concerning the blacks against the Junker Wenzel von Tronka before the court. With a rapid glance the Prince took Kohlhaas in from head to foot, then looked through the papers in the wallet; had him explain the meaning of a certificate from the court at Lützen acknowledging a deposit in favor of the Electoral treasury; and, after asking him all sorts of questions about his children, his means, and the kind of life he intended to lead in the future, so as to see the kind of man he was, and concluding that they might set their minds at rest about him in all respects, gave him back his papers and said that nothing now stood

in the way of his suit, and that all he need do to commence proceedings was to apply directly himself to the Lord High Chancellor of the Tribunal, Count Wrede. "In the meantime," said the
Prince after a pause, as he crossed over to the window and looked
out in astonishment at the crowd in front of the house, "you must
have a guard for the first few days to protect you in your house
and when you go out."

Kohlhaas looked down, disconcerted, and said nothing.

"Well then, never mind," said the Prince, coming away from the
window. "If anything happens, you have only yourself to blame
for it," and he turned to the door to leave. Kohlhaas, who had
had some second thoughts, said, "My Lord, do as you like! If you
give me your word the guard will be withdrawn whenever I wish
it, I have no objection." The Prince replied that that was understood; and after telling the three lansquenets detailed for the duty
that the man whose house they were staying in was completely at
liberty and that it was merely for his own protection that they were
to follow him when he went out, he saluted the horse dealer with
an easy wave of the hand and left.

Toward midday, escorted by his three lansquenets and trailed
by an immense crowd whom the police had warned against offering him any harm, Kohlhaas went to visit the Lord Chancellor,
Count Wrede. The Chancellor received him with great kindness in
his antechamber and, after talking with him two whole hours and
hearing Kohlhaas' story from beginning to end, he referred him to
a celebrated lawyer in the city, one who was a colleague of the
court, so that he might have the complaint drawn up and immediately presented. Kohlhaas did not lose a minute in going to the
lawyer's house; and after having the suit drawn up exactly like the
one which had been quashed—he asked for punishment of the
Junker according to the law, restoration of the horses to their previous condition, and compensation for his damages and also for
those suffered by his man Herse, who had fallen at Mühlberg, the
latter to be paid to the groom's old mother—he returned home,
still followed by the gaping crowd, his mind made up never to quit
the house again unless his affairs absolutely required it.

Meanwhile, the Junker had been released from his prison in
Wittenberg and, after getting over a dangerous attack of erysipelas
that had inflamed his foot, he had been peremptorily summoned

to appear before the Dresden court to answer the charges made against him by the horse dealer Kohlhaas concerning a pair of black horses that had been unlawfully taken from him and ruined by overwork. The two brothers von Tronka, cousins of the Junker, at whose house he came to stay, received him with the greatest bitterness and contempt; they called him a worthless wretch who had brought shame and disgrace on the whole family, told him he was sure to lose his suit, and to get ready to produce the pair of blacks which he would be condemned to fatten to the accompaniment of the scornful laughter of the world. The Junker answered in a weak and quavering voice that he was the most pitiable man alive. He swore he had known very little about the whole damned business that had brought him so much misfortune, and that the castellan and the steward were to blame for everything, for they had used the horses to get the harvest in without his remotest knowledge or consent and worked them until they were skin and bones, part of the time too in their own fields. Sitting down as he said this, he begged them not to abuse and insult him and plunge him back into the illness from which he had only recently recovered. The next day the lords Hinz and Kunz, who owned property in the vicinity of the ruins of Tronka Castle, wrote, at the urging of their cousin the Junker, since there was nothing else to do, to ask their steward and tenants for information about the two black horses that had disappeared on that unhappy day without being heard of since. But because the castle had been completely destroyed and most of its inhabitants massacred, all they could discover was that a stable boy, beaten with the flat of the incendiary's sword, had rescued them from the burning shed, and that afterwards, when the boy had asked him where to take the horses and what to do with them, the crazy fellow had answered him with a kick. The Junker's gouty old housekeeper, who had fled to Meissen, assured him, in reply to his written inquiry, that on the morning after that terrible night the stable boy had gone off with the horses toward the Brandenburg border; but all the inquiries made there proved vain, and anyhow there seemed to be an error at the bottom of this information, since none of the Junker's people came from Brandenburg or even from somewhere along the road to it. Some men from Dresden who had been in Wilsdruf a few days after the burning of Tronka Castle said that a groom had turned up there about that time leading two horses by the halter, and, since the animals were on their last legs and could not go any further, he had left them with a shepherd who had offered to feed them back to health in his cow-barn. For a variety of reasons, it semed quite probable that these were the pair of blacks in question; but the shepherd of Wilsdruf, according to people who had just come from there, had already disposed of them again, no one knew to whom; and according to a third rumor, whose author could not be discovered, the two horses had simply gone to their eternal rest and were buried in the Wilsdruf boneyard.

The lords Hinz and Kunz found this turn of affairs extremely welcome, as can readily be imagined, for it spared them the necessity (since their cousin the Junker no longer had any stables of his own) of fattening the horses in theirs, but they wanted to verify the story so as to be absolutely sure. Consequently Junker Wenzel von Tronka, as lord of the demesne, liege lord, and lord justice, addressed a letter to the magistrates at Wilsdruf minutely describing the horses, which he said had been placed in his care and accidentally lost, and requesting them to be so good as to ascertain their present whereabouts and to urge and admonish their owner, whoever he might be, to deliver them to the stables of the Chamberlain Sir Kunz in Dresden, where he would be generously reimbursed for all his costs. And a few days later the man to whom the shepherd at Wilsdruf had sold the horses did in fact appear with them, cadaverous creatures stumbling at the tail of his cart, and led them to the Dresden market place; but as the bad luck of Sir Wenzel and still more of honest Kohlhaas would have it, he turned out to be the knacker of Döbbeln.

As soon as the rumor reached Sir Wenzel, in the presence of his cousin the Chamberlain, that a man had arrived in the city with the two black horses that had escaped from the Tronka Castle fire, the two of them, after hurriedly rounding up some servants from the house, went down to the palace square where the fellow was, intending, if the animals proved to be Kohlhaas', to pay him the money he had spent on them and take the horses home with them. But the knights were taken aback to see a crowd, whom the spectacle had attracted, already gathered around the two-wheeled cart to which the horses were tied and getting bigger by the minute; laughing uproariously, the people shouted to one another that the

horses on whose account the foundations of the state were totter-
ing were already in the knacker's hands! The Junker, after walking
around the cart and staring at the miserable creatures who looked
as if they were going to die any minute, mumbled in embarrassment: they were not the horses he had taken from Kohlhaas; but
Sir Kunz the Chamberlain, throwing him a look of speechless rage,
which if it had been made of iron would have smashed him to bits,
and flinging back his cloak to show his orders and his chain of
office, strode over to the knacker and said: were those the black
horses that the shepherd of Wilsdruf had got hold of and that the
Junker Wenzel von Tronka, to whom they belonged, had com-
mandeered from the magistrate of that place? The knacker, who
had a pail of water in his hand and was giving a drink to the fat
and sturdy nag that drew his cart, said, "The blacks?" Then, putting down the pail and slipping the bit out of the horse's mouth,
he said that the pair of blacks tied to the back of the cart had been
sold to him by the swineherd of Hainichen. Where the latter had
got them, and whether they came from the shepherd at Wilsdruf,
he didn't know. He had been told, he said, taking up the pail again
and propping it between the cart shaft and his knee—he had been
told by the messenger from the Wilsdruf court to take the horses
to the Tronka residence in Dresden; but the Junker he had been
told to go to was named Kunz. And, turning away, he emptied the
water his animal had left in the pail onto the pavement. The
Chamberlain found it impossible to get the fellow, who went about
his business with phlegmatic diligence, to look at him, and said,
amid the stares of the jeering crowd, that he was the Chamberlain
Kunz von Tronka; the pair of blacks he was looking for were the
ones belonging to his cousin, the Junker; they had been given to
the shepherd at Wilsdruf by a groom who ran away from Tronka
Castle at the time it was sacked, and originally they had belonged
to the horse dealer Kohlhaas. He asked the fellow, who stood there
with his legs astraddle, hitching up his pants, whether he didn't
know something about all this. Hadn't the swineherd from Hainichen perhaps bought the horses from the Wilsdruf shepherd—for
everything depended on that—or from a third person who had got
them from the shepherd?

The knacker, after leaning up against the cart and passing water,
said he had been told to go to Dresden with the horses where he

could get the money for them at the Tronka house. He didn't understand what the Chamberlain was talking about; whether Peter or Paul or the shepherd of Wilsdruf had owned them before the swineherd in Hainichen was all one to him so long as they hadn't been stolen. And, cocking his whip across his broad back, he shambled off toward a public house that stood in the square, with the intention, since he was hungry, of getting himself some breakfast. The Chamberlain, who did not for the life of him know what to do with the horses the swineherd of Hainichen had sold to the knacker of Döbbeln, unless they were the ones the devil himself was galloping around Saxony on, asked the Junker to say something; but when the latter replied, with white and quivering lips, that the best thing to do under the circumstances was to buy the blacks whether they were Kohlhaas' or not, the Chamberlain flung his cloak back and, cursing the father and mother who had made him, strode out of the crowd, absolutely at a loss to know what he should do. He called over Baron von Wenk, a friend of his who happened to be riding along the street, and asked him to stop by at the house of the Lord Chancellor Count Wrede and have the latter arrange for Kohlhaas to come out to examine the pair of blacks; for he was stubbornly determined not to quit the square just because the mob were looking at him mockingly, their handkerchiefs crammed into their mouths, and only waiting for him to leave, it seemed, to burst out laughing. Now it so happened that Kohlhaas was at the Lord Chancellor's, where he had been summoned by a court messenger to explain some matters in connection with the deposit he had made in Lützen, when the Baron entered the room on his errand; and when the Chancellor got up from his chair with a look of annoyance, leaving the horse dealer standing with his papers to one side, the Baron, who did not know Kohlhaas, explained the difficulty in which the lords von Tronka found themselves. The knacker from Döbbeln, he said, acting on a defective requisition of the Wilsdruf court, had turned up with a pair of horses in such hopeless condition that it was no wonder the Junker Wenzel hesitated to recognize them as Kohlhaas'; but if they were going to be accepted from the knacker notwithstanding and an attempt made to put them in shape again in the knights' stables, an ocular inspection by Kohlhaas was needed so as to remove all doubt. "Will you therefore be good enough," he concluded, "to have a guard fetch the horse dealer from his house and conduct him to the market place where the horses are?" The Lord Chancellor took his glasses from his nose and said to the Baron that he was laboring under a double misapprehension: first, in thinking that the question of the horses' ownership could only be decided by an ocular inspection by Kohlhaas; and then in imagining that he, the Chancellor, possessed the authority to have Kohlhaas taken by a guard to wherever the Junker happened to wish. Whereupon he introduced him to the horse dealer standing behind him and asked him, as he sat down and put his glasses back on, to apply to the man himself in the matter.

Kohlhaas, whose expression gave no hint of what was passing in his mind, said that he was ready to follow the Baron to the market place to inspect the knacker's horses. As the latter faced around to him in surprise, Kohlhaas went up to the Chancellor's table again, gave him, with the help of the papers in his wallet, the information he needed about the deposit in Lützen, and said goodbye; the Baron, who with a crimson face had walked over to the window, likewise took his leave; and the two men, escorted by the Prince of Meissen's three lansquenets, made their way, with a crowd of people at their heels, to the palace square. The Chamberlain Sir Kunz, who meanwhile, over the protests of several friends who had joined him, had been standing his ground among the people opposite the knacker of Döbbeln, accosted the horse dealer as soon as he appeared with the Baron and asked him, as he tucked his sword with haughty ostentation under his arm, whether the horses standing at the cart tail were his. The horse dealer, after turning diffidently toward the unknown gentleman who had asked the question and touching his hat, moved over without answering to the knacker's cart, followed by all the knights; and, stopping twelve paces off from where the animals stood on unsteady legs with their heads bowed to the ground, refusing the hay the knacker had pitched out for them, he gave them one look, turned back to the Chamberlain, and said, "My lord, the knacker is quite right: the horses tied to his cart are mine." And then, looking around the circle of knights, he touched his hat again and left the square with his guard.

As soon as he heard this, the Chamberlain went across to the knacker at a jump that set his helmet plume nodding and tossed him a bag of money; and while the latter scraped the hair back from his forehead with a lead comb and stared at the money in his hand, Sir Kunz ordered a servant to untie the horses and lead them home. The man left a group of his family and friends in the crowd at his master's summons and did, in fact, with a red face, step over a large pile of dung at the horses' feet and go up to their heads; but he had hardly taken hold of the halter to untie them when Master Himboldt, his cousin, grabbed him by the arm, and crying: "Don't you touch those knacker's nags!" pulled him away from the cart. Then stepping precariously back over the dung pile, the Master turned to the Chamberlain, who stood there speechless with surprise, and said: he must get a knacker's man to do him a service like that! The Chamberlain, livid with rage, looked at the Master for a second and then turned and shouted over the heads of the knights for the guard; and when, at Baron von Wenk's command, an officer emerged from the castle at the head of some of the Elector's gentlemen-at-arms, he gave him a brief account of the shameful way in which the burghers of the city were inciting to rebellion and called on him to arrest the ringleader, Master Himboldt. Catching the Master by his shirt, he accused him of mistreating the servant he had ordered to untie the black horses and pushing him away from the cart. The Master twisted skillfully out of the Chancellor's grasp and said, "My lord, showing a boy of twenty what he ought to do is not inciting to revolt! Ask him if he wants to go against everything that's customary and decent and meddle with those horses tied to the cart. If after what I've said his answer is yes, it's all right with me, he can start skinning them right now for all I care!"

The Chamberlain turned to the groom and asked him if he had any objection to carrying out his order to untie Kohlhaas' horses and lead them home; when the fellow, retreating into the crowd, timidly replied: the horses must be made decent and respectable again before that could be expected of him, the Chamberlain came right after him, knocked off his hat in which he wore the badge of the Tronka house, trampled it under his feet, and, drawing his sword, drove him from the square and out of his service. Master Himboldt cried, "Down with the murderous tyrant!" And while his fellow citizens, outraged by this scene, pressed shoulder to shoulder and forced back the guard, he knocked the Chamberlain down from behind, ripped his cloak, collar, and helmet off, wrenched the sword from his hand, and with a violent motion sent it clattering across the square. The Junker Wenzel, escaping from the tumult, called to the knights to go to his cousin's aid, but to no avail: before they were able to take a step toward him, they were scattered by the rush of the mob, and the Chamberlain, who had hurt his head in falling, was exposed to their full fury. The only thing that saved him was the appearance of a troop of mounted lansquenets who happened to be crossing the square and whom the officer commanding the Elector's men called over to help him. The officer, after dispersing the crowd, seized the enraged Master and had some troopers lead him off to prison, while two of the Chamberlain's friends lifted the latter's blood-spattered form from the ground and carried him home. Such was the unhappy conclusion of the well-meant and honest attempt to procure the horse dealer satisfaction for the injustice done him. The Döbbeln knacker, as his business was done and he wished to be off, tied the horses to a lamp post when the crowd began to disperse and there they stayed the whole day through, without anybody's bothering about them, objects of ridicule for the ragamuffins and the idlers; but finally the police took charge of them for want of anybody else to care for them and toward evening they got the knacker of Dresden to carry them off to his yard outside the city until their disposition was decided.

The riot in the palace square, as little as Kohlhaas was to blame for it, nevertheless aroused a feeling through the land, even among the more moderate and better class of people, that was highly dangerous to the success of his suit. It was felt the state had got itself into an intolerable position vis-à-vis the horse dealer, and in private houses and public places alike the opinion grew that it would be better to do the man an open wrong and quash the whole proceedings again, than to see that justice, extorted by violence, was done him in so trivial a matter, just to satisfy his crazy obstinacy. To complete poor Kohlhaas' ruin, it was the Lord Chancellor himself, with his rigid honesty and his hatred of the Tronka family which sprang from it, who helped strengthen and spread this sentiment. It was most unlikely that the horses now in the hands of the Dresden knacker would ever be restored to the shape they were in when they left the stables at Kohlhaasenbrück, but even if this were possible through skillful, unremitting care, the disgrace that had fallen on the Junker's family as a result of everything that had happened was so great that nothing seemed fairer and more reasonable to people—seeing the important place the von Tronkas occupied in the government as one of the oldest and noblest houses in the country—than that they should pay Kohlhaas a money amends for the horses. Yet a few days later, when the President, Count Kallheim, acting for the Chamberlain who was laid up with his injuries, sent a letter to the Chancellor making just such a proposal, and even though the Chancellor wrote to Kohlhaas warning him against declining such an offer if one were made to him, he himself wrote the President a curt, barely civil reply asking to be excused from any private commissions in the matter, and advising the Chamberlain to address himself directly to the horse dealer, whom he described as a very reasonable and modest man. The horse dealer, whose will had in fact been broken by the incident in the market place, was ready, following the advice of the Chancellor, to meet any overture from the Junker or his kinsmen half way, with perfect willingness and forgiveness for everything that had happened; but just such an overture was more than the proud knights could stomach; and highly indignant at the answer they had received from the Lord Chancellor, they showed it to the Elector the next morning when he came to visit the Chamberlain in the room where he was laid up with his wounds. The Chamberlain, in a voice that illness made weak and pathetic, asked the Elector whether, after risking his life to settle the business according to his sovereign's wishes, he must also expose his honor to the censure of the world by going hat in hand to beg indulgence from a man who had already heaped every imaginable shame and disgrace on him and his family. The Elector, after reading the letter, asked Count Kallheim in embarrassment if the court did not have the right, without consulting further with Kohlhaas, to take its stand on the fact that the horses were past recovery and bring in a verdict for a money amends, just as if the horses were already dead.

"Your Highness," the Count replied, "the horses *are* dead, legally dead because they have no value any more, and they will be physically dead before any one can get them from the knacker's yard to the knights' stables"; upon which the Elector tucked the letter in his pocket, said that he would speak to the Lord Chan-

cellor about it himself, spoke reassuringly to the Chamberlain who
had raised himself on his elbow and seized his hand in gratitude,
and, after recommending him to watch his health, he rose with a
benign air from his chair and left the room.

So matters stood in Dresden when poor Kohlhaas found himself
the center of another, even more serious storm that came up from
the direction of Lützen, and whose lightning the crafty knights were
clever enough to draw down on his unlucky head. A man called
Johann Nagelschmidt, one of the band whom the horse dealer had
collected and then dismissed again after the Electoral amnesty, had
seen fit some weeks later to round up a part of this rabble, which
shrank from nothing, on the Bohemian border, with the intention
of carrying on for himself the trade Kohlhaas had taught him. This
ruffian announced, partly to scare the sheriff's officers on his heels,
and partly to get the peasantry to take a hand in his rascalities as
they had done with Kohlhaas, that he was Kohlhaas' lieutenant;
had it spread about, with a cleverness learned from his master, that
the amnesty had been broken in the case of several men who had
gone quietly back to their homes; that Kohlhaas himself, indeed,
with a perfidiousness that cried aloud to heaven, had been arrested
on his arrival in Dresden and placed under guard; the result of this
being that the incendiary crew were able to masquerade, in manifestoes very much like Kohlhaas' that Nagelschmidt had posted up,
as honest soldiers assembled together for the sole purpose of serving God and watching over the Elector's promised amnesty—all
this, as has just been said, done not at all for the glory of God nor
out of attachment to Kohlhaas, whose fate the outlaws did not care
a straw about, but to enable them to burn and plunder with the
greater impunity and ease. When the first word of this reached
Dresden, the knights could not conceal the joy they felt over a development that seemed to put such a different face on things. With
knowing glances of feigned displeasure they recalled what a mistake it had been, in spite of their earnest and repeated warnings,
to grant Kohlhaas an amnesty, going on as if there had been a deliberate intention to give every scoundrel in the country the signal
to follow in the horse dealer's footsteps; and not content with ac-
cepting Nagelschmidt's claim that he had taken up arms only to
defend his oppressed master, they expressed the certain opinion that
his appearance on the scene was nothing but a plot on Kohlhaas'

part to scare the government and hasten and assure a verdict that would satisfy his mad obstinacy down to the last detail. Indeed the Cupbearer, Sir Hinz, went so far as to say to some courtiers and hunting companions who had gathered around him after dinner in the Elector's antechamber that the disbanding of the brigands in Lützen had been nothing but a damned trick; and, while making fun of the Lord Chancellor's love of justice, he cleverly concatenated various facts to prove that the band was still intact in the forests of the Electorate and only waited for a signal from the horse dealer to burst forth afresh with fire and sword.

Prince Christiern of Meissen, who was highly displeased with this new turn of affairs, which threatened so much damage to his sovereign's reputation, went at once to the palace to see the Elector; and, clearly perceiving how the knights would wish to encompass Kohlhaas' ruin by convicting him of new offenses, he asked permission to question the horse dealer without delay. The horse dealer, not a little surprised at the summons, appeared at the Government House under a constable's escort with his two little boys, Heinrich and Leopold, in his arms—for his five children had arrived the day before with Sternbald from Mecklenburg where they had been staying, and considerations too numerous to detail here moved Kohlhaas, when the two burst into childish tears on his getting up to leave and begged to be taken along, to pick them up and carry them to the hearing. The Prince, after looking benevolently at the children whom their father had seated beside him and asking them their names and ages with friendly interest, told Kohlhaas about the liberties that his old follower Nagelschmidt was taking in the valleys of the Erzgebirge; and, handing him the latter's so-called manifestoes, he asked him what he had to say in his own defense. The horse dealer, though indeed he showed extreme dismay when confronted with these treasonable documents, had little difficulty in satisfying a man as upright as the Prince that the accusations leveled against him were baseless. He not only did not see how he needed the help of a third person, as matters stood now, to obtain a judgment in his suit, which was progressing entirely satisfactorily, but he had papers with him which he showed to the Prince that made it appear most unlikely that Nagelschmidt should ever wish to give him such help: for shortly before the dispersal of his band at Lützen he had been on the point of hanging the fellow, for a rape committed in open country and other outrages, when the publication of the Electoral amnesty severed their connection and saved Nagelschmidt's life; the next day they had parted deadly enemies.

With the Prince's approval, Kohlhaas sat down and wrote a letter to Nagelschmidt, in which he called the latter's claim to having taken up arms to enforce the amnesty a shameless and wicked fabrication; on his arrival in Dresden, he told him, he had neither been jailed nor put under guard, also his lawsuit was progressing just as he wished; and he gave him over, because of the acts of arson Nagelschmidt had committed in the Erzgebirge after publication of the amnesty, to the full vengeance of the law, as a warning to the rabble around him. Extracts from Kohlhaas' trial of Nagelschmidt in the castle at Lützen on account of the above-mentioned crimes were appended to the letter, to inform the people about this scoundrel who already at that time was destined for the gallows and owed his life, as we have mentioned, only to the Elector's edict. Upon which the Prince soothed Kohlhaas' resentment over the suspicions that under pressure of circumstances were inevitably expressed at the hearing; promised him that as long as he remained in Dresden the amnesty granted him would not be violated in any way; shook the boys' hands again as he made them a present of some fruit on the table; and said goodbye to Kohlhaas. Nevertheless, the Lord Chancellor recognized the danger hanging over the horse dealer's head and did everything in his power to press the lawsuit to a conclusion before new circumstances arose to complicate and confuse it; but to complicate and confuse the case was exactly what the crafty knights desired and intended. They no longer silently acknowledged the Junker's guilt and limited their efforts to obtaining a milder sentence for their cousin, but instead began to raise all sorts of cunning arguments and quibbling objections, so as to deny his guilt entirely. Sometimes they would pretend that Kohlhaas' horses had been detained at Tronka Castle by the castellan's and the steward's arbitrary action, and that the Junker had known little if anything about it; at other times they claimed the animals had been sick with a violent and dangerous cough when they arrived at the castle, and promised to produce witnesses to confirm the truth of what they said; and when, after lengthy investigations and explanations, they were forced to abandon these arguments, they fell back on an Electoral edict of twelve years' standing that in fact forbade importing horse stock from Brandenburg to Saxony on account of a cattle disease: clear proof that the Junker had not only the right but even the duty to seize the horses Kohlhaas had brought across the border.

Meanwhile Kohlhaas, who had repurchased his farm at Kohlhaasenbrück from the honest bailiff, paying him a small additional sum to reimburse him for the loss he suffered thereby, wished to leave Dresden for a few days and pay a visit to his home, apparently in order to settle this matter legally—in which decision, however, the above-mentioned consideration, pressing as it may actually have been on account of the need to sow the winter crop, undoubtedly played less part than did a wish to test his position in the strange and dubious circumstances prevailing; and he may also have been influenced by still other reasons that we shall leave to those who know their own hearts to divine. Accordingly, leaving at home the guard which had been detailed to watch him, he went to the Lord Chancellor and, with the bailiff's letters in his hand, explained that if he was not needed in court now, as seemed to be the case, he would like to leave the city and travel to Brandenburg for some eight to twelve days, within which period he promised to return. The Lord Chancellor, looking down with an annoyed and doubtful face, expressed the opinion that Kohlhaas' presence was more necessary than ever just then, as the court required statements and explanations from him on a thousand and one points that might come up, to counter the cunning shifts and dodges of his opponent; but when Kohlhaas referred him to his lawyer, who was thoroughly posted on the case, and pressed his request with modest persistence, promising to limit his absence to a week, the Lord Chancellor, after a pause, only said, as he dismissed him, that he hoped he would apply to Prince Christiern of Meissen for a pass.

Kohlhaas, who could read the Lord Chancellor's face very well, was only strengthened in his determination and, sitting down on the spot and giving no reason, he asked the Prince of Meissen, as Chief of the Government, for a week's pass to Kohlhaasenbrück and back. In reply, he received an order from the Governor of the Palace, Baron Siegfried von Wenk, to the effect that his request to visit Kohlhaasenbrück would be laid before his Serene Highness the Elector, and as soon as the latter's consent was forthcoming the pass would be sent to him. When Kohlhaas asked his lawyer how the order came to be signed by a Baron Siegfried von Wenk and not by Prince Christiern of Meissen, to whom he had addressed his request, he was told that the Prince had left for his estates three days ago and that during his absence the affairs of his office had been turned over to the Governor of the Palace, Baron Siegfried von Wenk, a cousin of the gentleman of the same name whom we have already encountered.

Kohlhaas, whose heart began to pound uneasily amid all these complications, waited several more days for an answer to his request, which had been submitted to the sovereign with such surprising formality; but when a week and more had passed without either his receiving a reply or the court's handing down a judgment in his case even though it had been promised him without fail, he sat down on the twelfth day, his mind made up to force the Government to reveal its intentions toward him, whatever they might be, and earnestly petitioned the Government once again for a pass. But on the evening of the following day, which had likewise passed without his getting the answer he was expecting, going over to the window of his little back room with his mind very much on his present situation and especially the amnesty Dr. Luther had got for him, he was thunderstruck to see no sign, in the little outbuilding in the yard which was their quarters, of the guard assigned him on his arrival by the Prince of Meissen. Thomas, his old servant, whom he called to him and asked the meaning of this, said with a sigh: "Sir, there's something wrong; there were more lansquenets here today than usual and at nightfall they posted themselves around the whole house: two of them, with their shields and pikes, are standing out in the street in front of the house door; two more are at the back door in the garden; and still another pair are stretched out on some straw in the entrance hall where they say they are going to spend the night."

Kohlhaas' face paled; turning away, he said it didn't really matter, as long as they were already there; when Thomas went down again, he should put a light in the hall so they could see. And, after he had opened the front shutters on the pretext of emptying a pot and convinced himself of the truth of Thomas' words, for just at that moment he saw the guard silently being changed—something

no one had ever thought of doing since the arrangement existed—
he went to bed, even though he did not feel much like sleeping,
with his mind instantly made up about what he would do the next
day. For what he disliked most about the regime he had to deal
with was the show of justice it put on, at the same time that it
went ahead and broke the amnesty which he had been promised;
if he was in fact a prisoner, as he could no longer doubt, he was
going to make them say so straight out. Accordingly, the next
morning he had Sternbald hitch up his wagon and bring it around
to the door; he meant, he said, to drive to Lockewitz to see the
steward there, an old friend of his who had spoken to him a few
days before in Dresden and invited him to pay him a visit with his
children. The lansquenets, having watched with huddled heads the
stir these preparations made in the household, secretly sent one of
their number into town, and a few minutes later an official of the
Government marched up at the head of some constables and went
into the house across the way as if he had business there. Kohlhaas was busy getting his children's clothes on, but he did not miss
these goings-on and purposely kept the wagon waiting in front of
the house longer than was really necessary; as soon as he saw the
police had taken up their posts, he came out in front of the house
with his children, told the lansquenets in the doorway as he went
by that they needn't bother to come along, lifted the boys into the
wagon, and kissed and comforted his tearful little girls whom he
had ordered to stay behind with the old servant's daughter. No
sooner had he himself climbed into the wagon than the official with
his following of constables came out of the house across the way
and asked him where he was going. On Kohlhaas' answering that
he was going to Lockewitz to see his friend the steward, who a
few days ago had invited him and his two boys to visit him in the
country, the official said that in that case he must ask Kohlhaas to
wait a minute or so, as he would be accompanied by some mounted
lansquenets in obedience to the Prince of Meissen's orders. Kohlhaas looked down with a smile from the wagon and asked him if
he thought his life would not be safe in the house of a friend who
had invited him to share his board for the day. The official replied
good-humoredly that the danger was certainly not very great, adding that the soldiers were not to incommode him in any way.
Kohlhaas, now looking grave, answered that on his coming to

Dresden the Prince of Meissen had left it up to him as to whether he should have the guard or not; when the official expressed surprise at this, and in carefully chosen words reminded him that he had been accompanied by the guard all the time he had been there, the horse dealer described the circumstances under which the soldiers had been put into his house. The official assured him that by order of the Governor of the Palace, Baron von Wenk, who was at the moment chief of police, he must keep an uninterrupted watch over his person; if he would not consent to the escort, would he be good enough to go to the Government House himself to clear up the misunderstanding that must certainly exist. Kohlhaas, giving the man a knowing look, and his mind now made up to settle the matter once and for all, said that he would do just that; got down from his wagon with beating heart; gave the children to the servant to take back into the house; and, leaving the groom waiting in front of the house with the carriage, went off to the Government House with the official and his guard.

When the horse dealer entered with his escort, he found the Governor of the Palace, Baron von Wenk, in the midst of looking over a group of Nagelschmidt's men who had been captured near Leipzig and brought to Dresden the evening before, while the knights with him were questioning them about a great many things on which information was wanted. The Baron, as soon as he caught sight of the horse dealer, went up to him in the silence that followed the sudden cessation of the interrogation and asked him what he wanted; and when the horse dealer respectfully explained his intention of going to dine at midday with the steward at Lockewitz, and said he wished to leave the lansquenets behind since he did not need them, the Baron changed color and, seeming to swallow something that he was about to say, told Kohlhaas that he would do well to stay quietly at home and postpone the spread at the Lockewitz steward's for the present. Then, turning to the official and cutting short the colloquy, he told him that the orders he had given him about Kohlhaas still held good and that the latter was not to leave the city unless accompanied by six mounted lansquenets. Kohlhaas asked him if he was a prisoner, and if he was to understand that the amnesty solemnly granted him before the eyes of the whole world was now broken, upon which the Baron wheeled around suddenly, thrust his face, which had flushed a fiery red, up to Kohlhaas', said, "Yes! Yes! Yes!"—turned his back on him again, left him standing where he was, and went back to Nagelschmidt's men. Thereupon Kohlhaas left the room, and although he realized that what he had done had made the only possibility now remaining to him—flight—much more difficult, nevertheless he did not regret it because he now felt released from any further obligation to observe the terms of the amnesty. Arriving home, he had the horses unharnessed and, feeling depressed and upset, went to his room, still accompanied by the official; and while the latter assured the horse dealer, in a way that sickened him, that all the trouble must be due to some misunderstanding which would shortly be cleared up, he signed to the constables to bolt all the doors leading to the courtyard; but the main entrance, he hastened to say, was still open for him to use as he pleased.

Meanwhile Nagelschmidt had been so hard pressed from every side by sheriff's men and lansquenets in the forests of the Erzgebirge that the idea occurred to him, seeing how he lacked all means to carry through the kind of role he had undertaken, of actually getting Kohlhaas to help him; and since a traveler passing that way had given him a fairly accurate notion of how matters stood with Kohlhaas' lawsuit in Dresden, he thought he could persuade the horse dealer, in spite of the open enmity between them, to seal a new alliance with him. He therefore sent one of his fellows to him with a letter, written in almost unreadable German, that said: if he would come to the Altenburg and resume command of the band they had got together there from the remnants of his dispersed troops, he, Nagelschmidt, was ready to help him escape from Dresden by furnishing him with horses, men, and money; at the same time he promised Kohlhaas to be more obedient, indeed better behaved in every respect, in the future than he had been in the past; and to prove his faithfulness and attachment, he pledged himself to come in person to the outskirts of Dresden in order to rescue Kohlhaas from jail. Now the fellow whose job it was to deliver this letter had the bad luck, in a village right near Dresden, to fall down in a violent fit of a kind he was susceptible to from childhood; the letter that he was carrying in his tunic was discovered by the people who came to his aid, while he himself, as soon as he had recovered consciousness, was arrested and, followed by a large crowd, carried to the Government House under guard. As soon as Baron von Wenk had read the letter, he went to see the Elector at the Palace, and there he also found Sir Kunz (who was now recovered from his injuries), Sir Hinz, and the President of the Chancery of State, Count Kallheim. It was these gentlemen's opinion that Kohlhaas should be arrested without delay and tried for secretly conspiring with Nagelschmidt; for they pointed out that such a letter could not have been written unless there had been earlier letters from the horse dealer and unless a criminal compact had been concluded by the two for the purpose of hatching fresh iniquities. But the Elector steadfastly refused to violate, on the sole grounds of this letter, the safe-conduct he had solemnly promised Kohlhaas; he himself was inclined to think that Nagelschmidt's letter indicated there had been no previous connection between the two; and all he would consent to do to get to the bottom of the matter, though only after long hesitation, was, following the President's proposal, to let the letter be delivered to Kohlhaas by Nagel-schmidt's man, just as if he had never been arrested, and see whether Kohlhaas would answer it. The next morning, accordingly, the fel-low, who had been put in jail, was brought to the Government House where the Governor of the Palace gave him back the letter and ordered him to deliver it to the horse dealer as if nothing had happened, in return for which he promised him his freedom and to let him off the punishment he had earned. The fellow lent him-self to this base deception forthwith, and in apparently mysterious fashion, on the pretext of selling crabs (which the official supplied him with from the market) he gained admission to Kohlhaas' room. Kohlhaas, who read the letter while the children played with the crabs, in other circumstances would certainly have seized the ras-cal by the collar and handed him over to the lansquenets at his door; but in the present temper of men's minds even such a step was liable to misconstruction, and anyhow he was fully convinced that nothing in the world could ever rescue him from the business in which he was entangled: so, looking mournfully into the fel-low's face which he knew so well, he asked him where he was staying and told him to come back in an hour or so when he would let him know his decision. At his bidding Sternbald, who hap-pened to come in the door of his room, bought some crabs from the man; when this was done, and both men had left without rec-ognizing one another, Kohlhaas sat down and wrote Nagelschmidt as follows: First, that he accepted his offer to take command of the band in Altenburg; that Nagelschmidt should therefore send a wagon with two horses to Neustadt-near-Dresden so that he could be freed from the temporary confinement in which he and his five children were being held; that, to get away faster, he would also need another team of two horses on the road to Wittenberg which, though a roundabout way, was the only one he could take to come to him, for reasons it would require too long to explain; that he thought he could bribe the lansquenets who were guarding him, but in case force was necessary he would like to be able to count on finding a pair of stout-hearted, capable, and well-armed fellows in Neustadt; that he was sending him twenty gold crowns by his messenger to pay the cost of all these preparations, and he would settle with him afterwards about the sums actually paid out; and that as for the rest, he requested Nagelschmidt not to come to Dresden to take a personal part in the rescue as it was unnecessary, indeed he explicitly ordered him to stay behind in Altenburg in temporary command of the band, which could not be left without a chief.

When the messenger returned in the evening Kohlhaas gave him the letter, accompanied by a generous tip, and warned him to guard it carefully.

Kohlhaas' intention was to go to Hamburg with his five children and there embark for the Levant or the East Indies or wherever the blue sky looked down on people entirely different from the ones he knew: for quite apart from his reluctance to make common cause with Nagelschmidt, in the despair and anguish of his soul he had given up hope of ever seeing his pair of blacks fattened by the Junker.

No sooner had the fellow delivered the horse dealer's answer to the Governor of the Palace than the Lord Chancellor was deposed, the President, Count Kallheim, was appointed head of the court in his place, and, by an order in council of the Elector, Kohlhaas was arrested, put in chains, and thrown into the Dresden dungeon. On the evidence of the letter, a copy of which was posted at every street corner, he was brought to trial; and when he answered "Yes!" to a councilor who held the letter up in front of him at the bar and asked him if he acknowledged the handwriting as his own, but looked down at the ground and said "No!" when he was asked if he had anything to say in his own defense, Kohlhaas was condemned to be tortured with red-hot pincers by knackers' men, to be drawn and quartered, and his body burned between the wheel and the gallows.

Thus matters stood with poor Kohlhaas in Dresden when the Elector of Brandenburg intervened to pluck him from the fist of arbitrary power; in a note presented to the Chancery of State in Dresden, he claimed him as a subject of Brandenburg. For the honest City Governor, Sir Heinrich von Geusau, during a walk on the banks of the Spree, had told the Elector the story of this strange person who was really not a bad man, and when closely questioned by the astonished sovereign about it he could not avoid indicating the heavy responsibility which his own royal person bore for the improper way in which his Archchancellor, Count Siegfried, had conducted himself. The Elector, extremely angry, called the Archchancellor to account, and, finding that his kinship with the house of Tronka was to blame for it all, he immediately relieved him of his post, with more than one token of his displeasure, and appointed Sir Heinrich von Geusau to his place.

Now just at this time the Polish crown was involved in a dispute with the House of Saxony, over what we do not know, and pressed the Elector of Brandenburg repeatedly to make common cause with them against the Saxons; and in this situation the Archchancellor, Sir Heinrich who did not lack for skill in such matters, saw an opportunity to satisy his sovereign's desire to see justice done Kohlhaas without imperiling the peace of the whole realm more than consideration for one individual warranted. Accordingly, the Archchancellor not only insisted on Saxony's immediately and unconditionally surrendering Kohlhaas on account of the arbitrary proceedings used against him, which were an offense against God and man, so that the horse dealer, if he were guilty of a crime, could be tried according to the laws of Brandenburg on charges preferred by the Dresden court through an attorney in Berlin; but Sir Heinrich even demanded a passport for an attorney whom the Elector of Brandenburg wished to send to Dresden to see that justice was done Kohlhaas in the matter of the black horses that the Junker Wenzel von Tronka took from him on Saxon territory, as well as other flagrant instances of ill-usage and acts of violence. The Chamberlain, Sir Kunz, who had been appointed President of the State Chancery in the change of posts in Saxony, and who in his present hard-pressed circumstances had a number of reasons for not wishing to offend the Berlin court, replying in the name of his sovereign, whom the note from Brandenburg had very much cast down, said: he wondered at the unfriendliness and the unfairness which Brandenburg showed in challenging the right of the Dresden court to judge Kohlhaas according to its laws for crimes he had committed on Saxon ground, since the whole world knew that the horse dealer owned a large piece of property in the capital and did not himself dispute the fact that he was a citizen of Saxony. But since the Polish crown was already assembling an army of five thousand men on the Saxon frontier to press their claims by arms, and since the Archchancellor, Sir Heinrich von Geusau, announced that Kohlhaasenbrück, the place after which the horse dealer was named, lay in Brandenburg and they would consider the execution of the death sentence on him as a violation of the law of nations, the Elector of Saxony, following the advice of the Chamberlain Sir Kunz himself (who wanted to withdraw from the whole business), summoned Prince Christiern of Meissen from his estates and decided, after a few words with this prudent man, to heed the Berlin court's demand and give Kohlhaas up. The Prince, little pleased with all the improprieties committed in the Kohlhaas affair but required by his hardpressed sovereign to take over its direction, asked the Elector on what grounds he now wished to act against the horse dealer in the High Court at Berlin; and since they could not base their case on Kohlhaas' unfortunate letter to Nagelschmidt because of the questionable and obscure circumstances under which it had been written, nor on all of Kohlhaas' earlier acts of depredation and arson for which he had been pardoned by edict, the Elector decided to furnish His Majesty the Emperor in Vienna with an account of Kohlhaas' armed invasion of Saxony, accuse him of breaking the Emperor's peace, and appeal to His Majesty, who was of course not bound by any amnesty, to have Kohlhaas arraigned by the Imperial prosecutor for these crimes before the High Court at Berlin. A week later the horse dealer, still in chains, was packed into a wagon by the Knight Friedrich von Malzahn, whom the Elector of Brandenburg had sent to Dresden with six horsemen, and, reunited with his five children who had been collected at his plea from various foundling homes and orphan asylums, he was carried toward Berlin.

Now just at this time the Elector of Saxony, at the invitation of the High Bailiff, Count Aloysius von Kallheim, who in those days owned broad estates along the Saxon border, had gone to a great stag hunt at Dahme that had been got up for his entertainment, and in his company were the Chamberlain Sir Kunz and his wife Lady Heloise, daughter to the High Bailiff and sister to the President, not to mention other brilliant lords and ladies, hunting pages, and courtiers. Under the shelter of tents decked with pennants and pitched right across the road on a hill, the entire company, still covered with the dust of the hunt, were seated at table and being served by pages, while lively music sounded from beneath an oak tree, when Kohlhaas and his escort of horsemen came riding slowly up the road from Dresden. For the illness of one of his little children, who were quite frail, had made it necessary for the Knight of Malzahn to hold up for three days in Herzberg; a measure which, as he was answerable only to the Prince he served, the Knight had seen no need to inform the Dresden government about. The Elector, with his shirt open at the throat and his feathered hat stuck with sprigs of fir in hunter's fashion, was seated beside the Lady Heloise, who had been the first love of his youth, and the gaiety of the fête having put him in a high good humor, he said, "Let's go and offer this goblet of wine to the unfortunate fellow, whoever he may be." Lady Heloise, giving him a radiant look, immediately got up and levied tribute on the whole table to fill a silver dish handed her by a page with fruit, cakes, and bread; and the entire company had already streamed out of the tent with refreshments of every kind in their hands when the High Bailiff came toward them in evident embarrassment and begged them to stay where they were. When the Elector asked him in surprise what had happened to throw him into such confusion, the Bailiff, looking at the Chamberlain, stammered out that it was Kohlhaas who was in the wagon; at this piece of news, which none could understand, for it was public knowledge that the horse dealer had departed six days ago, the Chamberlain, Sir Kunz, turning back toward the tent, emptied his goblet of wine into the sand. The Elector, flushing violently, set his goblet down on a plate that a page held out to him at a sign from the Chamberlain; and while the Knight Friedrich von Malzahn, respectfully saluting the company whom he did not know, passed slowly through the tent ropes running across the road and continued on his way toward Dahme, the ladies and gentlemen, at the Bailiff's invitation, returned inside the tent. The Bailiff, as soon as the Elector was seated again, secretly sent a messenger to Dahme to tell its magistrate to see to it that the horse dealer was speeded on his way; but as the day was too far gone and the Knight of Malzahn insisted on spending the night there, there was nothing for it but to put Kohlhaas up, very quietly, at one of the magistrate's farmhouses, which lay hidden in the thickets off the main road. Toward evening, when all recollection of the incident had been driven from the lords' and ladies' minds by the wine and sumptuous desserts, the High Bailiff announced that a herd of stags had been sighted and proposed that they should take their stations again, a proposal that the whole company eagerly took up. Getting guns for themselves, they hurried in pairs, over ditches and hedges, into the nearby forest—which was how it happened that the Elector and the Lady Heloise, who had taken his arm to go and watch the sport, found to their astonishment that their guide had led them right into the yard of the house in which Kohlhaas and the Brandenburg horsemen were lodged. Lady Heloise, when she heard this, said, "Come, your Highness," playfully tucking the chain that hung around the Elector's neck inside his silk tunic, "let's slip inside the farmhouse before the crowd catches up and see what the strange man spending the night there is like!" The Elector, reddening, caught hold of her hand and said, "Heloise, what are you saying?" But when she looked at him in surprise and said there was no fear of his being recognized in the hunting clothes he was wearing, and pulled him along, and when at that very moment a pair of hunting pages who had already satisfied their curiosity came out of the house and reported that neither the Knight nor the horse dealer, thanks to the High Bailiff's efforts, knew who the company gathered in the neighborhood of Dahme were, the Elector pulled his hat down over his eyes with a smile and said, "Folly rules the world, and her throne is a pretty woman's lips!"

The nobleman and lady entered to find Kohlhaas sitting on a heap of straw with his back against the wall, in the midst of feeding bread and milk to the child who had fallen ill at Herzberg.

Lady Heloise, to start a conversation, asked him who he was and what was the matter with the child, and what he had done, and where were they taking him with such an escort, to all of which Kohlhaas, doffing his leather cap, gave short but sufficient answers as he went on feeding his child. The Elector, who was standing behind the hunters, noticed a little lead capsule hanging from a silk string around the horse dealer's neck, and for lack of anything better to say he asked him what it meant to him and what was in it. "The capsule, your Worship!" Kohlhaas replied, and he slipped it from around his neck, opened it, and drew out a little piece of paper sealed with gum—"There is a very strange story connected with this capsule. Seven months ago, I think it was, the very next day after my wife's funeral—I had left Kohlhaasenbrück, as you perhaps know, to capture the Junker von Tronka, who had done me a very grave injustice—the Elector of Saxony and the Elector of Brandenburg met to discuss some business, though exactly what it was I do not know, in the market town of Jüterbock, through which my expedition led me; and having satisfactorily settled matters between them by evening, they walked along in friendly conversation through the streets of the town to see the merrymaking at the fair, which happened to be taking place just then. In the market square they came upon a gypsy woman sitting on a stool, telling the fortunes of the people standing around her, and they asked her jokingly if she didn't also have something to tell them that they would like to hear. I had just dismounted with my men at an inn and was present in the square when all this happened, but as I was standing at the rear of the crowd, in the entrance to a church, I could not make out what the strange woman said to the two lords; and when the people, whispering laughingly to their neighbors that she did not share her knowledge with everybody, crowded in close to witness the scene about to take place, I got up on a bench behind me that was hewn out of the church entrance, really not so much because I was curious myself as to make room for the curious. No sooner did I catch an uninterrupted view, from this vantage point, of the two lords and the old woman, who was sitting on the stool in front of them and seemed to be scribbling something, than she stood up suddenly on her crutches and, searching around the crowd, fixed her eye on me, who had never exchanged a word with her nor ever in all my life desired to consult her art; making her way through the dense throng, she said, 'There! If the gentleman wishes to know his fortune he may ask you about it!' And with these words, Your Worship, she handed me this paper in her shriveled, bony hands. And when I said in astonishment, as all the people turned to look at me, 'Granny, what's this present you are giving me?' she answered, after mumbling a lot of stuff I couldn't make out, in the middle of which, however, I was flabbergasted to hear her say my own name, 'An amulet, Kohlhaas the horse dealer; take good care of it, some day it will save you your life!'—and she vanished. Well," Kohlhaas continued good-naturedly, "to tell the truth, I had a pretty close call in Dresden, but still I got off with my skin. But how I shall make out in Berlin, and whether the charm will come to my rescue there too, the future must show."

At these words the Elector dropped down on a bench; when Lady Heloise asked him anxiously what was the matter with him, he answered, "Nothing, nothing at all," only to collapse unconscious on the floor before she could spring forward and catch him in her arms. The Knight of Malzahn entered the room just then on an errand and said, "Good God, what's wrong with the gentleman?" Lady Heloise cried, "Fetch some water!" The pages lifted the Elector up and laid him on a bed in the next room; and the consternation reached its height when the Chamberlain, who had been summoned by a page, declared, after several vain attempts to restore him to consciousness, that he gave every sign of having suffered a stroke. The Bailiff, while the Cupbearer sent a courier on horseback to Luckau for the doctor, had the Elector, after he had opened his eyes, put in a carriage and carried at a walk to his hunting lodge nearby; but the ride was responsible for his falling into two more fainting fits after he had arrived there, and it was not until late the next morning, after the doctor from Luckau had arrived, that he recovered somewhat, though showing definite symptoms of the onset of a nervous fever. As soon as he was fully conscious again, the Elector raised himself on his elbow and his first question was: where was Kohlhaas? The Chamberlain, misunderstanding the question, took his hand and said he could set his mind at rest about that dreadful man: after that strange and inexplicable occurrence, he himself had given orders for Kohlhaas to remain where he was in the farmhouse at Dahme with his escort from Brandenburg. Assuring the Elector of his warmest sympathy, and protesting how bitterly he had taxed his wife for her irresponsible frivolity in bringing him together with that man, the Chamberlain asked his master what had produced such a strange and awful effect on him in the interview. He had to confess, the Elector replied, that it was the sight of an insignificant piece of paper the man carried about with him inside a lead capsule that was to blame for the whole unpleasant incident. He added a great deal more besides by way of explanation, which the Chamberlain could not understand; suddenly swore to him, as he clasped his hand in his own, that possession of the paper was of the utmost consequence to him; and begged him to mount that instant, ride to Dahme, and get it for him from the horse dealer at whatever cost. The Chamberlain, who had difficulty in concealing his dismay, assured him that if the piece of paper had the slightest value to him, nothing in the world was more essential than to hide that fact from Kohlhaas: if an indiscreet remark made the latter suspect something, all the Elector's riches would not suffice to buy it from that ferocious fellow with his insatiable vindictiveness. To reassure the Elector, he added that they must think of another way, and since the scoundrel probably did not set much store by the paper for its own sake, perhaps they could trick him into giving it up to some third person who had never had any part in the matter. The Elector, wiping his sweating face, asked if they might not send somebody to Dahme right away to try and do that, and meanwhile they could keep the horse dealer from going on until the paper was got hold of somehow. The Chamberlain, who could hardly believe his ears, answered that unfortunately, by every reckoning, the horse dealer must already have left Dahme and got across the border onto Brandenburg ground, where any attempt to interfere with his going on or to make him turn back would create exceedingly unpleasant and in all likelihood insurmountable difficulties. As the Elector fell back mutely on the pillow with a look of utter despair, the Chamberlain asked him what was in the paper and by what strange and inexplicable chance he had found out that the contents concerned himself. To this, however, the Elector gave no answer, only looking ambiguously at the Chamberlain, whose obligingness he was beginning to distrust; he lay there rigid, his heart beating nervously, staring down abstractedly at the corner of the handkerchief he was holding in his hands, when suddenly he asked the Chamberlain to summon the Junker von Stein, an energetic, clever young man whom he had often employed before in affairs of a secret nature, on the pretext that he had some other business to arrange with him. After explaining the matter to von Stein and impressing upon him the importance of the paper in Kohlhaas' possession, the Elector asked him if he wished to acquire an eternal claim on his friendship by getting hold of the paper for him before the horse dealer reached Berlin; and when the Junker, as soon as he had somewhat grasped the situation, which in truth was a very strange one, promised to serve him to the utmost of his ability, the Elector commanded him to ride after Kohlhaas and, since there was little likelihood of his being got at with money, to make him a shrewd speech and offer him his life and liberty in exchange for the paper—indeed, if Kohlhaas insisted on it, he should help him then and there, with horses, men and money, albeit prudently, to escape from the Brandenburg horsemen who were escorting him. The Junker, after requesting a letter of credentials which the Elector wrote out for him, immediately set out with several men, and, as he did not spare the horses, he was lucky enough to overtake Kohlhaas in a border village where the horse dealer, his five children, and the Knight von Malzahn were eating their midday meal in the open air before the door of a house. The Knight of Malzahn, on the Junker's introducing himself as a passing stranger who wished to catch a glimpse of his extraordinary prisoner, at once made him acquainted with Kohlhaas and courteously invited him to be seated; and since the Knight was coming and going continually in his preparations to leave, and the troopers were eating their dinner on the other side of the house, the Junker soon found an opportunity to tell the horse dealer who he was and the special business he came to him on.

The horse dealer already knew the title and name of the man who had swooned in the farmhouse at Dahme at the sight of the lead capsule and all he needed to climax the excitement into which this discovery had thrown him was to open the paper and read its secrets; but this, for various reasons, he was determined not to do for mere curiosity's sake. Replying to the Junker, he said that, in view of the ungenerous and unprincely treatment he had been forced to endure in Dresden despite his entire willingness to make every possible sacrifice, he would keep the paper. When the gentleman asked him why he gave this strange refusal to a proposal involving nothing less than his life and liberty, Kohlhaas said, "Noble sir, if your sovereign should come to me and say, 'I'll destroy myself and the whole pack of those who help me wield the scepter'—destroy himself, mind you, which is the dearest wish of my soul—I would still refuse him the paper, which is worth more to him than his life, and say, 'You can send me to the scaffold, but I can make you suffer, and I mean to.' " And Kohlhaas, with death staring him in the face, called a trooper over and invited him to have the large portion of food left in his dish. And all the rest of the hour that he spent in the place he behaved as if the Junker sitting at the table were not there, only turning to give him a parting glance when he climbed into the wagon.

The Elector's condition took such a turn for the worse on his receiving this news that for three critical days the doctor feared for his life. But thanks to the fundamental soundness of his constitution he recovered at the end of several painful weeks on a sickbed; or at least he was well enough to be placed in a carriage amply supplied with pillows and robes and carried back to Dresden to take up the affairs of government again. No sooner did he arrive in the city than he summoned Prince Christiern of Meissen and inquired how far along the arrangements were for the departure for Vienna of the attorney Eibenmayer, whom the government intended sending there as its legal representative to accuse Kohlhaas before his Imperial Majesty of breach of the peace of the Empire. The Prince replied that, pursuant to the Elector's orders on his departing for Dahme, the attorney had left for Vienna immediately after the arrival in Dresden of the jurist Zäuner, whom the Elector of Brandenburg had commissioned to proceed against the Junker Wenzel von Tronka in the matter of Kohlhaas' black horses.

The Elector, walking over to his desk with a flushed face, expressed surprise at such haste, for he thought he had made it clear that he wanted Eibenmayer's departure postponed until after a consultation they needed to have with Dr. Luther, who had procured the amnesty for Kohlhaas, when he meant to issue a more definitive order. As he said this, he shuffled together some letters and documents lying on his desk with an expression of suppressed annoyance. The Prince, after a pause in which he looked at him in surprise, said that he was sorry if he had displeased him in this matter; however, he could show him the Council of State's decision requiring him to send the attorney off at the aforesaid time. He added that nothing had been said in the Council about a consultation with Dr. Luther; earlier in the affair it might perhaps have served some purpose to give consideration to the churchman's views because of his intercession on Kohlhaas' behalf, but this was no longer the case now that the amnesty had been broken before the eyes of the whole world and the horse dealer had been arrested and handed over to the Brandenburg courts for sentencing and execution. Well, the Elector remarked, the mistake of sending Eibenmayer off was really not too serious; however, for the present, until further orders from himself, he did not wish the man to bring the action against Kohlhaas in Vienna, and he requested the Prince to send a courier to him immediately with instructions to that effect. Unfortunately, the Prince replied, this order came a day too late, as Eibenmayer, according to a report he had just received, had already gone ahead and presented his complaint to the State Chancery in Vienna. "How was all this possible in so short a time?" the Elector asked in dismay, to which the Prince replied that three weeks had already passed since Eibenmayer's departure and his instructions had been to settle the business with all possible dispatch as soon as he arrived in Vienna. Any delay, the Prince added, would have been all the more unseemly, seeing how the Brandenburg attorney, Zäuner, was pressing his case against the Junker Wenzel von Tronka with stubborn persistence; he had already made a motion for the court to remove the horses from the hands of the knacker for the time being, with a view to their being ultimately restored to health, and, in spite of all his opponent's objections, he had won his point. The Elector rang the bell, saying never mind, it did not matter, and after turning back to the Prince and asking him, with a show of unconcern, how things were going in Dresden otherwise, and what had happened in his absence, he lifted his hand and, unable to conceal his inner distress, signalled him to go. That same day the Elector sent the Prince a note asking for the entire Kohlhaas file, on the pretext that the political importance of the case required him to give it his personal attention; and since he could not bear to think of destroying the one man who could tell him the paper's secrets, he wrote a letter in his own hand to the

Emperor beseeching him with all his heart, for weighty reasons that he would perhaps be able to explain at greater length a little later on, to be allowed to withdraw for a time the accusation made against Kohlhaas by Eibenmayer. The Emperor, in a note drawn up by the State Chancery, replied as follows: he was astonished at the Elector's apparently sudden change of mind; the report that Saxony had furnished him on the Kohlhaas case made it a matter for the entire Holy Roman Empire; he consequently felt it his duty as Emperor to appear as Kohlhaas' accuser before the House of Brandenburg; and since the Court Justiciary, Franz Müller, had already gone to Berlin as the Emperor's advocate for the purpose of accusing Kohlhaas of breach of the public peace, retreat was no longer possible and the affair must take its course according to the law.

The Emperor's letter disheartened the Elector completely. When word reached him privately from Berlin a short time after that the action had been commenced before the High Court, and that Kohlhaas would in all probability end on the scaffold, the unhappy prince, resolving on one more effort, wrote a letter in his own hand to the Elector of Brandenburg in which he begged him to spare the horse dealer's life. He gave the pretext that the amnesty granted the man did not, in justice, permit a death sentence to be executed on him; assured the Elector that, in spite of the apparent severity with which Kohlhaas had been treated in Saxony, it had never been his intention to let him die; and described how inconsolable he would feel if the protection Berlin had said it wished to extend to the man should, by an unexpected turn of events, prove worse for him in the end than if he had remained in Dresden and his case had been decided according to Saxon law. The Elector of Brandenburg, to whom much in this account seemed ambiguous and obscure, answered that the vigor with which His Majesty's counsel was proceeding made any departure from the strict letter of the law in order to satisfy his wish absolutely out of the question. The misgivings that he had expressed about the justice of the proceeding were really excessive: for though the Elector of Saxony had granted Kohlhaas an amnesty for the offenses of which he now stood accused before the High Court in Berlin, it was not he who was the accuser but the Supreme Head of the Empire, whom the amnesty in no way bound. At the same time he pointed out how necessary it was, in view of Nagelschmidt's continuing outrages, which the outlaw, with unheard of audacity, had even carried as far as Brandenburg, to make an example of Kohlhaas; and asked him, in case he was not swayed by these considerations, to appeal to the Emperor himself, since an edict of reprieve for Kohlhaas could only be proclaimed by His Majesty.

The Elector fell ill again from chagrin and vexation over all these unsuccessful efforts; and when the Chamberlain visited his bedside one morning, he was moved to show him the letters he had written to Vienna and Berlin in his efforts to obtain a reprieve for Kohlhaas and in that way gain some time in which to try to get hold of the paper in the latter's possession. The Chamberlain fell on his knees in front of him and pleaded in the name of everything he held sacred and precious to tell him what the paper said. The Elector asked him to bolt the door and sit on his bed; and after taking his hand and pressing it to his heart with a sigh, he began as follows: "Your wife, I gather, has already told you how the Elector of Brandenburg and I encountered a gypsy woman on the third day of our meeting in Jüterbock. Now the Elector, who has a very lively spirit, had decided to play a joke on the bizarre old woman and ruin her reputation for soothsaying, which had just been all the talk at dinner, in front of all the people. Walking up to her table with folded arms, he demanded a sign from her, one that could be put to the proof that very day, to confirm the truth of the fortune she should tell him; claiming that otherwise, though she were the Roman Sibyl herself, he could not believe one word she said. The woman, measuring us at a glance from head to foot, said that this was the sign: the big horned roebuck that the gardener's son was raising in the park would come to meet us in the market place where we were standing, before we should have gone away. Now the roebuck, you must understand, was intended for the Dresden kitchen and was kept under lock and key inside an enclosure surrounded by high palings and shaded by the oaks of the park; and since the park as a whole, as well as the garden leading into it, was also kept carefully locked because of the smaller game and the fowl they contained, it was impossible to see how the beast could fulfill the strange prediction and come to meet us in the square. Nevertheless, the Elector was afraid there was some trick in it, and after a short consultation with me, since he was absolutely bent on exposing the ridiculousness of everything she had to say, he sent to the castle and ordered the roebuck slaughtered then and there and the carcass dressed for dinner on one of the next days. Then, turning back to the woman, before whom all this had been openly done, he said, 'Well, now! What kind of fortune have you got to tell me?' The woman studied his palm and said, 'Hail, my Elector and Sovereign! Your Grace shall rule for many years, the house from which you spring shall endure for many years, and your descendents shall be great and glorious and more powerful than all the other princes and sovereigns of the earth!'

"For a brief moment the Elector looked thoughtfully at the woman, then muttered in an undertone, as he took a step toward me, that now he almost regretted sending a messenger to stop the prophecy from coming true; and while the knights who followed him, amid loud rejoicing, showered money into the woman's lap, to which he added a gold piece from his own pocket, he asked her whether the greeting that she had for me had as silvery a sound as his. The woman, after opening a box at her side, very deliberately arranging the money in it according to kind and quantity, and then closing it again, shaded her eyes with her hand as if the sun annoyed her and looked at me; and when I repeated the question to her, and jokingly added to the Elector, while she studied my hand, 'She has nothing very pleasant to say to me, it seems,' she seized her crutches, laboriously raised herself up from the stool by them, and, pressing close to me with her hands held out mysteriously in front of her, she whispered distinctly in my ear, 'No!'

" 'Is that so?' I said in confusion, recoiling a step before her cold and lifeless look, which seemed to come from eyes of marble, as she sat down again on the stool behind her. 'From what direction does the danger to my house come?' Taking charcoal and paper and crossing her knees, she asked whether she should write it down for me; and when I said, 'Yes, please do,' because I was really at a loss and there was simply nothing else for me to say under the circumstances, she replied, 'All right. I will write down three things for you: the name of the last ruler your house shall have, the year in which he shall lose his throne, and the name of the man who shall seize it for himself by force of arms.' And having done so under the eyes of the crowd, she arose, sealed the paper with gum that she moistened in her wrinkled mouth, and pressed it with a leaden signet ring that she wore on her middle finger. And when I reached for the paper, more curious than words can express, as you may well imagine, she said, 'No, no, no, your Highness!' turned, and pointed with one of her crutches. 'From that man there, the one with the feathered bonnet, standing on the bench in the church entrance, behind all the people—get the paper back from him, if you like!' And before I could quite understand what she was saying, she turned around and left me standing speechless with astonishment in the square; clapping shut the box behind her and slinging it over her shoulder, she vanished into the crowd, and that was the last I saw of her. But at that very moment, I confess to my immense relief, the knight whom the Elector had sent to the castle reappeared and reported to him, with a broad grin, that two hunters had killed the roebuck under his very eyes and hauled it off to the kitchen. The Elector jovially put his arm through mine with the intention of leading me from the square, and said, 'Well, do you see? Her prophecy was just an ordinary swindle, not worth the time and money it cost us!' But what was our surprise when a shout went up, even before these words were fairly out of his mouth, all around the square, and everybody turned to see a huge butcher's dog trotting toward us from the castle yard with the roebuck that he had seized by the neck in the kitchen as fair game; and, hotly pursued by the kitchen menials, he let it fall to the ground three paces from us—and so in fact the woman's prophecy, which had been her pledge for the truth of everything she said, was fulfilled, and the roebuck, dead though it was, to be sure, had come to meet us in the market place.

"The lightning that plummets from a winter's sky is no more devastating than this sight was to me, and my first endeavor, as soon as I got free of the people around me, was to discover the whereabouts of the man with the feathered bonnet whom the woman had pointed out to me; but none of my people, though they searched without stop for three days, could discover even the remotest trace of his existence. And then, friend Kunz, a few days ago, in the farmhouse at Dahme, I saw the man with my own eyes!" And letting go the Chamberlain's hand and wiping his sweating face, he fell back on the couch.

The Chamberlain, who thought it a waste of effort to try and convince the Elector of his own very different view of this incident, urged him to use any and every means to get hold of the paper, and afterwards to leave the fellow to his fate; but the Elector said that he saw absolutely no way of doing so, although the thought of having to do without the paper, or perhaps see all knowledge of it perish with the man, nearly drove him out of his mind. When his friend asked him if he had made any attempt to find the gypsy woman, the Elector said that he had ordered the Government to search for her, on some pretext or other, throughout the length and breadth of the Electorate, which they had been doing to this very day without result, but that for reasons he would rather not go into he doubted whether she could ever be found in Saxony. Now it happened that the Chamberlain intended to visit Berlin to see about a number of large properties in Neumark that his wife had inherited from Count Kallheim, whose death had followed upon his dismissal from the Chancellorship; and as he really loved the Elector, he asked him, after a moment's reflection, if he would allow him a free hand with the whole business. When his master pressed his hand warmly to his breast and said, "Be myself in this, and get me the paper!" the Chamberlain turned over his affairs of office, advanced his departure by several days and, leaving his wife behind, set out for Berlin accompanied only by a few servants.

Meanwhile Kohlhaas had arrived in Berlin, as we have said, and by special order of the Elector of Brandenburg was lodged in a knights' jail, where he and his five children were made as comfortable as circumstances permitted. As soon as the Imperial Attorney General from Vienna appeared, he was summoned to the bar of the High Court to answer the charge of breach of the peace of the Empire; and when he pleaded in his own defense that he could not be indicted for his armed invasion of Saxony and the acts of violence accompanying it because of the agreement he had made with the Elector of Saxony at Lützen, he was formally apprised that His Majesty the Emperor, whose Attorney General was the complainant in the case, could not give that any consideration. The matter having been explained to him in detail, however, and on his being assured that on the other hand full satisfaction would be given him in Dresden in his action against the Junker Wenzel von Tronka, he very soon yielded his defense. Thus it fell out that on the very day that the Chamberlain arrived in Berlin, sentence was pronounced and Kohlhaas was condemned to die on the block—a sentence which, in spite of its mercifulness, seeing how complicated the affair was, no one believed would be carried out, which indeed the whole city, knowing the goodwill the Elector bore Kohlhaas, confidently expected to see commuted to a simple, even if long and severe, term of imprisonment. The Chamberlain, who nevertheless understood that there was no time to be lost if he was to execute his master's commission, started out by showing himself to Kohlhaas in his ordinary court costume, clearly and close at hand, one morning when the horse dealer was standing at the window of his prison innocently studying the passers-by; and, concluding from a sudden movement of Kohlhaas' head that he had noticed him, and observing with particular satisfaction how his hand went involuntarily to the part of his chest where the capsule hung, he considered what had passed at that moment in Kohlhaas' soul as sufficient preparation for his going one step further in his attempt to get hold of the paper. He sent for an old woman that hobbled around on crutches selling old clothes, whom he had noticed in a crowd of other ragpickers in the streets of Berlin and who seemed to tally fairly well in her age and dress with the woman described to him by the Elector; and as he felt sure that the old gypsy woman's features had not impressed themselves very sharply on Kohlhaas' memory, since he had had only a fleeting glimpse of her as she handed him the paper, he decided to pass the one woman off as the other and have her masquerade, if possible, as the gypsy with Kohlhaas. To acquaint her with her part, he gave her a detailed account of everything that had taken place between the Elector and the gypsy woman, making sure, as he did not know how much the latter had revealed to Kohlhaas, to lay particular stress on the three mysterious items in the paper; and after explaining how she must mutter an incoherent and incomprehensible speech in which she would let it fall that schemes were afoot to get hold of the paper, on which the Saxon court set great importance, by force or cunning, he instructed her to pretend to Kohlhaas that the paper was no longer safe with him and to ask him to give it into her keeping for a few critical days. The old-clothes woman consented at once to do what was asked of her, provided she received a large reward, a part of which she insisted on the Chamberlain's paying her in advance; and since some months ago she had made the ac-

quaintance of the mother of Herse, the groom that fell at Mühlberg, and this woman had the Government's permission to visit
Kohlhaas occasionally, it was an easy matter for her, a few days
later, to slip something into the warder's palm and gain admission
to the horse dealer.

Kohlhaas, indeed, on the woman's entering and his seeing the
signet ring on her hand and a coral chain hanging around her neck,
thought he recognized the same old gypsy woman who had handed
him the paper in Jüterbock; but probability is not always on the
side of truth, and something had happened here which we must
perforce record but which those who may wish to question are
perfectly free to do: the Chamberlain had committed a most co-
lossal blunder, and in the old-clothes woman whom he had picked
up in the streets of Berlin to impersonate the gypsy woman he had
stumbled upon that very same mysterious gypsy woman whom he
wished to have impersonated. At any rate, the woman told Kohlhaas, as she leaned on her crutches and patted the cheeks of the
children, who, scared by her strange appearance, shrank back
against their father, that she had returned to Brandenburg from
Saxony some time ago, and hearing the Chamberlain incautiously
ask in the streets of Berlin about the gypsy woman who had been
in Jüterbock in the previous spring, she had immediately pressed
forward and offered herself, under a false name, for the business
that he wanted done. The horse dealer was so struck by the un-
canny likeness he discovered between her and his dead wife that
he was inclined to ask the old woman whether she was Lisbeth's
grandmother; for not only did the features of her face, as well as
her still well-shaped hands and the way she gestured with them as
she spoke, remind him vividly of Lisbeth, but he even noticed a
mole on her neck just like the one Lisbeth had had. Amid a confusion of thoughts such as he had seldom experienced, the horse
dealer invited her to sit down and asked what business of the
Chamberlain's she could possibly have with him. The Chamberlain, she said, as Kohlhaas' old dog sniffed around her knees and
wagged his tail when she scratched his head, had instructed her to
disclose to the horse dealer the three questions that were so important to the Saxon court, the mysterious answers to which were
contained in the paper; to warn him of an envoy who was in Berlin for the purpose of obtaining it; and to ask him for the paper

on the pretext that it was no longer safe in his bosom where he carried it. But, she said, the real reason for her coming was to tell him that the threat to get the paper away from him by force or cunning was an absurd and empty one; that he need not have the least fear for its safety while he was in the custody of the Elector of Brandenburg; that the paper, indeed, was much safer with him than with her; and that he should take care not to give it up to anybody, regardless of who it was or what the pretext. Nevertheless, she said in conclusion, he would be wise, in her opinion, to use the paper for the purpose she had given it to him at the Jüterbock fair: let him lend a favorable ear to the offer that the Junker von Stein had made him on the frontier and surrender the paper to the Elector of Saxony in return for his life and liberty. Kohlhaas, who exulted in the power given him to wound his enemy mortally in the heel at the very moment that it was treading him in the dust, replied, "Not for the world, Granny, not for the world!" squeezed the old woman's hand, and only wanted to know what the paper's answers were to the awful questions. The old woman lifted the youngest child, who had been squatting at her feet, onto her lap and said, "Not for the world, Kohlhaas the horse dealer, but for this pretty little fair-headed boy!" and she smiled at the child and petted him as he looked at her wide-eyed, and with her bony hands gave him an apple from her pocket. Kohlhaas, disconcerted, said that the children themselves, when they were grown, would approve his conduct, and that he could do nothing better for them and for their grandchildren than to keep the paper. Besides, he asked, after what had happened to him, who was there to guarantee him against his being deceived a second time, and would he not in the end be fruitlessly sacrificing the paper to the Elector just as he had recently done his band of men at Lützen? "Once a man has broken his word to me, I never trust him again. Only a clear and unmistakable request from you can part me from this bit of writing, through which satisfaction has been given me so wonderfully for all that I have suffered." The old woman, putting the child down again, said that in many respects he was right and he could do just as he pleased. And she took hold of her crutches to leave. Kohlhaas again asked her what was in that marvelous paper; he was eager, he said—as she quickly interjected that of course he could open it, but it would be pure curiosity on his part—to find out about a thousand other things before she left: who she really was, how she had come by the knowledge she possessed, why she had refused to give the paper to the Elector, for whom it had been written, after all, and among so many thousands of people had handed it just to him, Kohlhaas, who had never wanted anything from her skill.

But just at that moment some police officers were heard mounting the stairs and the old woman, alarmed lest she be discovered in the place, said, "Goodbye, Kohlhaas, goodbye till we meet again, when there won't be one of these things you shall not know!" And turning toward the door, she cried, "Farewell, children, farewell!" kissed the little people one after the other, and vanished.

Meanwhile the Elector of Saxony, a prey to his despairing thoughts, had called in two astrologers, named Oldenholm and Olearius, who then enjoyed a considerable reputation in Saxony, to ask their advice about the mysterious piece of paper that was so important to him and his posterity; but when, after an earnest investigation lasting several days that they conducted in the Dresden palace tower, the men could not agree as to whether the prophecy aimed at the centuries to come or at the present time, with perhaps the Polish crown being meant, with whom relations were still very warlike, the uneasiness, not to say despair, in which this unhappy lord found himself, being only intensified by such learned disputes, finally reached a pitch that was more than his spirit could bear. And on top of it all, just at this time the Chamberlain sent word to his wife, who was about to follow him to Berlin, to break the news discreetly to the Elector before she left that after an unsuccessful attempt he had made with the help of an old woman who had not been heard of since, their hopes of ever getting hold of the paper in Kohlhaas' possession seemed very dim, seeing that the death sentence pronounced on the horse dealer had now at last been signed by the Elector of Brandenburg, after a complete review of the file of the case, and the day of execution fixed for the Monday after Palm Sunday—at which news the Elector shut himself up in his room like a lost soul, his heart consumed by grief, but on the third day, after sending a short note to the Government House that he was going to the Prince of Dessau's to hunt, suddenly disappeared from Dresden. Where he actually went, and whether in fact he arrived in Dessau, we shall not attempt to say, as the chronicles which we have compared oddly contradict and cancel one another on this point. This much, however, is certain: that at this very time the Prince of Dessau lay ill in Brunswick at his uncle Duke Heinrich's residence and was hardly in a state to go hunting, and that the next evening Lady Heloise arrived in Berlin to join her husband Sir Kunz the Chamberlain in the company of a certain Count von Königstein, whom she introduced as her cousin.

Meanwhile, at the Elector of Brandenburg's order, the death sentence was read to Kohlhaas, his chains were struck off, and the property deeds taken from him in Dresden were returned; and when the counselors assigned him by the court asked what disposition he wished to make of his possessions, he drew up a will, with the help of a notary, in favor of his children and appointed his honest friend the bailiff of Kohlhaasenbrück to be their guardian. Nothing could match the peace and contentment of his last days; for soon after, a special Electoral decree unlocked the prison chamber in which he was kept to all his friends, of whom he had a great many in the city, who were free to visit him day and night. Indeed, he even had the satisfaction, one day, of seeing the theologian Jacob Freising enter his jail with a letter for him from Dr. Luther in the latter's own hand—without doubt a most remarkable missive, all trace of which, however, has been lost; and from the hands of his minister, in the presence of two Brandenburg deans who assisted him, he received the blessing of the Holy Communion.

And now the fateful Monday after Palm Sunday arrived, on which Kohlhaas was to make atonement to the world for his all too rash attempt to take its justice into his own hands, amid a general commotion in the city which could not disabuse itself even yet of the hope of seeing him saved by an Electoral pardon. Just as he was passing out of the gate of the jail under a strong escort, with the theologian Jacob Freising leading the way and his two little boys in his arms (for he had expressly asked this favor at the bar of the court), the castellan of the Electoral palace came up to Kohlhaas through the crowd of grieving friends around him who were shaking his hand and saying goodbye, and with a haggard face handed him a paper that he said an old woman had given him. Kohlhaas stared in surprise at the man, whom he hardly knew, and opened the paper; its gum seal bore an impression that instantly recalled the gypsy woman. But who can describe the astonishment that gripped him when he read the following communication: "Kohlhaas, the Elector of Saxony is in Berlin; he has already gone ahead of you to the place of execution and can be recognized, if that is of any interest to you, by the hat with blue and white plumes he has on. I don't have to tell you what his purpose is: as soon as you are buried he is going to dig the capsule up and read the paper inside it. Your Elizabeth."

Kohlhaas, completely dumbfounded, turned to the castellan and asked him if he knew the mysterious woman who had given him the note. But just as the castellan answered: "Kohlhaas, the woman——" and then halted strangely in the middle of his sentence, the procession, starting up again, swept the horse dealer along and he was unable to make out what the man, who seemed to be trembling in every limb, was saying.

When he arrived at the scaffold, he found the Elector of Brandenburg and his suite, which included the Archchancellor Sir Heinrich von Geusau, sitting their horses in the midst of an immense crowd of people; on the Elector's right stood the Imperial Attorney General, Franz Müller, with a copy of the death sentence in his hand; on his left, his own attorney, Anton Zäuner, with the Dresden court's decree; in the center of the half-open circle, which the crowd completed, stood a herald with a bundle of articles in his hand, and the two black horses, sleek with health and pawing the ground with their hooves. For the action that the Archchancellor Sir Heinrich had started at Dresden in his master's name against the Junker Wenzel von Tronka having triumphed in every point, without the slightest reservation, a banner had been waved over the horses' heads to make them honorable again, they had been removed from the knacker's care, fattened by the Junker's men, and handed over, in the Dresden market place, to the horse dealer's attorney in the presence of a specially appointed commission. When Kohlhaas, with his guard, advanced up the knoll to the Elector, the latter said, "Well, Kohlhaas, this is the day on which justice is done you. Look here, I am giving you back everything that was taken from you by force at Tronka Castle, which I as your sovereign was duty bound to restore to you: the two blacks, the neckerchief, gold gulden, laundry—everything down to the money for the doctor's bills for your man Herse who fell at Mühlberg. Now are you satisfied with me?"

At a sign from the Chancellor the decree was handed to Kohlhaas, who set down on the ground the two children he was carrying and read it through with sparkling eyes; and when he found that it contained a clause condemning the Junker Wenzel von Tronka to two years' imprisonment, his feelings overcame him and, crossing his hands on his breast, he knelt down from afar before the Elector. Rising again and putting his hand in his bosom, he joyfully assured the Archchancellor that his dearest wish on earth had been fulfilled; walked over to the horses, examined them and patted their plump necks; and, coming back to the Chancellor, cheerfully announced that he was giving them to his two sons Heinrich and Leopold! The Archchancellor, Sir Heinrich von Geusau, looking down at him kindly from his horse, promised in the name of the Elector that his last wish would be held sacred, and also asked him if he would not dispose as he thought best of the things in the bundle. Kohlhaas thereupon called Herse's old mother, whom he had caught sight of in the square, out of the crowd, and, giving her the things, he said, "Here, Granny, these belong to you!"—adding the sum he had received as damages to the money in the bundle, as a gift to help provide for her in her old age.

The Elector called out, "Kohlhaas the horse dealer, now that satisfaction has been given you in this wise, you on your side prepare to satisfy His Majesty the Emperor, whose attorney stands right here, for breach of the public peace!" Taking off his hat and tossing it on the ground, Kohlhaas said he was ready to do so; he lifted the children from the ground one more time and hugged them tightly; then, giving them to the bailiff of Kohlhaasenbrück, who, weeping silently, led them away from the square with him, he advanced to the block. He had just unknotted his neckerchief and opened his tunic when he gave a quick glance around the circle formed by the crowd and caught sight, a short way off, of a figure that he knew with blue and white plumes, standing between two knights whose bodies half hid him from view. Kohlhaas, striding up in front of the man with a suddenness that took his guard by surprise, drew out the capsule, removed the paper, unsealed it and read it through; and looking steadily at the man with the blue and white plumes, in whose breast fond hopes were already beginning to spring, he stuck the paper in his mouth and swallowed it. At this sight the man with the blue and white crest was seized by a fit and fell unconscious to the ground. Kohlhaas, however, while his dismayed companions bent over him and raised him from the ground, turned around to the scaffold where his head fell under the executioner's ax.

So ends the story of Kohlhaas. Amid the general lamentation of the people, his body was laid in a coffin; and while the bearers lifted it from the ground to carry it to the graveyard in the outskirts of the city for decent burial, the Elector of Brandenburg called the dead man's sons to him and, instructing the Archchancellor to enroll them in his school for pages, dubbed them knights on the spot. Shortly thereafter the Elector of Saxony returned to Dresden, shattered in body and soul; what happened subsequently there must be sought in history. Some hale and hearty descendants of Kohlhaas, however, were still living in Mecklenburg in the last century.

Translated by Martin Greenberg

The Earthquake in Chile

Heinrich von Kleist

In Santiago, the capital of the kingdom of Chile, at the moment of the great earthquake of the year 1647 in which many thousands lost their lives, a young Spaniard called Jeronimo Rugera, who had been accused of a crime, was standing beneath one of the pilasters of his prison cell and was about to hang himself. A year or so previously Don Henrico Asteron, one of the richest noblemen of the city, had expelled him from his house where he had been employed as a tutor, because he had been intimate with Donna Josepha, his employer's only daughter. After an explicit warning, a secret appointment, revealed to the old man by his proud son whose malice made him watchful, aroused his indignation to such an extent that he placed her in the Carmelite convent of Our Lady of the Mountain.

A happy chance had enabled Jeronimo to resume the liaison in this very place; and on a silent night he had made the convent garden the scene of his complete happiness. It was the feast of Corpus Christi and the solemn procession of nuns, followed by the novices, was just beginning when the unfortunate Josepha, now in the pangs of childbirth, collapsed on the Cathedral steps amidst the pealing of bells.

This occurrence made an extraordinary stir. Without consideration for her condition, the young sinner was at once taken to prison; and she had hardly begun her confinement when, at the bishop's command, a most rigorous trial was opened. The scandal was discussed with such bitterness in the city, and the whole convent in which it had taken place was attacked by so many sharp tongues that neither the appeal of the Asteron family, nor even the wish of the abbess, who had taken a liking to the young girl on account of her otherwise irreproachable conduct, could soften the severity with which she was threatened by monastic law. All that could be done—and this to the great resentment of the matrons and virgins of Santiago—was to induce the Viceroy to commute the sentence of death by burning into one of decapitation.

Windows were hired out in the street through which the culprit was due to pass to her execution, the roofs of houses were pulled down, and the pious daughters of the city invited their girl friends to attend at their sisterly sides the spectacle offered to divine vengeance.

Jeronimo, who meanwhile had also been put in prison, almost lost consciousness when informed of this monstrous turn of events. In vain he pondered how he might rescue her; everywhere, though borne on the pinions of reckless thought, he ran into bolts and walls, and an attempt to file through the prison bars only ended in discovery and even closer confinement. He fell on his knees in front of an image of the Holy Mother of God, who alone could offer salvation now, and prayed to her with boundless fervor.

Yet the fearful day appeared and with it the conviction of the utter hopelessness of his position. The bells, which accompanied Josepha's passage to the place of execution with their ringing, could be heard clearly in the cell, and despair seized his soul. Life began to be odious to him and he resolved to kill himself with a rope that had been left by chance in his cell. At this moment, as was already mentioned, he was standing beneath a pilaster fastening the rope, which was to take him out of the clutches of this wretched world, to an iron bracket attached to the cornice, when suddenly the greater part of the city caved in with a crack, as if the firmament itself had collapsed, and buried all the living under its rubble. Jeronimo Rugera was stiff with horror and, as though his consciousness had been wholly shattered, he now clung to the pilaster on which he had intended to die to keep himself from falling. The ground swayed under his feet. The prison walls cracked, and the whole building leaned as if it were about to crash down into the street. Only the fall of the house opposite prevented total collapse of the prison by partly supporting it. Trembling, his hair on end, his knees threatening to give way, Jeronimo slipped down the steeply inclined floor toward the opening made in the prison's front by the collision of the two buildings.

He was scarcely outside when a second tremor completely demolished the buildings still remaining on the shaken street. Without thinking how he might save himself from the general doom, he hurried on over debris and beams to the nearest city gate, while death launched attacks against him from all directions. Here another house caved in and, hurling rubble about, drove him into a side street. There the flame, flashing in clouds of smoke, curled out of every gable and drove him, terrified, into another street. Here, the Mapocho River, lifted out of its banks, rolled toward him with a roar and swept him into a third. Here lay a heap of corpses; here people shouted on burning roof-tops; there men and animals struggled with the waves; here a brave rescuer endeavored to help; there stood another man pale as death, and silently extended his trembling hands to heaven.

When Jeronimo had reached the gate and climbed a hill beyond it, he fainted.

He had lain there, completely unconscious, for a quarter of an hour or so when he recovered and half raised himself up, his back turned to the city. He touched his forehead and chest, not knowing what to make of his situation, and an unspeakable feeling of bliss came over him when the west wind from the sea fanned his returning life and his eyes wandered in all directions over the fertile environs of Santiago. Only the crowds of bewildered people, now visible everywhere, oppressed him; he could not understand what had brought them and him to this place, and only when he turned round and saw the city razed behind him did he remember the most horrible moment of his life. He bowed so low that his forehead touched the ground as he thanked God for his miraculous escape and, just as if the impression of his one horrible experience had removed all traces of the earlier ones, he wept with joy at the thought that life and all its various delights had not been taken from him.

But a ring on his finger recalled Josepha and, together with her, his prison, the bells he had heard there and the moments which preceded the collapse of the building. Deep sorrow filled him again; he began to regret his prayer and thought that it was a terrible being who ruled above the clouds. He joined the people occupied with the salvaging of their property, who poured out of the gates. Not without timidity, he ventured to ask them about Asteron's daughter and whether the execution had taken place; but no one gave him detailed information. A woman who carried an incredible load of household goods on her back, bent almost to the ground, with two small children clinging to her waist, said in passing, as though she herself had witnessed it, that Josepha had been beheaded. Jeronimo turned back; and since, when he calculated the time, he himself could not doubt the execution of the sentence, he sat down in a deserted wood and abandoned himself entirely to his grief. He wished that the destructive violence of nature might overwhelm him once more. He could not grasp why he had escaped that death which his afflicted soul desired, at the very moment when it had been freely offered to him on all sides. He firmly resolved not to hesitate if even now the oaks were uprooted and their crests came crashing down upon him.

Later, when he had wept long enough, and hope had returned in the midst of his tears, he got up and searched the fields. He visited every hill-top on which people were assembled. On every road along which the stream of refugees still swept he went out to meet them. His trembling legs carried him wherever a woman's dress flapped in the wind, but none covered the beloved daughter of Asteron. The sun was going down, and with it his hope, when he stepped on to the edge of a rock and the view into a wide valley opened out to him. Few people were to be seen. Not sure what he should do next, he let his eyes stray over the isolated groups and was about to turn away when suddenly he observed a young woman near the stream which irrigates the valley; she was washing a child. His heart leapt at the sight. Filled with presentiments, he jumped down over the rocks, calling out, "Most holy Mother of God!" and recognized Josepha when, shyly, she looked round at the sound. How blissfully they embraced, these wretches saved by a heavenly miracle!

Josepha's fatal procession had taken her quite close to the place of execution, when the whole assembly was violently scattered by the crashing buildings. Her first fearful footsteps impelled her toward the nearest gate; but she soon regained control of her senses and turned back to the convent, where she had left her helpless little son. She found the whole convent already in flames and the abbess, who had promised to take care of the infant during those minutes which were to be Josepha's last, was at the entrance, crying out for help to save him. Fearlessly, Josepha rushed into the smoke which poured out at her, into the collapsing building and, just as if all the angels of heaven were protecting her, appeared again at the portal with the child. She was about to embrace the abbess, who was covering her head with her clasped hands, when this lady was struck and killed by a falling gable, together with nearly all her nuns. Josepha retreated trembling at this sight; she hastily closed the abbess's eyes and fled, utterly terrified, to deliver the precious child whom heaven had restored to her from the present danger.

She had taken only a few paces when she ran into the Archbishop's crushed body which had just been pulled out of the debris of the Cathedral. The Viceroy's Palace had collapsed, the law courts in which sentence had been passed on her were in flames and in the place where her father's house had stood there was a lake which emitted reddish vapors. Josepha summoned all her strength to sustain her. She hardened herself against all this wretchedness, bravely walked on from street to street with her prize and was already near the gate when she saw the nearly demolished prison in which Jeronimo had languished. The sight of this made her reel and she would have fallen down in a swoon in some corner, had not the collapse of a building weakened by the tremors driven her on again and strengthened her resistance. She kissed the child, wiped the tears out of her eyes and, no longer aware of the surrounding horrors, reached the gate. When she found herself in the open country, she soon gathered that not everyone who had been inside a demolished building had necessarily been crushed beneath it.

At the next crossroads she paused and waited to see whether perhaps another, dearest to her after little Philip, would appear. Since he did not come, and the pushing mob grew in size, she went on, turned back again, waited again and, shedding many tears, crept into a dark, pine-shaded valley to pray for his soul, since she believed him to be dead. But here in the valley she found her lover, and such joy that it might have been the Valley of Eden.

In a voice filled with emotion, she told all this to Jeronimo and when she had finished, gave him the boy to kiss. Jeronimo took him, fondled him with a father's unspeakable joy, and when his stranger's face made the infant cry, caressed him till he was silent.

Meanwhile the loveliest of nights had descended on them, full of marvelously gentle fragrance, silvery and still as only a poet might dream of it. Everywhere along the banks of the stream people had sat down in the glittering moonlight and were preparing soft beds of moss and foliage to rest upon after the terrors of that day. And since the poor creatures were still lamenting, one the loss of his house, another that of his wife and child, and a third of everything, Jeronimo and Josepha crept away to a denser thicket so that the secret exultation of their souls would not give offense to anyone. They found a splendid pomegranate tree with outspread branches full of scented fruit, and the nightingale piped his voluptuous song on the tree's crest. Here Jeronimo seated himself, leaning against its trunk; Josepha on his lap and Philip on hers, they sat and rested, wrapped in his cloak.

The tree's shadow passed over them with its scattered lights and the moon was already fading as the dawn grew red before they went to sleep. For they had endless things to talk over, about the convent garden and the prisons, and what they had suffered for the other's sake, and they were deeply moved at the thought of how much misery had to be brought into the world so that they might be happy!

They planned to go to Concepción as soon as the tremors had ceased, for an intimate friend of Josepha's, from whom they hoped to obtain a small loan, lived there. With this sum they would embark for Spain, where Jeronimo's relatives on his mother's side were living, there to conclude their happy lives. Thereupon, amidst many kisses, they went to sleep.

When they awoke the sun was high in the sky, and they found several families busily preparing a small breakfast at the fire. Jeronimo was just wondering how to obtain food for his own, when a well-dressed young man with a child in his arms approached Josepha and asked her modestly whether she would feed at her breast this poor little wretch whose mother lay injured under those trees. Josepha was a little confused when she recognized him to be an acquaintance; but since, misinterpreting her uneasiness, he continued, "It will only be for a few minutes, Donna Josepha, and this child has not been fed since that hour which made us all unhappy," she said, "The reason for my silence—was a different one,

Don Fernando; in these terrible times no one refuses to let others share whatever he may possess." She handed her own child to its father, took the little stranger and put him to her breast.

Don Fernando was very grateful for this kindness and asked her to come with him to his own party who were preparing breakfast. Josepha answered that she would accept the offer with pleasure. Since Jeronimo made no objection, she followed him to his family, where she was received in the most tender and affectionate manner by Don Fernando's two sisters-in-law whom she knew to be very worthy young ladies.

Donna Elvira, Don Fernando's wife, who was lying on the ground, her feet seriously injured, drew Josepha down toward her in a most friendly way when she saw her own weakened boy at her breast. Don Pedro too, his father-in-law, who was wounded in the shoulder, nodded to her affably.

In the minds of Jeronimo and Josepha strange thoughts began to stir. They found themselves treated with so much candor and kindness, that they did not know what to think of their past. The scaffold, the prison and the bells—had they only dreamed of these? It seemed as if the minds of these people, after the terrible blow which had shaken them to their foundations, were ready for reconciliation. Their memories could not penetrate beyond it. Only Donna Elizabeth, who had been invited by a friend to yesterday's spectacle, but had refused the invitation, sometimes directed a dreamy and lingering look at Josepha; but new reports of some gruesome misfortune soon recalled her spirit to the present from which it had scarcely escaped.

They heard how, immediately after the first main tremor, the city was full of women who were delivered in the sight of all the men; how the monks had run about with crucifixes in their hands, shouting that the end of the world had come; how a guard, who at the Viceroy's order had demanded that a church be cleared of people, had received the reply that there was no longer a Viceroy of Chile! How, at the most frightful moments, the Viceroy had been obliged to erect gallows to end the outbreak of looting, and an innocent man who was leaving a burning house by the back door had been seized by the owner in excessive haste and immediately strung up.

Donna Elvira, with whose injuries Josepha was much occupied, had chosen the moment when these stories were being bandied in the most lively fashion to ask Josepha how she had fared on this most fearful day. And when Josepha, with terror in her voice, told her some of the main features of her story she had the supreme satisfaction of seeing tears in this lady's eyes. Donna Elvira grasped her hand, pressed it and intimated that she should be silent. Josepha felt as if she were among the blessed. A feeling which she could not repress gave to the preceding day, however much misery it had brought into the world, the appearance of a blessing such as heaven had never yet bestowed on her. And indeed, in the midst of this catastrophe in which all the earthly possessions of men had perished and the whole of nature was threatened with burial, the human spirit seemed to unfold like a lovely flower. In the fields, as far as the eye could reach, men and women of all classes could be seen lying about together, princes and beggars, noble matrons and peasant women, government officials and day laborers, friars and nuns, pitying one another, helping one another, gladly giving away anything they had saved for the preservation of life, as if the general calamity had welded all those who had escaped it into one family.

Instead of the meaningless conversations, for which at other times the world of tea tables had provided the subject matter, they now discussed examples of tremendous deeds: men who formerly had received little attention from society had shown a Roman greatness of character. There were innumerable instances of fearlessness, of joyful contempt for danger, of self-denial and divine self-sacrifice, even of the throwing away of life itself as though it were the most trivial of possessions and could be replaced without difficulty. Indeed, since there was no one who on that day had not experienced some stirring incident or had not himself performed some generous action, the pain in every human heart was mingled with so much sweetness and delight that, she thought, it was difficult to say whether the sum of general well-being had not increased on the one hand by as much as it had lost on the other.

Jeronimo took Josepha's arm after they had silently exhausted themselves in making these observations, and inexpressibly at peace, he walked with her under the shady leaves of the pomegranate trees. He told her that in view of the general state of mind and the total upheaval of the social order, he was giving up his intention of embarking for Europe; that, should the Viceroy still be alive, he would risk a personal appeal to him. The Viceroy had always been favorably disposed toward his cause. He hoped (at this moment he kissed her) to remain with her in Chile. Josepha replied that similar thoughts had occurred to her; that she too did not doubt her father's readiness to forgive her, if he was still alive; but that she advised him to go to Concepción and to address a written appeal to the Viceroy, rather than throw himself at his feet, since in any case they would then be near the harbor and at best, if their business achieved the desired results, could easily return to Santiago. After brief consideration, Jeronimo expressed his approval of this prudent precaution, walked on a little through avenues of trees, anticipating the happy moments of their future, and returned with her to the company.

Meanwhile the afternoon had come. Since the tremors were now less violent, the minds of the swarming fugitives had at last been somewhat calmed, when it was reported that in the Dominican Church, the only one which the earthquake had spared, a solemn mass would be read by none other than the prior of the monastery with the purpose of imploring heaven to prevent further misfortunes.

Already everywhere the groups were breaking up and people were streaming toward the city. In Don Fernando's party someone raised the question whether they too should not participate in this solemnity and join the general rush? Donna Elizabeth, with some embarrassment, recalled the mischief which had been done in the church only yesterday, that such services of thanksgiving would certainly be repeated and that then, with the danger less fresh in their minds, they would be able to respond more gladly and more easily to the mood of thankfulness. Josepha, getting up at once, remarked with some enthusiasm that she had never felt a stronger urge to lay her face in the dust before her Maker than at this very time, when His incomprehensible and sublime power was so clearly revealed. Donna Elvira vigorously seconded Josepha's opinion. She insisted that they should hear the mass and called upon Don Fernando to lead the party, whereupon all of them, even Donna Elizabeth, rose from their seats. However, the latter was seen to hesitate. Her breast was working violently as she made her little preparations for departure. To the question, what was wrong with her, she replied that she could not tell what unhappy presentiment oppressed her. Donna Elvira thereupon calmed her and suggested that she remain behind with her and with her sick father.

Josepha said, "In that case, Donna Elizabeth, you will perhaps relieve me of this little darling who, as you see, has again found his way to me."

"Gladly," Donna Elizabeth replied, and reached out for him; but when he cried piteously at this injustice and would not consent to it on any terms, Josepha said with a smile that she would keep him, and kissed him till he was silent.

Then Don Fernando, who was pleased with her dignified and graceful bearing, offered her his arm. Jeronimo, who was carrying little Philip, escorted Donna Constanza. The remaining members who had joined the party followed behind, and in this order they proceeded to the city.

They had scarcely walked fifty paces when they heard Donna Elizabeth, who meanwhile had talked excitedly and secretively with Donna Elvira, shouting, "Don Fernando!" and saw her running after them as if troubled in some way. Don Fernando stopped and turned round, waited for her without releasing Josepha and, when she remained standing some distance away, as if waiting for him to meet her, asked her what she wanted. Donna Elizabeth approached him, though, it seemed, with reluctance, and whispered some words in his ear in such a way that Josepha could not hear them.

"Well," Don Fernando asked, "and what harm can come of that?"

Donna Elizabeth continued to whisper into his ear, her face distorted with anxiety; Don Fernando's flushed with irritation. He replied, "That's enough," said that Donna Elizabeth should calm herself, and proceeded with his lady.

When they arrived in the Dominican Church, the organ's musical splendor met them, and an immeasurable crowd surged inside the church. The throng extended far beyond the portal into the square outside and on the walls, high up in the niches framing the pictures, boys were clinging, their caps in their hands, and an expectant look on their faces. All the chandeliers burnt brightly, the columns cast mysterious shadows in the gathering dusk, the large rose window in the extreme back of the church, with its stained glass, glowed like the very evening sun that lit it up and, now that the organ was silent, stillness reigned in the whole assembly as if no one were capable of making a sound. Never did such a flame of zeal rise to heaven from a Christian cathedral as on that day, in the Dominican Church at Santiago, and no human breast contributed a warmer glow than those of Jeronimo and Josepha.

The service began with a sermon delivered from the pulpit by one of the oldest Canons, in full ceremonial array. Raising his trembling arms high up to heaven with the wide folds of his surplice flowing around them he began at once with praise, glorification and thanksgiving. Still, even in this part of the world that had crumbled to ruins, there were men able to raise up their faltering voices to God. He described what had happened at a sign given by the Almighty. Judgment Day could not be more terrible. And when, pointing at a fissure in one of the Cathedral walls, he called the earthquake a mere presage of doom, a shudder passed through the whole flock. From this point the current of priestly eloquence bore him on to the subject of the city's moral depravity; abominations such as Sodom and Gomorrah had never witnessed had been punished here, and only God's infinite, long-suffering patience had preserved the city from total destruction.

But the hearts of our two unfortunates, already quite rent by the sermon, were pierced as by a sword when the Canon dwelled in detail on the offense committed in the convent garden of the Carmelites, called the indulgence with which it had been treated by the world a godless one, and in a digression filled with imprecations, delivered the souls of the culprits, whom he mentioned by name, to all the princes of hell! Plucking at Jeronimo's sleeve, Donna Constanza called out, "Don Fernando!" The latter, however, replied as emphatically and, at the same time, as secretively as possible, "You will be silent, Donna, you will not stir, not even the pupil of your eye, and will pretend that you are about to faint, whereupon we shall leave the church." But before Donna Constanza could execute this artful strategem, devised to secure their escape, a voice interrupted the Canon's sermon, crying out, "Keep well away, citizens of Santiago, here are the godless creatures!" and when another voice terrifyingly asked, "Where?" while a wide circle of horror formed around them, a third replied, "Here!" and, filled with holy fanaticism, pulled Josepha by the hair so that she would have fallen down with Don Fernando's son if Don Fernando had not supported her.

"Are you mad?" the young man cried out and put his arm around Josepha. "I am Don Fernando Ormez, son of the Town Commandant whom you all know."

"Don Fernando Ormez?" cried a near-by cobbler, who had worked for Josepha and knew her as well at least as he knew her small feet. "Who is this child's father?" he asked, turning to Asteron's daughter with scornful insolence.

Don Fernando went pale at this question. Now he glanced shyly at Jeronimo, now he scanned the congregation to see if there was no one who knew him.

Josepha, compelled by the horrible situation, called out, "This is not my child, Master Pedrillo, as you think," and, looking at Don Fernando with infinite terror in her soul, "This young gentleman is Don Fernando Ormez, son of the Town Commandant, whom you all know."

The cobbler asked, "Which of you, citizens, knows this young man?" And several of the bystanders repeated, "Who knows Jeronimo Rugera? Let him step forward?"

Now it so happened that at this very moment little Juan, frightened by the uproar, showed his desire to leave Josepha's breast and take refuge in Don Fernando's arms. At once a voice yelled out, "He is the father!" and another, "He is Jeronimo Rugera," and a third, "These are the blasphemers!" and "Stone them! Stone them!" cried all the Christians assembled in that temple of Jesus.

Then Jeronimo intervened, "Stop, you inhuman creatures! If you are looking for Jeronimo Rugera: here he is. Set free that man, who is innocent."

The furious mob, confused by Jeronimo's words, hesitated. Several hands let go of Don Fernando. At that moment a naval officer of high rank approached hurriedly. Pushing his way through the crowd, he asked, "Don Fernando Ormez! What have they done to you?" Now quite free, Don Fernando replied with truly heroic presence of mind, "Yes, look at the murderous villains, Don Alonzo! I should have been lost if this worthy man hadn't given himself out to be Jeronimo Rugera in order to calm the raging mob. Be so kind as to take him into protective custody, as well as the young lady; and as for this good-for-nothing"—taking hold of Master Pedrillo—"who started this uproar, arrest him!"

The cobbler exclaimed, "Don Alonzo Onoreja, I ask you on your conscience, is not this girl Josepha Asteron?"

When Don Alonzo, who knew Josepha well, withheld his reply, and several voices, fanned by this into a new blaze of fury, called out, "It is, it is she!" and, "Kill her!" Josepha placed little Philip, whom Jeronimo had been carrying, in Don Fernando's arms, together with little Juan, and said, "Go now, Don Fernando, save your two children and leave us to our fate!"

Don Fernando took the two children and said he would sooner perish than allow anyone in his company to suffer harm. He offered Josepha his arm, after asking the naval officer for his sword, and told the other couple to follow him. They did in fact get out of the church since under these circumstances the people made way for them with an adequate show of respect, and thought themselves saved. But they had hardly reached the equally crowded square when a voice, one of the furious mob who had pursued them, cried, "This is Jeronimo Rugera, citizens, for I am his own father!" and struck him down at Constanza's side with a powerful blow of his club.

"Jesus Maria!" Donna Constanza cried out, and fled to her brother-in-law. But already, "Convent whore!" rang out, and with it the second blow of a club from the other side which left her stretched out lifeless beside Jeronimo.

"Monster!" a stranger called out, "this was Donna Constanza Xares!"

"Why did they lie to us?" the cobbler replied.

"Look for the right one, then, and kill her!"

Seeing Constanza's corpse, Don Fernando glowed with rage; he drew his sword and aimed such a blow at the fanatical, murderous villain who was the cause of these atrocities that he would have split him in two if the cobbler had not avoided the furious blow with a quick movement. He could not overpower the surging mass that advanced against him. "Farewell, Fernando! Farewell, children!" Josepha called out. "Here, murder me, you bloodthirsty tigers!" and she voluntarily hurled herself amongst them to put an end to the fight.

Master Pedrillo struck her down with his club. Then, spattered with her blood, he shouted, "Send the bastard after her to hell!" and thrust himself forward once more, his lust for murder not yet sated. Don Fernando, this godlike hero, now stood with his back to the church. With his left hand he held the children, with his right the sword. With every blow he struck one of them down, his sword flashing like lightning; a lion could not have defended himself better. Seven bloodhounds lay dead in front of him, the prince of the satanic rabble himself was wounded. But Master Pedrillo would not rest till he had snatched one of the children from Don Fernando's breast, seized it by one leg, swung it around over his head and dashed it against the edge of a church buttress.

Now everything was silent and everyone moved away. Don Fernando, seeing his little Juan lying in front of him with his brains gushing out, raised his eyes to heaven, his grief beyond description. The naval officer rejoined him, tried to console him and assured him that his own inaction during those unhappy moments, though justified by several circumstances, was causing him remorse. But Don Fernando said that he was beyond reproach and only asked him to help now with the removal of the corpses. They were all carried to Don Alonzo's house in the obscurity of dusk, and Don Fernando followed, weeping copiously over the face of little Philip. He spent the night at Don Alonzo's and for a long time failed to inform his wife of the full extent of the calamity. He deliberately falsified the facts, firstly, because his wife was ill, and secondly, because he did not know how she would judge his conduct in this matter. But soon after this, having been accidentally informed by a visitor of all that had occurred, this excellent lady silently wept away her maternal grief, and one morning put her arms round his neck, with the remnant of a shining tear in her eye, and kissed him. Don Fernando and Donna Elvira decided to adopt the little stranger; and when Don Fernando compared Philip with Juan, and the ways in which he had acquired each of them, it almost seemed to him that he had reason to be glad.

Translated by Michael Hamburger

Betrothal in Santo Domingo

Heinrich von Kleist

At Port au Prince, in the French part of the island of Santo Domingo, on the plantation of Monsieur Guillaume de Villeneuve, there lived at the beginning of this century, when the blacks were murdering the whites, a fearsome old Negro by the name of Congo Hoango. This man, who came originally from the Gold Coast of Africa, and who in his youth seemed of a loyal and upright nature, had been overwhelmed by his master with innumerable benefactions, because he had saved his life on a voyage to Cuba. Not only did M. Guillaume give him his freedom on the spot and assign him a house and holdings upon his return to Santo Domingo; he also made him a few years later, and contrary to the custom of the country, the overseer of his very considerable estates, and, since he did not wish to re-marry, gave him instead of a wife an elderly mulatto from his plantation by the name of Babekan, with whom he was distantly related through his deceased first wife. Indeed when the Negro had reached his sixtieth year he retired him on a handsome pension and crowned his beneficent deeds by remembering him in his testament with an inheritance. And yet all these proofs of gratitude were not able to shield M. Villeneuve from the wrath of this fierce man. In the general frenzy of revenge ignited by the ill-considered actions of the French National Assembly, Congo Hoango was one of the first to seize a gun, and, remembering the tyranny that had torn him from his homeland, he put a bullet through the head of his master. He set fire to the house in which the latter's wife and her three children, together with the rest of the whites in the settlement, had taken refuge, ravaged the whole plantation, to which the heirs, who lived in Port au Prince, could have laid claim, and, when all the buildings belonging to the estate had been razed, marched about the neighborhood with the Negroes he had gathered and armed, to help his brothers in their fight against the whites. He would sometimes ambush travelers going about the land in armed groups, sometimes attack in broad daylight the planters themselves, barricaded in their settlements, and put to the sword everyone he found there. In his inhuman lust for vengeance he even demanded that old Babekan and her daughter, a fifteen year old mestiza named Toni, should take part in his grim struggle, which had thoroughly rejuvenated him, and because the main building of the plantation, which he had spared and now used as his own dwelling, lay on a lonely stretch of road and was frequently visited during his absence by white and Creole refugees seeking food or shelter, he instructed his women to detain these white dogs, as he called them, by all possible kindnesses until he returned. Babekan, who, as the result of some terrible punishment inflicted upon her in her youth, suffered from consumption, was accustomed in such cases to dress young Toni, who, because of her high-yellow complexion was especially suited for this gruesome ruse, in her best clothes; she encouraged the girl to refuse the strangers no caress except the ultimate one, which was forbidden her on pain of death: and when Congo Hoango returned from his punitive expeditions in the surrounding countryside with his troop of Negroes, immediate death was the lot of those poor devils who had allowed themselves to be taken in by these tricks.

Now it is common knowledge that in the year 1803, when General Dessalines was advancing on Port au Prince with 30,000 Negroes, everyone with a white skin rushed into the town in order to defend it. For it was the last stronghold of French power on the island, and, if it fell, all the whites living there were lost to the last man. Under such circumstances and precisely during the absence of old Hoango, who had set out with his blacks to bring a transport of powder and shot to General Dessalines through the midst of the French outposts, it chanced that on a stormy, rainy night someone knocked at the back door of Hoango's house. Old Babekan, who was already in bed, got up, throwing only a skirt about her hips, opened the window and asked who was there. "In the name of Mary and all the saints," said the stranger softly, taking a stand beneath the window: "answer me first one question!" And so saying, he stretched out his hand in the darkness of the night to grasp that of the old woman and asked: "Are you a black?" Babekan said: "Well, you're certainly a white, since you'd rather look this pitch-black night in the face than you would a black woman! Come in," she added, "and fear nothing; a mulatto lives here, and the only other person in the house is my daughter, a mestiza!" With this she closed the window as though she were going down to open the door for him; but, pretending she could not immediately find the key, she first slipped up to the bedroom with some clothes which she had snatched out of a closet and waked her daughter. "Toni!" she said: "Toni!"—"What is it, Mother?"— "Quick!" she said. "Get up and dress! Here are clothes, white linen and stockings! There's a white man, on the run, standing at the door asking to be let in!" "A white man?" Toni asked, half-raising herself in bed. She took the clothes the old woman was holding out to her and asked: "Is he alone, Mother? And have we nothing to fear if we let him in?"—"Nothing, nothing!" the old woman replied, lighting a candle. "He's alone and unarmed, and the fear that we may harm him trembles through his every limb!" And, while Toni drew on a skirt and stockings, she lighted a big lantern that was hanging in a corner of the room, quickly tied up the girl's hair on top of her head, according to the custom of the country, and after lacing her bodice, covered her head with a hat, put the lantern in her hand and ordered her to go down to the courtyard and bring in the stranger.

Meanwhile, the barking of the farm dogs had awakened a boy named Nanky, who was an illegitimate offspring of Hoango and a Negro woman and who slept in one of the outbuildings with his brother Seppy; when by the light of the moon he saw a man standing alone on the back steps of the house, he at once hurried, as he had been instructed to do in such instances, to lock the courtyard gate, through which the man had entered. The stranger, who did not grasp the significance of these actions, asked the boy, in whom, at closer range and to his horror, he recognized a Negro: who lived in this settlement? And when the boy answered that the property, since the death of M. Villeneuve, had come into the possession of the Negro Hoango, he was on the point of throwing him to the ground, tearing the key to the main gate from the boy's hand and taking to his heels, when Toni, lantern in hand, stepped out of the house. "Quick!" she said, taking his hand and pulling him towards the door: "Come in here!" As she said this, she was careful to hold the lantern so that its full beam fell on her face. Resisting, the stranger cried, "Who are you?" and, taken aback for more than one reason, gazed meanwhile on her young, lovely form. "Who lives in this house, in which you tell me I am to find refuge?"—"No one, by the light of the sun," said the girl, striving to pull him along with her, "but my mother and myself!" "What, no one!" cried the stranger, freeing his hand and retreating a step: "Didn't this boy just say that a Negro named Hoango lives here?"—"I say no!" said the girl, stamping her foot with impatience; "and even though the house does belong to a savage creature by that name, he is absent at the moment and thirty miles away!" And with this she drew the stranger with both hands into the house, ordered the boy to tell no one who had arrived, took the stranger's hand, after she had reached the door, and led him up the stairs to her mother's room.

"Well," said the old woman, who had listened to the whole conversation from the upstairs window and had noticed by the light of the lantern that the man was an officer: "what's the meaning of the sword you're carrying under your arm, ready to draw? We have allowed you," she continued, adjusting her spectacles, "at the risk of our lives a refuge in our house; have you entered it to repay this good deed with treachery, according to the custom of your countrymen?"—"Heaven forbid!" the stranger replied, stepping closer to her armchair. He grasped the old woman's hand, pressed it to his heart, and, casting apprehensive glances about the room, unbuckled the sword he wore at his side, saying: "In me you see the most miserable of men, but not an evil or an ungrateful one!"—"Who are you?" the old woman asked, then shoved a chair over to him with her foot and told the girl to go to the kitchen and do what she could to prepare supper for him. The stranger answered: "I am an officer with the French forces, but, as you can no doubt see for yourself, no Frenchman. My fatherland is Switzerland and my name Gustav von der Ried. Would that I had never left my homeland for this unhappy island! I come from Fort Dauphin, where, as you know, all the whites have been slain, and I am trying to reach Port au Prince before General Dessalines succeeds in cut-

ting it off and besieging it with the troops under his command."—
"From Fort Dauphin!" cried the old woman. "And you have managed, with your complexion, to cover such an enormous distance
through the very midst of a land inhabited by blacks in the throes
of rebellion?" "God and all the saints have protected me," replied
the stranger. "And I am not alone, my good woman; in my company, which I left behind, there is a venerable old man, my uncle,
with his wife and five children, not to mention several servants,
men and women, who belong to the family; a company of twelve
persons, whom I, with the help of two miserable mules, have to
take along with me on indescribably difficult night marches, since
we do not dare show ourselves by day on the military road." "Good
heavens!" cried the old woman, shaking her head in sympathy as
she took a pinch of snuff. "And where is the rest of your company
at this moment?" "You," replied the stranger, after he had thought
a bit, "you I can trust; from your face shines a ray of my own
color. You must know then that the family is only three miles from
here, near Gull Pond, on a mountain in the midst of the woods:
hunger and thirst forced us to seek refuge there yesterday. In vain
did we send out our servants last night to try to find a little bread
and wine at the houses of the natives; fear of capture and death
prevented them from taking any decisive action, so that today I
saw myself forced at the risk of my life to try my own luck. And,
unless all appearances deceive me," he went on, pressing the old
woman's hand, "heaven has led me to people with compassion,
who do not share that cruel and unheard-of bitterness that has seized
all the inhabitants of this island. Be so kind as to fill a few baskets
with food and drink for me; I will reward you well. We have only
a five days' journey to Port au Prince, and if you provide us with
the means of reaching that city, we will regard you as our sav-
iors."—"Yes, this insane bitterness," said the old woman hypo-
critically. "Is it not as if the hands of *one* body, or the teeth of *one*
mouth, were seeking to destroy each other, because *one* member
is not made like the other? How can I, whose father came from
Santiago de Cuba, help the shimmer of light that appears in my
face when day breaks? And can my daughter, who was conceived
and born in Europe, help it that the bright day of that part of the
world is reflected in hers?"—"What?" cried the stranger, "do you
mean to say that you, who have the features of a mulatto and thus

must be of African origin, that you and your daughter, the lovely young mestiza who led me into the house, are damned together with us Europeans?"—"By heaven!" replied the old woman, taking her spectacles from her nose, "do you think that the bit of property we have acquired by the work of our hands through toilsome, miserable years does not tempt this pitiless, hell-born mob of robbers? If we did not know how to protect ourselves from their persecution through cunning and the whole range of sly tricks with which self-defense endows the weak: the shadow of kinship that you see in our faces, of that you may rest assured, will not do it!"— "It can't be possible!" cried the stranger; "and who on the island is persecuting you?" "The owner of this house," answered the old woman; "the Negro Congo Hoango! Since the death of M. Guillaume, the former owner of this plantation, who fell by Hoango's merciless hand at the outbreak of the revolt, we who, as his relatives, run things for him are completely delivered up to his arbitrariness and violence. Every bite of bread, every swallow of water that we, out of common humanity, give to any of the refugees who pass this way, he holds against us and abuses us with curses and mistreatment; and there is nothing he wants more than to call down the wrath of the blacks on us white and Creole halfdogs, as he calls us, in part simply to get rid of us, because we censure him for his savagery against the whites, partly in order to be able to take possession of the bit of property we would leave."—"How unfortunate you are and how much to be pitied!" exclaimed the stranger. "And where is this madman at the moment?" "With the army of General Dessalines," answered the old woman, "to whom he and the other blacks who belong to this plantation are bringing a transport of powder and shot the general needed. We expect him back, in case he doesn't embark on some other undertaking, in ten or twelve days; and if then, which God forbid, he should discover that we had given shelter and protection to a white man on his way to Port au Prince, while he himself was engaged in the business of wiping the whole race from the island, we would all, as you can well imagine, be as good as dead."—"Heaven, which loves humanity and compassion," answered the stranger, "will protect you in your endeavor to help an unfortunate man.—And since in this case you will have called down Hoango's wrath anyway," he added, moving his chair closer to the old woman, "and your obedience, even if you were to renew it, would be of no help to you, you can surely—for any reward you may care to ask—make up your mind to give my uncle and his family, who are exhausted from their terrible journey, shelter in your house for one or two days, so that they can recover a little?"—"Young man!" said the old woman, taken aback, "what are you asking? How is it possible, in a house lying on the main road, to shelter a group of that size without someone betraying the fact to those who live nearby?"—"Why not?" the stranger urged: "If I were to go immediately to Gull Pond myself and lead them here to the settlement before day-break; if one were to house all of them, the masters and the ser-vants, in one and the same room, and if, to guard against the worst eventuality, one took the further precaution of carefully closing all the doors and windows?——" The old woman replied, after she had considered the proposal a while, that, if he should undertake to lead this group from their mountain gully to the plantation that very night, he would inevitably meet on his way back a troop of armed Negroes whose march along the main road had been an-nounced by a small advance party of sharpshooters.—"Very well!" replied the stranger: "then we will be satisfied for the time being with sending those poor unfortunates a basket of provisions and postpone the business of leading them here until the following night. Will you do that, my good woman?"—"Well," said the old woman, as the stranger's lips rained kisses on her bony hand, "for the sake of the European who was the father of my daughter I will grant his afflicted countrymen this favor. Sit down at daybreak and write your people a note telling them to come here to the plantation; the boy you saw in the courtyard can deliver the note, together with some provisions, then, for their own safety, stay with them over-night in the mountains; at dawn of the following day, if they ac-cept the invitation, he can serve to guide them here."

Meanwhile Toni had returned with a meal she had prepared in the kitchen and, flirtatiously glancing toward the stranger while she laid the table, asked the old woman: "Well, tell me, Mother, has the gentleman recovered from the fright that came over him at our door? Is he convinced that neither poison nor knife is waiting for him and that the Negro Hoango is not at home?" The mother an-swered with a sigh: "My child, you know the proverb: once burned, twice cautious. The gentleman would have acted foolishly if he had ventured into the house before he knew to what race its inhabitants belong." The girl came and stood before her mother and told her how she had held the lantern so that its full beam fell in her face. But his imagination, she said, was so filled with Negroes and blackamoors that if a lady from Paris or Marseilles had opened the door to him, he would have thought it was a black woman. The stranger, putting his arm gently about her waist, said with embarrassment that the hat she had been wearing had hindered him from seeing her face. "Had I been able to look into your eyes," he continued, pressing her vigorously to his breast and blushing at his own words, "as I can now, I would have been willing, even if all the rest of you had been black, to drink with you out of a poisoned cup." The mother urged him to sit down; Toni sat beside him at the table and, cupping her chin in her hands, gazed into the stranger's face while he ate. He asked her how old she was and the name of her native city, whereupon the mother intervened and said that Toni was conceived and born fifteen years ago in Paris on a trip that she had made with the wife of her former master, M. Villeneuve. She added that the Negro Komar, whom she had later married, had indeed adopted her, but that her real father was a rich merchant of Marseilles by the name of Bertrand and that her own name was therefore Toni Bertrand. Toni asked him whether he knew such a gentleman in France. The stranger answered: no, France was a big country and during his short stay there before embarking for the West Indies he had not met anyone by that name. The old woman volunteered the information that, according to fairly certain news she had received, M. Bertrand no longer lived in France. "His ambitious and adventurous nature," she said, "was not satisfied with the humdrum round of middle class life; at the outbreak of the Revolution he became involved in politics, in the year 1795 went with a French embassy to the Turkish court and, so far as I know, has not yet returned." The stranger smiled and said to Toni, taking her hand, that in that case she must be a rich and distinguished person. He encouraged her to make use of these advantages and said he thought she had every prospect of being introduced one day by her father into more brilliant circumstances than those in which she now lived. "Hardly," interposed the old woman with suppressed irritation. "During my pregnancy in Paris, M. Bertrand denied in court that he was the father of his child, because he was ashamed to admit it before his rich young fiancée. I shall never forget the oath which he had the audacity to take in my very presence; I got a bilious fever as a result and soon afterwards sixty lashes by order of M. Villeneuve, in consequence of which I suffer from consumption to this very day."—Toni, her head laid pensively in her hand, asked the stranger: who he was anyway, where he came from and where he was going? The latter, after a short embarrassed silence occasioned by the old woman's embittered outburst, answered that he came from Fort Dauphin with the family of Herr Strömli, his uncle, and that he had left them in the forest near Gull Pond under the protection of two young cousins. At the girl's request, he related a number of incidents connected with the revolt that had broken out in Fort Dauphin; how, at midnight, when everyone was asleep, at a signal treacherously given, the slaughter of the whites by the blacks had begun, how the leader of the blacks, a sergeant in the French engineer corps, had been so malicious as to burn immediately all the ships in the harbor in order to cut off the flight of the whites to Europe; how the family had barely had enough time to escape from the city with a few belongings and how, since the revolt had flared up simultaneously all along the coast, they had had no other recourse than, with the help of two mules they had managed to find, to start out overland, across the whole island, for Port au Prince, which, protected by a strong French army, was the only place still capable of offering resistance to the numerically superior forces of the blacks.— Toni asked: how the whites had made themselves so hated?—The stranger answered, taken aback: "Through the general relationship that they, as masters of the island, had with the blacks, and which I, to tell the truth, would not undertake to defend, but which had existed thus for centuries! The mad rage for freedom that seized all these plantations drove the Negroes and the Creoles to break the chains that bound them and to take revenge on the whites for the frequent and blameworthy mistreatment they had suffered at the hands of some evil members of the race.—I was particularly horrified and impressed," he continued after a short silence, "by the deed of one girl. Just at the time the revolt flared up, this girl, a Negro, was lying sick of the yellow fever, which had broken out in the town, doubling its misery. Three years before she had been the slave of a white planter, who, offended because she would not yield to his desires, had treated her harshly and later sold her to a Creole planter. When, on the day of the general revolt, the girl learned that the planter, her former master, had taken refuge in a nearby stable to escape the wrath of the Negroes, she, remembering how she had been mistreated, sent her brother to him at dusk to invite him to spend the night with her. The unlucky man, who neither knew that the girl was unwell nor of what disease she was suffering, came and took her in his arms, full of gratitude for his salvation. But scarcely had he spent half an hour tenderly caressing her in her bed when suddenly, with an expression of wild, cold rage, she raised herself up and said: "You have kissed one who bears death in her bosom: I have the plague! Go and give the yellow fever to all your kind!" The officer, while the old woman loudly expressed her abhorrence of such a deed, asked Toni: whether *she* would be capable of such an act? "No!" said Toni, looking down in confusion. The stranger, laying his napkin on the table, said: it was his heartfelt conviction that no tyranny the whites had ever committed could justify a betrayal so vile and abhorrent. The vengeance of heaven, he said, standing up with a passionate gesture, was disarmed by such a deed: incensed, the angels themselves would take the part of those in the wrong and, to uphold human and divine order, defend their cause! With these words, he stepped to the window for a moment and looked out into the night where storm clouds were passing across the moon and the stars; and, since it seemed to him that mother and daughter were exchanging glances, although he did not by any means notice that they were giving each other signals, an unpleasant feeling of annoyance came over him; he turned aside and begged them to show him the room where he could sleep.

The mother remarked, looking at the wall-clock, that it was indeed almost midnight, and picking up a candle asked the stranger to follow her. She led him down a long corridor to the room intended for him; Toni carried his cloak and the other things he had taken off; the mother showed him a bed comfortably piled with bolsters, where he was to sleep, and after she had told Toni to prepare the gentleman a footbath, she bade him good night and left. The stranger stood his sword in a corner and laid on the table a pair of pistols he was carrying in his belt. While Toni pushed out the bed and spread a white sheet over it, he looked about the room and, since he soon concluded from the luxury and taste with which it was appointed that it must have been the room of the former owner of the plantation, a sense of unrest settled like a vulture about his heart and he wished he were back in the forest with his own people, hungry and thirsty as when he came. Meanwhile the girl had fetched from the nearby kitchen a basin with warm water, fragrant with aromatic herbs, and invited the officer, who was leaning at the window, to refresh himself with a footbath. Silently freeing himself of his neckcloth and vest, the officer sat down on a chair, began to remove his boots and, while the girl knelt before him making final preparations for the bath, he contemplated her attractive figure. Her luxurious black hair had rolled down onto her young breasts; a look of exceptional grace played about her lips and over the long lashes of her downcast eyes; except for the color of her skin, which was repellent to him, he would have sworn that he had never beheld anything more beautiful. At the same time, a distant resemblance—he himself did not know with whom, though he had noticed it even when he entered the house—struck his attention and won him over to her heart and soul. When she stood up from her task, he seized her by the hand, and since he quite rightly concluded that there was only one way to find out whether she had a heart or not, he pulled her down on his lap and asked: whether she were already engaged? "No!" the girl lisped, bashfully casting down her large black eyes. She added, without stirring from his lap that Konelly, a young Negro neighbor, had in fact asked for her hand three months ago, but she had turned him down because she was too young. The stranger, who was holding her slim body with both hands, said: in his native land, according to a proverb current here, a girl of fourteen years and seven weeks was old enough to marry. He asked, while she examined a small gold cross he wore on his breast, how old she was?—"Fifteen," Toni replied. "So, you see!" said the stranger,—"Is it that Konelly doesn't have the means to set up the kind of household you would like?" Toni, without raising her eyes, answered: "O no!—on the contrary," she said, dropping the cross she was holding in her hand, "since the recent turn of events; he has become a rich man; the whole settlement that formerly belonged to his master, the planter, has now fallen to Konelly's father."—"Then why did you refuse him?" asked the stranger. He gently stroked her hair back from her forehead and said: "Perhaps you didn't like him?" The girl laughed and shook her head; to the stranger's question, whispered jestingly in her ear: whether perhaps it would take a white man to win her favor? she suddenly, after a fleeting, dreamy pause and with an exquisite blush that suffused her sunburned face, laid herself on his breast. The stranger, touched by her grace and loveliness, called her his dear girl and as though a divine hand had released him from every care took her in his arms. It was impossible for him to believe that all these emotions he perceived in her could be merely the wretched expression of monstrous, calculated treachery. The thoughts that had perturbed him now departed like an army of ghastly birds; he blamed himself for having even for a moment misinterpreted her heart, and while he rocked her on his knees and drew in the sweet breath she sent up to him, he pressed a kiss on her brow, as a sign, so to speak, of reconciliation and forgiveness. Meanwhile the girl, suddenly becoming strangely alert as though she heard someone approaching the door from the corridor, had straightened up; pensively and dreamily she adjusted the kerchief that had become disarranged over her bosom, and only when she saw that she had been mistaken did she turn back to the stranger with a serene look and remind him that the water, if he didn't use it soon, would get cold.—"Well?" she said, puzzled when the stranger remained silent and gazed at her thoughtfully: "Why are you looking at me so attentively?" She tried to cover the embarrassment that had come over her by busying herself with her bodice, and cried, laughing: "Strange man, what so strikes your attention when you look at me?" The stranger, who had rubbed his hand over his brow, said, suppressing a sigh as he lifted her down from his lap: "A remarkable similarity between you and a young woman friend of mine I once knew!" Toni, seeing that his good humor had fled, took him kindly and sympathetically by the hand and asked: "What young woman?" Whereupon the stranger, after a short pause, resumed and said: "Her name was Mariane Congreve and she lived in Strassburg. Shortly before the outbreak of the Revolution I had become acquainted with her in that city, where her father was a merchant, and had been fortunate enough to gain her consent to marriage and, tentatively, also that of her mother. Oh, she was the most loyal soul under the sun, and the terrible and touching circumstances under which I lost her return to my mind with such force when I look at you that I can't resist weeping for sorrow." "What?" said Toni, pressing up against him sweetly and ardently, "she's no longer alive?"—She died," the stranger answered, "and only with her death did I come to know the essence of all human worth and kindness. God knows," he continued, bowing his head in pain on her shoulder, "how I could have been so indiscreet as to allow myself one evening in a public place to express opinions concerning the fearful Revolutionary Tribunal which had just been established. I was informed against, they were searching for me, and, since I had been lucky enough to find a hiding place in the suburbs, my rabid pursuers, who had to have a victim, proceeded, when I could not be found, to the house of my fiancée and, because of her truthful assertion that she did not know where I was, dragged her, instead of me, claiming that we were fellow conspirators, with wanton irresponsibility to the place of execution. Scarcely had this shocking news reached my ears when I at once stepped forth from my hiding place and, breaking through the crowd, rushed to the scaffold, crying: 'Here, you inhuman beasts, here I am!' But she, who was already standing beside the guillotine, when questioned by some judges to whom I was unfortunately a stranger, answered, as she turned away from me with a look that is indelibly imprinted in my soul: 'I do not know this man!' Whereupon, a few minutes later amidst drumming and shouting instigated by these wolves impatient for blood, the knife fell and severed her head from her body.—How I was saved, I do not know; a quarter of an hour later I found myself in the home of a friend, where I fell into one swoon after another, and, half out of my senses, was loaded toward evening on a wagon and brought across the Rhine."—With these words the stranger released the girl and stepped to the window, and when she saw how moved he was and how he was pressing his face in his handkerchief, she was overcome by a sense of compassion, awakened by various causes; she quickly went up to him, threw her arms about his neck and mingled her tears with his.

What followed we need not recount, since anyone who has read this far can supply it for himself. The stranger, when he had again collected himself, did not know whither the deed he had committed would lead him; meanwhile he saw that he was saved for the time being and need fear nothing in this house, at least from the girl. When he saw her lying on the bed weeping, her arms folded across her bosom, he tried in every possible way to console her. He took from his breast the small gold cross, a gift from his deceased fiancée, the faithful Mariane, and bending over her with infinite tenderness hung it as a bridal gift, as he called it, about her neck. Since she, dissolved in tears, did not heed his words, he sat down on the edge of the bed and told her, stroking and kissing her arm: that in the morning he would ask her mother for her hand. He described to her the small property, free and unencumbered, which he owned on the banks of the Aar; a house comfortable and roomy enough to shelter her and her mother, if the latter's health would permit her to undertake such a journey; fields, gardens, meadows, vineyards; and an old venerable father, who would receive them gratefully and kindly, because she had saved the life of his son. Since her tears continued to flow down onto the pillows, he clasped her in his arms and asked her, himself overcome with emotion: how he had harmed her and whether she could forgive him? He swore that his love for her would never leave his heart and that only the tumult of his strangely confused senses, the mixture of desire and fear with which she had inspired him, had led him to commit such an act. Finally, he reminded her that the morning stars were already shining and that, if she tarried longer in bed, her mother would come in and surprise them in it; he urged her, for the sake of her health, to get up and rest a few hours in her own bed; he asked her, plunged in terrible anxiety by her state, whether he should perhaps carry her in his arms to her room; but since she made no reply to anything he proposed, and, moaning softly, hid her head in her arms without stirring and remained there on the rumpled pillows, there was finally nothing else for him to do, since day was now beginning to shimmer through both windows, but to lift her up without more ado and carry her, hanging over his shoulder like a lifeless corpse, up the stairs to her bedroom and, after he had laid her on the bed and repeated with endless caresses all that he had already told her, he called her his dear bride, pressed a kiss on her cheek and hurried back to his room.

As soon as it was full day, old Babekan went up to her daughter and, sitting down on her bed, explained to her what plan she had in mind for the stranger and his company. She said that since the Negro Congo Hoango would not return before two days were up, everything depended on luring the stranger to stay in the house during this time, but without admitting his companions, whose presence in such numbers could become dangerous. To this end, she said, she had decided to delude the stranger by pretending that, according to news she had just received, General Dessalines and his army were about to march through this region and that in a situation of such extreme danger one would therefore only be able to grant his wish and admit the family to the house on the third day, after Dessalines had passed through. The company itself, she concluded, must in the meantime be furnished with provisions so that they would not continue their journey, and further, so that one could seize them later, be kept under the impression that they were to find refuge in the house. She remarked that this was an important matter because they were probably carrying considerable possessions with them and she urged her daughter to support her with all the wiles at her command in the scheme she had outlined. A blush of indignation suffused Toni's face as, half sitting up in bed, she replied: that it was mean-spirited and shameful to abuse the rights of hospitality in this way with persons one had lured into one's house. She said that a refugee, who had entrusted himself to their protection, should be doubly secure with them, and vowed that if she, Babekan, did not renounce this bloody design, she would at once go and reveal to the stranger what a den of murderers the house was in which he had thought to find salvation. "Toni!" said the mother, looking at her wide-eyed, her arms akimbo.—"Indeed, I will!" replied Toni, lowering her voice. "What has this young man, who is not even a Frenchman by birth, but, as we have seen, a Swiss, done to harm us, that like robbers we should want to attack him, kill him and plunder him? Are the complaints urged against the planters here also valid in the part of the island he comes from? Does not everything rather point to his being the noblest and most excellent person? Surely, whatever injustices the blacks may accuse his race of do not apply to him!" The old woman, contemplating the girl's strange expression, merely said with trembling lips that she was astounded. She asked what the young Portuguese had done whom they had lately clubbed to the ground in the gateway? She asked what crime had been committed by the two Dutchmen, who had been shot to death by the Negroes three weeks ago in the courtyard? She wanted to know what blame could be laid to the three Frenchmen and so many other individual refugees who had been executed in the house with guns, spears, and knives since the outbreak of the revolt? "By the sun's light," said the daughter, getting out of bed in a rage, "you are wrong indeed to remind me of these atrocities! The inhuman actions in which you force me to take part have long incensed my inmost feelings; and to reconcile myself with God's wrath for all that has occurred I swear to you that I will rather suffer death ten times over than permit anyone to touch even a hair of this young man's head as long as he is in our house."—"Very well," said the old woman, suddenly compliant: "then let the stranger go his way! But when Congo Hoango returns," she added, rising and preparing to leave the room, "and discovers that a white man has spent the night in our house, then you can take the responsibility for the compassion that moved you, against his express command, to allow the white man to depart."

This utterance, in which, in spite of all seeming charitableness, the old woman's fury was apparent, left the girl in no little dismay. She knew her hatred of the whites too well to believe that she would pass up such an opportunity to satiate it. The fear that she might send to the neighboring plantations and call in Negroes to overpower the stranger moved her to get dressed and at once follow her mother to the downstairs sitting room. While the latter in agitation left the cupboard, where she had apparently been occupied, and sat down at the spinning wheel, Toni stood looking at the order nailed to the door, according to which all blacks were forbidden on pain of death to give aid and comfort to whites: and, as though seized by fright, she now recognized the wrong she had done, she suddenly turned and threw herself at her mother's feet, knowing that the latter had been observing her out of the corner of her eye. Clasping her knees, she begged her to forgive the mad things she had said in favor of the stranger; she gave her as an excuse the half-dreaming, half-waking state in which, still lying in bed, she had been surprised by the proposal to deceive him, and said she was willing to surrender him without reservation to the law of the land, which had determined upon his extermination. The old woman, after a pause, in which she regarded the girl steadily, said: "By heavens, this declaration of yours will save his life for today! For, since you threatened to protect him, there was already poison in his food, which would at least have delivered him dead into Congo Hoango's hands, according to his order." And with this she rose and poured out of the window a jug of milk that was standing on the table. Toni, who could not believe her eyes and ears, stared at her mother horrorstruck. The old woman, sitting down again and lifting up the girl who was still lying on her knees, asked: what had so changed her mind in the course of the night? Had she stayed with him long the night before after preparing his footbath? Had she had an extended conversation with the stranger? But Toni, whose breast was heaving, did not answer these questions, or at least she said nothing definite; her eyes on the floor, she stood holding her head and excused herself by saying she had had a dream; but one glance at the breast of her unhappy mother, she said, bending quickly to kiss her hand, recalled to memory all the inhumanity of the race to which this stranger belonged: turning aside and burying her face in her apron, she vowed that, as soon as the Negro Hoango returned, her mother would see what kind of daughter she had in her.

Babekan was still sitting lost in thought, wondering about the reason for the girl's strangely passionate behavior, when the stranger entered with a note he had written in the bedroom, inviting the family to spend a few days at the plantation of the Negro Hoango. He greeted mother and daughter very cheerfully and affably and, handing the old woman the note, begged them to send someone to Gull Pond at once to look after his traveling companions as promised. Babekan rose and said with an uneasy air as she laid the note in the cupboard: "Sir, we must ask you to return to your room at once. The road is full of scattered Negro troops who tell us that General Dessalines is going to head this way with his army. This house, which is open to everyone, cannot provide you security unless you hide in your bedroom, which opens on the courtyard, and carefully close all doors and shutters."—"What?" said the stranger, taken aback: "General Dessalines . . ."—"Don't ask!" interrupted the old woman, rapping her cane three times on the floor: "In your bedroom, to which I will follow you, I will explain everything." Urged out of the room by the old woman's anxious gestures, he turned again in the doorway and cried: "But won't you at least have to send a message to the family, who are waiting for me, to tell. . ." "Everything will be taken care of," the old woman broke in, as the bastard boy, whom we already know, entered, summoned by her rapping. Then she instructed Toni, who, turning her back on the stranger, had stepped in front of the looking-glass, to pick up a basket of provisions standing in the corner, and mother, daughter, the stranger, and the boy went up to the bedroom.

Here the old woman, comfortably settling herself in an armchair, told how the whole night through they had seen watchfires burning on the mountains on the horizon: this was indeed the case, although up to that moment not a single Negro of Dessalines' army, which was advancing on Port au Prince from the Southwest, had shown himself in the region. Thus she succeeded in plunging the stranger into a turmoil of disquiet, though she also knew how to calm him afterwards by assuring him that she would do everything possible to rescue him, even in the unhappy event that they had troops quartered on them. At his fervently reiterated plea, in this case to at least help out the family with some provisions, she took the basket from her daughter's hand and giving it to the boy told him he should go the woods beyond Gull Pond and deliver it to the family of the foreign officer he would find there. The officer himself, he was to tell them, was in good health; friends of the whites, who themselves had much to suffer from the blacks because of their partisanship, had kindly received him in their home. She concluded that, just as soon as the road was again free of the armed band of Negroes they were expecting, arrangements would immediately be made to accommodate them, the family, in the house too. —"Do you understand?" she asked when she had finished. The boy, putting the basket on his head, replied: that he knew Gull Pond very well, he and his friends sometimes went fishing there, and that he would deliver the message to the family of the foreign gentleman that had spent the night here, just as he had told him. The stranger, upon the old woman's question: whether he had anything to add? took a ring from his finger and handed it to the boy with instructions to give it to the head of the family, Herr Strömli, as a sign that the message he brought was in order. Hereupon the mother made several arrangements, intended, as she said, to assure the stranger's safety: she ordered Toni to close the shutters and, not without difficulty, for the tinder would not catch she herself struck a light with a flint lying on the mantelpiece, in order to disperse the darkness that now pervaded the room. The stranger took advantage of this moment to put his arm gently around Toni's waist and whisper in her ear: how she had slept? and: whether he shouldn't inform her mother of what had happened? But Toni did not answer the first question, and to the other she replied, freeing herself from his embrace: "No, if you love me, not a word!" She suppressed the anxiety that all these deceitful arrangements aroused in her, and, with the excuse that she had to fix the stranger some breakfast, rushed quickly downstairs into the living room.

From her mother's cupboard she took the letter in which the stranger in his innocence had invited the family to follow the boy to the plantation and, trusting to luck whether her mother would miss it or not, but resolved, if worst came to worst, to suffer death with him, she flew down the road after the boy. For she now saw the young man, in the eyes of God and her heart, no longer as merely a guest to whom they had given protection and shelter but as her promised husband, and she was determined, just as soon as his party had reached sufficient strength in the house, at all costs to tell her mother, on whose utter dismay under such circumstances she reckoned, of their engagement. "Nanky," she said, as she breathlessly caught up with the boy on the road, "Mother has changed her plan about Herr Strömli's family. Take this letter! It's addressed to Herr Strömli, the head of the family, and contains an invitation for him and all those with him to spend a few days at our plantation.—Use your wits and add all you can think of to persuade them to accept the invitation. Congo Hoango, the Negro, will repay you for it when he returns!" "All right, all right, Cousin Toni," answered the boy. Carefully wrapping up the letter and sticking it in his pocket he asked: "And I'm to act as their guide on their way here?" "Of course," replied Toni, "that's understood, because they don't know the country. But you are not to start out before midnight because of possible troop movements on the road; but then make haste and see to it you arrive here before daybreak.—Can I rely on you?" "Rely on Nanky!" answered the boy; "I know why you're luring these white people to the plantation, and the Negro Hoango will be satisfied with me!"

Toni returned to the house and served the stranger his breakfast, and when the table had been cleared, mother and daughter retired to the front living room to pursue household tasks. It was inevitable that some time afterward the mother should go to the cupboard and only natural that she should miss the letter. Not trusting her memory, she laid her hand to her forehead and asked Toni: where she could have laid the letter the stranger gave her? Toni answered after a short pause during which she stared at the floor: that the stranger, as she remembered, had put it back in his pocket again and then torn it to pieces upstairs in his room in the presence of both of them! The mother looked at the girl wide-eyed; she said she distinctly remembered taking the letter from his hand and putting it in the cupboard, but since she couldn't find it in spite of searching and since she mistrusted her memory because of similar occurrences, there was nothing for her to do but believe what her daughter told her. Meanwhile she could not suppress her lively displeasure about this incident, and said that the letter would have been of the greatest importance to the Negro Hoango, in order to get the family to come to the plantation. At noon and in the evening, while Toni was serving the stranger his meals, Babekan kept him company at a corner of the table and several times took the opportunity of asking him about the letter; but Toni was clever enough, every time the conversation took this dangerous turn, to change the subject or confuse the issue, so that it never became clear to the mother from the stranger's explanations what had actually happened to the letter. Thus the day passed; after supper the mother locked the stranger's room—as a precautionary measure, she said—and after she and Toni had considered by what ruse they could come into possession of such a letter on the next day, she retired and told the girl to go to bed likewise.

As soon as Toni, who had awaited this moment with longing, had reached her bedroom and convinced herself that her mother was asleep, she placed the image of the Virgin that hung beside her bed on a chair and knelt down before it with folded hands. She implored the Savior, Her divine son, in a prayer full of infinite fervor, to give her the courage and constancy to confess to the young man to whom she had given herself the misdeeds that weighed on her bosom. She vowed to conceal from him nothing, however much it might cost her heart, not even the intention, pitiless and horrifying, with which she had yesterday lured him into the house; but for the sake of the steps she had already taken for his salvation she hoped that he would forgive her and take her with him to Europe as his faithful wife. Wonderfully strengthened by her prayer, she rose and took the skeleton key that opened all the chambers in the house and slowly proceeded, without a light, down the narrow corridor that ran through the house to the stranger's bedroom. She softly opened the door and stepped in front of his bed where he lay in deep sleep. The moonlight shone on his fresh young face and the nocturnal breeze that came through the opened windows played in the hair on his forehead. Inhaling his sweet breath, she tenderly bent over him and called his name, but a deep dream, of which she seemed to be the object, held his mind: at any rate she repeatedly heard from his glowing, trembling lips the whispered word: Toni! An indescribable tenderness came over her; she could not bring herself to tear him from the heaven of his sweet imaginings into the depths of a common and wretched reality, and, in the certainty that he was bound to awaken sooner or later of his own accord, she knelt beside his bed and covered his dear hand with kisses.

But who can depict the horror that a few minutes later seized her heart when she suddenly heard in the courtyard the sounds of men, horses, and weapons, and among them clearly distinguished the voice of the Negro Congo Hoango, who had unexpectedly returned with his whole gang from the camp of General Dessalines. Carefully avoiding the moonlight that threatened to betray her, she rushed behind the curtains of the window and already heard how her mother was giving the Negro an account of everything that had taken place during his absence, including the presence of a European refugee in the house. In a subdued voice, the Negro ordered his men to keep quiet. He asked the old woman where the stranger was to be found at the moment? whereupon the latter designated the room to him and immediately seized the opportunity to inform him of the strange and striking conversation she had with her daughter concerning the stranger. She assured the Negro that the girl was a traitress and their whole scheme for seizing the white man in danger of miscarrying. That sly little wretch, she said, had slipped into his bed at nightfall, where she was calmly taking her ease at this very moment, and probably, unless the stranger had already fled, he was now being warned and the means of expediting his escape were being discussed. The Negro, who had already tested the girl's loyalty in similar cases, answered: "It can't be possible!" Then: "Kelly!" he shouted, in a rage, "Omra! Take your rifles!" And without saying another word he began to ascend the stairs accompanied by all his Negroes and headed for the stranger's bedroom.

Toni, before whose eyes, in the course of a few minutes, this whole scene had taken place, stood there, paralyzed in every limb, as though struck by lightning. She thought for a moment of wakening the stranger, but on the one hand she saw that, because of the men in the courtyard, it was impossible for him to flee, and on the other hand she knew that he would reach for his sword and, given the numerical superiority of the blacks, would be felled immediately. Indeed, the terrible realization to which she was forced to come was this: that the unfortunate man himself, if he were to find her in these circumstances beside his bed, would think her a traitress, and, instead of heeding her advice, in a mad, unthinking rage would senselessly run into the arms of the Negro Hoango. In her indescribable anguish, she caught sight of a cord which, heaven knows by what chance, was hanging on a peg on the wall. God himself, she thought, taking it down, had put it there for her friend's salvation. With it she tied the young man by the hands and feet, making many knots, and, paying no attention to his struggles, pulled the ends together and fastened him to the bedstead, then, rejoicing at having mastered the situation, she pressed a kiss on his lips and hurried to meet the Negro Hoango, who was already stamping up the stairs.

The Negro, who still did not believe the old woman's report about Toni, when he saw her coming out of the room in question came to a standstill in the corridor, nonplussed and bewildered, his gang with torches and arms crowding behind him. "That faithless, lying girl!" he cried, and turning to Babekan, who had taken a few steps toward the stranger's door, he asked: "Has he escaped?" Babekan, who had not looked into the room, but had seen that the door was open, cried out as she returned in a fury: "The cheat, she's let him get away! Hurry, block the exits before he reaches the open!" "What's the matter?" asked Toni, looking at Hoango and the blacks surrounding him with an expression of astonishment. "What's the matter?" returned the Negro, seizing her by the chest and dragging her toward the room. "Are you crazy?" cried Toni, shoving the old man away as he froze at the sight that presented itself to his eyes. "There lies the stranger, tied to his bed by me, and, by heavens, it's not the worst deed I've done in my life!" With these words, she turned her back and sat down at a table, as though weeping. The old man turned to the mother, who was standing at one side in confusion, and said: "Babekan, what fairy tale have you been telling me?" "Heaven be praised," the mother answered, embarrassedly investigating the cords that bound the stranger; "he's there all right, though I don't know how it came about." The Negro, returning his sword to its scabbard, stepped up to the bed and asked the stranger: who he was? where he came from and where he was going? But since the latter, struggling and twisting to free himself, did not answer except to moan pitifully and painfully: "O Toni! O Toni!"—the mother intervened and explained that he was a Swiss by the name of Gustav von der Ried and that he came, with a whole family of European dogs who at this moment were hiding in the caves near Gull Pond, from the coastal settlement Fort Dauphin. Hoango, seeing the girl sitting there holding her head in her hands in such a melancholy way, went up to her and called her his dear child, patted her on the cheek and begged her to forgive him for his overhasty suspicions. The old woman, who had likewise gone up to the girl, placed her hands on her hips and asked, shaking her head: why she had tied up the stranger, who after all knew nothing about the danger he was in? Toni, now openly weeping from rage and anguish, answered, suddenly turning on her mother: "Because you have no eyes and ears! Because he *did* know the danger he was in! Because he wanted to escape; because he had begged me to help him flee; because he was planning to take your own life and would undoubtedly have done so at daybreak if I had not bound him in his sleep." The old man caressed and calmed the girl and ordered Babekan to hold her peace about the matter. He summoned a couple of riflemen to immediately carry out the law to which the stranger's life was forfeit, but Babekan whispered to him secretively: "No, for heaven's sake, Hoango!" She took him aside and explained: Before he was executed, the stranger must compose an invitation by means of which the family, whom it would be dangerous to try to capture in the woods, could be lured to the plantation.—Hoango, realizing that the family would probably not be unarmed, approved this proposal; it was too late to have the letter written now; he left two guards beside the white fugitive, and, after he had, for safety's sake, examined his bonds, and finding them too loose, had called a couple of his men to tighten them, he left the room with his whole gang and everybody, gradually, went to rest.

But Toni, who had only made a pretense of going to bed after she had said good-night to the old man, who had extended his hand to her once more, got up again as soon as she saw that all in the house was quiet, slipped out through the back door into the open field and ran, wild despair in her heart, on a path that crossed the main road in the direction from which Herr Strömli's company had to come. For the looks full of contempt that the stranger had cast at her from his bed had pierced her heart like knives; a feeling of hot bitterness mingled with her love for him, and she rejoiced in the thought of dying in this effort she was undertaking for his rescue. In her fear of missing the family, she took up a position under a pine tree by which the family, if they had accepted the invitation, would have to pass, and, in accordance with their agreement, scarcely had the first gleams of light appeared on the horizon than the voice of the boy Nanky, who was conducting the company, became audible from a distance beneath the trees.

The group consisted of Herr Strömli and his wife, who was riding on a mule, their five children, of whom two, Adelbert and Gottfried, youths of 18 and 17 years of age, were walking beside the mule, three serving men and two maids, of whom one, a nursing child at her breast, was riding on the other mule: in all, twelve persons. They were proceeding slowly along the path, which was encumbered with pine roots, toward the tree where Toni was standing: she, as noiselessly as was necessary not to frighten anyone, stepped forth from the shadow of her tree and cried: "Halt!" The boy recognized her at once and in answer to her question: where Herr Strömli was? the boy happily presented her to the venerable head of the family, while men, women, and children all crowded about her. "Noble sir!" said Toni, interrupting the old man's ceremonious greetings with a firm voice: "The Negro Hoango has unexpectedly returned to the settlement with all his men. You can't stop there now without the greatest danger to your lives; in fact, your cousin, who, to his misfortune, was received there, is lost, unless you take up arms and follow me to the plantation to free him from the arrest in which the Negro Hoango is holding him!" "God in heaven!" exclaimed all the members of the family, seized by sudden fright; and the mother, who was ill and exhausted by the journey, fell from her mule in a swoon to the ground. While the maids, summoned by Herr Strömli, hastened to assist their mistress, Toni, overwhelmed with questions by the young people, led the other men and Herr Strömli, out of fear of Nanky, to one side. She told the men, not restraining her tears of shame and remorse, everything that had happened; how matters had stood when the young man came to the house; how the private conversation she had had with him had changed things in a quite inexplicable fashion; what she, in her wild anxiety, had done when the Negro returned, and how she was now willing to risk her life to free him from the captivity into which she herself had delivered him. "My gun!" cried Herr Strömli, running to his wife's mule and taking down his rifle. He said, while Adelbert and Gottfried, his sturdy sons, and the three stouthearted servants armed themselves: "Cousin Gustav has saved the life of more than one of us; now it's our turn to do the same for him," and with these words he lifted his wife, who had recovered, back onto her mule, had them bind the hands of the boy Nanky, out of precaution, as a kind of hostage; sent the whole company of women and children, under the sole protection of his thirteen-year-old son, Ferdinand, who was also armed, back to Gull Pond, and, after he had questioned Toni, who had herself taken a helmet and spear, about the strength of the blacks and their position in the courtyard, and had promised her to spare Hoango and her mother if at all possible, trusting in God, he spiritedly placed himself at the head of his small band and set out for the plantation, led by Toni.

As soon as the band had stolen in through the back gate, Toni pointed out to Herr Strömli the room in which Hoango and Babekan were sleeping, and, while Herr Strömli silently entered the open house with his men and seized all the stacked arms of the Negroes, she slipped aside into the stable in which Nanky's five-year-old halfbrother Seppy was sleeping. Nanky and Seppy, both bastard children of old Hoango, were very dear to him, especially Seppy, whose mother had lately died, and since, even if they succeeded in freeing the captive, the retreat to Gull Pond and the flight from there to Port au Prince, which Toni intended to join, were still subject to many difficulties, she concluded quite rightly that the possession of the two boys, as a kind of security, would be of great advantage to the family, should the blacks set out in pursuit. She managed to lift the boy out of bed without being seen and to carry him in her arms, half awake, half asleep, into the main building. In the meantime, Herr Strömli had crept with his band as secretively as possible up to Hoango's chamber door; but instead of finding him and Babekan, as he had expected, in bed, they were standing there, although half-naked and helpless, in the middle of the room. Herr Strömli, rifle in hand, cried out for them to surrender or be killed, but Hoango, instead of answering, seized a pistol from the wall and fired it into the crowd, grazing Herr Strömli's head. At this signal, Herr Strömli's band furiously attacked the Negro, Hoango, after firing a second shot, which pierced the shoulder of one of the servants, was wounded in the hand by a sabre stroke and both he and Babekan were overpowered and bound with ropes to the leg of a large table. In the meanwhile, Hoango's blacks, numbering twenty or more, awakened by the shots, had swarmed out of the stables and, hearing old Babekan screaming in the house, were pressing toward it to take possession of their weapons again. In vain did Herr Strömli, whose wound was of no consequence, post his men at the windows to fire among the attackers and keep them in check; they paid no attention to two of their dead who were already lying about the courtyard, and were in the process of fetching axes and crowbars to break down the door, which Herr Strömli had bolted, when Toni, trembling in every limb, entered Hoango's room with Seppy in her arms. Herr Strömli, who was extremely glad to see her, tore the boy from her arms; drawing his hunting knife, he turned to Hoango and swore he would kill the boy on the spot, if he did not order his blacks to desist from their undertaking. Hoango, whose strength was broken by the blow across three fingers of his right hand and who would have risked his own life had he refused, replied after some hesitation, letting himself be raised from the floor: that he would do this. Led by Herr Strömli, he placed himself at the window and signaling with his handkerchief, which he held in his left hand, out across the courtyard, he called to the Negroes: that no help was necessary to save his life and that they should leave the door alone and return to the stables. Hereupon the struggle calmed down somewhat; Hoango, at Herr Strömli's request, sent a Negro who had been captured in the house to repeat the order to the band still tarrying and taking counsel in the courtyard, and since the blacks, as little as they understood the matter, had to obey the words of this official messenger, they gave up their attack, for whose execution everything was already prepared, and gradually, though grumbling and cursing, returned to the stables. Herr Strömli, as he had the boy Seppy's hands bound before Hoango's eyes, said to the latter: that his object was none other than to free his cousin, the officer, from the arrest imposed upon him in the plantation and that, if no obstacles were placed in the way of his flight to Port au Prince, nothing was to be feared either for his, Hoango's, life nor for that of his children, who would be restored to him. When Toni approached Babekan and with emotion she could not suppress was about to take her hand in farewell, the old woman violently shoved her hand away. She called her base and traitorous and said, twisting around on the leg of the table to which she was bound: God's vengeance would overtake her before she had time to rejoice in her shameful deed. Toni answered: "I have not betrayed you; I am white and engaged to marry the young man you hold captive; I belong to those on whom you openly wage war and will know how to answer to God for taking their side." Hereupon Herr Strömli placed a guard on the Negro Hoango, whom he had had fettered again for security and bound to the doorposts; he had the servant, who was lying unconscious on the floor with a shattered shoulder-blade, lifted up and carried away, and, after he had told Hoango that in a few days he could fetch both children, Nanky as well as Seppy, from Sainte Luze, where the first French outposts were stationed, he took Toni, who, besieged by various conflicting feelings, could not suppress her tears, by the hand and led her, followed by the curses of Babekan and old Hoango, out of the bedroom.

Meanwhile Herr Strömli's sons, Adelbert and Gottfried, had hastened, at their father's orders, directly after the cessation of the main skirmish fought beneath the windows, into the room of their cousin Gustav and had been fortunate enough, after a hard struggle, to overpower the two blacks who were guarding him. One lay dead in the room, the other, with a serious gunshot wound, had dragged himself into the corridor. The brothers, of whom one, the elder, had been wounded, although only lightly, in the thigh, untied their beloved cousin: they embraced him with kisses and urged him, shouting triumphantly as they gave him a gun and side arms, to follow them to the room in the front of the house where, since the victory had been secured, Herr Strömli was probably already making preparations for their retreat. But Cousin Gustav, half sitting up in bed, only pressed their hands in a friendly way; otherwise, he was quiet and distracted and, instead of taking the pistols offered him, raised his right hand and, with an expression of unutterable grief, rubbed his brow. The two youths, who had sat down beside him, asked: what was the matter with him? and, since he put his arm about them and silently leaned his head on the shoulder of the younger one, Adelbert, thinking he was going to faint, was just getting up to fetch him a drink of water: when Toni, the boy Seppy on her arm, and led by Herr Strömli, stepped into the room. At this sight, Gustav's face changed color; he rose, supporting himself on the shoulders of his cousins, as though about to swoon; and before the youths knew what he meant to do with the pistol he now seized from their hands, he fired it, gnashing his teeth with rage, at Toni. The shot pierced her in the middle of the breast, and when, with a broken cry of pain, she advanced toward him a few steps and handing the boy to Herr Strömli, sank down at his feet, he flung the pistol away across her body, kicked her from him and, calling her a whore, threw himself again on the bed. "You monster!" cried Herr Strömli and his two sons. The youths threw themselves down beside the girl and, raising her up, summoned one of the old servants who had in a number of similar desperate cases served in the capacity of doctor; but the girl, who was convulsively holding the wound with her hand, shoved the friends aside and: "Tell him . . . !" she gasped, pointing to him who had shot her, and again: "Tell him . . .!" "What are we to tell him?" asked Herr Strömli as death robbed her of speech. Adelbert and Gottfried rose and cried out to the incomprehensibly horrible murderer, asking him whether he knew that the girl was his savior, that she loved him and that it had been her intention to flee with him, for whom she had sacrificed everything, parents and property, to Port au Prince?—They thundered in his ears: "Gustav!" and asked him if he couldn't hear? They shook him and pulled his hair, but he continued to lie on the bed, unfeeling. Gustav raised himself up. He cast a glance at the girl wallowing in her own blood and the rage that had led him to do the deed gave way, in a natural fashion, to a sense of common pity. Herr Strömli, weeping hot tears into his handkerchief, asked: "Why did you do that, wretched man?" Cousin Gustav, who had gotten up from his bed and was gazing at the girl as he wiped the sweat from his brow, answered: that she had treacherously bound him while he slept and delivered him over to the Negro Hoango. "Oh!" cried Toni, extending her hand toward him with an indescribable look in her eyes: "I bound you, dear friend, because . . ." But she could not speak and could not reach him with her hand; her strength suddenly slackened and she fell back again into Herr Strömli's lap. "Why?" asked Gustav, growing pale and kneeling down to her. Herr Strömli, after a long pause interrupted only by Toni's death rattle, during which he vainly hoped for an answer from her, said at last: "Because, after the arrival of Hoango, there was no other way to save you, unhappy man; because she wanted to avoid the fight that you would have inevitably begun, because she wanted to gain time until we, who were already, thanks to her intervention, hurrying here, could rescue you by force of arms." Gustav covered his face with his hands. "Oh!" he cried without looking up and felt as if the earth was sinking beneath his feet: "Is what you tell me true?" He put his arms about her body and looked with piteously torn heart into her face. "Oh," cried Toni, and these were her last words: "You shouldn't have mistrusted me!" And with this she breathed out her pure soul. Gustav pulled his hair. "Of course!" he said, as his cousins tore him away from the body, "I shouldn't have mistrusted you; for you were betrothed to me by an oath, although we had exchanged no vows!" Sobbing, Herr Strömli pulled down the bodice from the girl's bosom. He urged the servant, who was standing beside him with some makeshift instruments, to extract the bullet which, he thought, must be lodged in her breastbone; but all efforts, as we have said, were useless, the ball had pierced her completely and her soul was already fled to better stars.—In the meantime, Gustav had gone to the window, and while Herr Strömli and his sons were trying to decide what to do with the body and whether to call in the mother, Gustav blew out his brains with the other pistol. This new act of violence robbed the relatives of their last trace of composure. Their help was now directed to their cousin, but since the wretched man had placed the pistol in his mouth, his skull was utterly shattered and pieces of it

were hanging about on the walls. Herr Strömli was the first to col-
lect his wits again. For, since the day was already shining brightly
through the windows and reports were coming in that the blacks
were beginning to show themselves again in the courtyard, there
was nothing else to do but plan an immediate retreat. They laid
the two corpses, which they did not wish to leave to the wanton
desecration of the blacks, on a board, and, after reloading their
guns, set off in sad procession for Gull Pond. Herr Strömli, the
boy Seppy on his arm, marched in front; he was followed by the
two strongest servants carrying the corpses on their shoulders; the
wounded man came reeling along behind supporting himself on a
staff, while Adelbert and Gottfried, rifles cocked, walked along at
the side of the slowly moving funeral procession. The blacks, when
they perceived that the band was so weak, came out of the stables
armed with goads and pitchforks and seemed about to attack, but
Hoango, whom they had had the foresight to untie, stepped out
on the stoop of the house and signaled the Negroes to be calm.
"In Sainte Luze!" he called to Herr Strömli, who was already in
the gateway with the bodies. "In Sainte Luze!" answered the latter, whereupon the procession came out into the open without being
pursued and reached the wooded area. At Gull Pond, where they
found the rest of the family, they dug with many tears a grave for
the bodies and, after they had exchanged the rings each wore on
their hands, lowered them with silent prayers into the dwelling place
of eternal peace. Five days later, Herr Strömli was fortunate enough
to reach Sainte Luze with his wife and children; where he left the
two Negro boys, as he had promised. He arrived in Port au Prince
shortly before the beginning of the siege, in which he fought on
the walls for the white cause and, when the city, after a stubborn
defense, surrendered to General Dessalines, he fled with the French
army onto the English fleet, whence he crossed to Europe with his
family, all of whom reached their fatherland, Switzerland, without
further incident. Here Herr Strömli bought, with the little that remained of his fortune, some property in the neighborhood of the
Rigi and in the year 1807 there was still to be seen beneath the
bushes of his garden a monument which he had had erected to
Gustav, his cousin, and to Gustav's bride, his faithful Toni.

Translated by Robert M. Browning and Frank G. Ryder

The Life of Maria Wuz, the Merry-Hearted Dominie of Auenthal

A KIND OF IDYLL

Jean Paul

Gentle and calm as a summer sea were thy life and death, thou merry-hearted Dominie, Maria Wuz. The mild heaven of a Martinmas summer spread over thy life no clouds, but a balmy haze; thy climacterics were the tremors, and thy death the decline of a lily, whose leaves drop on standing flowers, and even on this side the grave thou wast softly sleeping.

But, first of all, my friends, you must move your chairs to the fire, and push the table with my glass of water closer to me; draw the curtains, and put on your slippers; forget all about the *grand monde* over the way and the Palais Royal, because I am going to tell you the simple story of the merry-hearted Dominie. And you, dear Christian, my friend whose heart is ever open to receive the only joys of life that are fire-proof, the joys of home, sit you down on the arm of the old arm-chair, from which I am going to tell my tale, and never fear if you lean upon me now and again—you will not put me out.

Ever since the Swedish Wars, a Wuz had been schoolmaster in the village of Auenthal, and I do not think that the parson or the parish ever had a complaint against any one of the family. Invariably, eight or nine years after the marriage of a Wuz, he and his eldest boy were found conscientiously performing the duties of their office. *Our* Maria Wuz taught the alphabet under his father the very week in which he was himself learning the art of spelling—

that profiteth nothing. The character of our Wuz, like the teaching of other school-men, had something playful and childish about it; but it partook of the pleasures, not the pains of childhood. Even as a child he was somewhat childish. For you know, there are two kinds of children's games, the childish and the serious. The serious are imitations of grown-up people—playing at buying and selling, at soldiers, or artisans; the childish, the mimicry of animals. In playing, Wuz was always a hare, a turtle-dove or its young one, a bear, a horse, or even the cart. Take my word for it, a seraph sees in our university lectures and lecture-rooms no work, but only play; and, if he opens his eyes wide, these two kinds of play.

However, Wuz too, like all philosophers, had his serious business and serious hours. Had he not already—long before the grown-up Brandenburg clergy had put on a shred of parti-colored vestments—shown himself superior to deep-rooted prejudices, by donning, in the morning, a blue apron (a color seldom affected by the "poor parson of a town," but in most cases the magic Dr. Faustus' mantle on which they are spirited into a living), and in this sky-blue surplice he would point out to the maid-of-all-work the many sins that might endanger her eternal salvation. Nay, he even attacked his own father, but that was after dinner. When he read to him Kober's "Family Preacher," it was his chief delight to put in here and there two or three words, or even lines, cut of his own head, and to read this interpolation with the text, as if Herr Kober himself was addressing his father. I think these reminiscences will throw much light on our friend, and on a joke which he used to practice at a later time of his life in the pulpit, when he took the afternoon's service for the minister, and read a sermon out of the "Postilla," with so many additions of his own manufacture that he woke up the sleepy congregation, and did some damage to the Adversary. "Justina, my dear," he would say to his wife at four o'clock, when the service was over, "you can't think down below there, in your pew, how grand it is up in the pulpit, especially during the hymn before the sermon."

We can easily learn from his riper years what he was as a fledgling. In after life he used always to call for candles in December an hour after dusk, because he lived his childhood over again during that hour, taking each day another day of the past. When the wind darkened his windows with curtains of snow, and the fire peeped at him through the chinks in the stove, he would shut his eyes and let the long-buried spring descend again in dew upon the frozen meadows. Then he built once more a nest for himself and his sister in the hay-cock out in the field, and riding home on the top of the towering dome of the hay cart, with closed eyes, tried to guess what spot they were passing. In the cool of the evening, whilst the swallows were skirmishing overhead, delighted at the freedom from his nether garments, and the "déshabillé" of his legs, he flitted about as a twittering swallow, and by help of a wooden bill constructed a mud rotunda for himself and his young one—a wooden Christmas cock with feathers stuck into it—and then brought to the nest straw and feathers for bedding. In the palingenesis of another winter evening he celebrated a splendid Trinity Sunday—(I wish there were 365 Trinity Sundays in the year!)—when with Spring ringing in him and around him he strutted in the morning, with his jingling bunch of keys, through the village into the garden, cooled himself in the dew, thrust his glowing face through the dripping currant bushes, measured himself with the tall grass, and with a pair of weak fingers twisted off the roses for the rector's pulpit. On this same Trinity Sunday—and this was the second course of this same December evening feast—with the sunshine on his back, he squeezed into or rather *off* the organ-keys (that is all he can manage) the hymn, "Give honor to our heavenly King," and made vain efforts to reach the pedals with his short legs, whilst his father drew the right stops out for him. Had he in the two hours of this December evening recalled the December of his childhood, it would indeed have been a jumble of memories; but he was too prudent not to leave to a third hour the recollection of his boyish delight at the fastening of the shutters, when he could crouch securely in the lamp-lit room, for he did not like to look too long into the room outside in the darkness, which the reflection of the bright window panes revealed. He remembered how he, with his brothers and sisters, watched, assisted, and interrupted their mother in cooking the family supper, and how he and they, behind the ramparts of their father's legs, pressing their fingers to their eyes, waited to be dazzled by the advent of the candle; how warm, and comfortable, and happy they felt in this narrow room, cut out of, or built into, the infinite vault of the universe.

And every year, as often as he undertook this backward journey to the days of his childhood, and the wolf's month (December), he would forget, and, when the lamp was lit, be startled to find himself sitting in that very room which he had brought over, like a Loretto cell, from the Canaan of his infancy. So, at least, he himself describes those High Operas of memorable recollections in his "Promenades à la Rousseau," which I keep open before me that I may tell no untruths.

But I shall get entangled in a wilderness of roots and brambles, unless I extricate myself by cutting out of his advanced age, and at once expounding, a certain extremely important circumstance. After that, I mean to begin in due order "à priori," and accompany our schoolmaster slowly up the three ascending, and down again on the other side the three descending stages of life; until at last, at the foot of the lowest step, Wuz will sink into the grave before us.

I would I had not fallen upon this simile. Whenever I have looked into Lavater's "Fragments" or Comenius's "Orbis Pictus," or hung up on the wall the dismal scaffold of the Seven Stages of Life, and seen how the painted creature, lengthening and stretching itself out, climbs up the pyramidal ant-hill, looks about on the top for three minutes, and, then contracting, descends on the other side, and finally tumbles over upon the generations of the dead which lie heaped around this Golgotha—if I then turn to the rosy face, so full of Spring, and thirsting to drink in a whole heaven of delights, and consider that, not thousands of years, but only a few decades, have dried it up into that shrunk and shrivelled parchment on the other side, full of outlived hopes . . . But while I grow sad over the fate of others, I myself am being carried up and down those steps, and—we must not make each other so serious.

The important circumstance, which we are so anxious to state in advance, is this:—Wuz had written for himself an entire library with his own hand. How could he possibly have bought one? His writing-desk was his pocket printing office. As soon as our schoolmaster saw that a new book had come out at the Leipzig Fair, it was as good as written, or bought; for he sat down forthwith and composed it, and added it to his extensive library, which, like those of the ancients, consisted of manuscripts only. For instance, scarcely had Lavater's "Physiognomical Fragments" made their appearance, when Wuz hastened to keep abreast of this fertile author, folded his foolscap in quarto, and, never leaving his stool for three weeks, travailed with his own brain, until he had produced his physiognomical fetus—its cradle was his book-shelf—and had thus overtaken the Swiss writer. These Wuzian fragments he labelled as Lavater's, and added in a note that he had no objection to the printed ones, but he hoped his hand-writing was as legible, if not better, than any pica type. *He* was no d—d literary pirate, who takes the original and often copies the greater part of it; *he* never touched the original. This explains two of his peculiarities: first, that he committed sometimes very curious mistakes, *e.g.,* in Feder's Treatise on Space and Time he touched on nothing but shipping *space* and "that *time* of the month" (as we say of women); secondly, that he came to believe that his copy-books were the genuine and canonical documents, and that the printed ones were only plagiarisms. But one thing, he said, he could not make out—not if he were offered a canonry—how and why the plagiarist always altered the text so much that anyone, if he did not know better, would swear that the printed and the writer's books had different authors.

It was too transparent a joke, if an author thought to put him out by writing profoundly, viz., in square folio, or flippantly, viz., in duodecimo. His fellow author, Wuz, was at once equal to the occasion, and folded his sheet square or cramped it into duodecimo.

There was only one book he admitted into his house: the catalogue of the Leipzig Book Fair. The best pieces in this inventory the Rector marked for him with a black index-hand on the margin, that he might be able to work them off fast enough to house the Easter Fair crop on his shelves before the aftermath of the Michaelmas Fair could spring up. I should be sorry to have to write his master-pieces. He suffered most grievously—constipation for weeks at a time and, for a change, the sniffles—when the Rector (his Friedrich Nicolai) marked too many good books for him to write, and thus spurred on Wuz's hand by the index-hand on the margin. His son often complained that there were years when his father scarcely allowed himself time to sneeze, owing to his labors in literary childbirth; for instance, when he had in one year to bring into the world Sturm's Reflections (the revised edition), Schiller's Robbers, and Kant's Critique of Pure Reason. This was done in the day-time. In the evening, after supper, the good man had to sail round the South Pole, and whilst he was engaged in Cook's Voyages Round the World, hardly found time to lift his head to speak three sensible words with his son in Germany. For, as our encyclopedist had never set foot in the interior of Africa, or in a Spanish mule-stable, nor ever talked to the natives of either, he had all the more leisure and ability to produce extensive descriptions of travels of these and of other countries—I mean the kind that a statistician, a Historian of Civilization, or I myself could work with—in the first place, because many travel writers do their journals without the journey; in the second, because travel literature cannot possibly be done in any other fashion, given the fact that no travel writer ever stood face-to-face with or on the soil of the country he was sketching. After all, no one is so stupid as not to have learned this much from Leibniz's pre-established harmony: that the soul, e.g. the souls of people like Forster or Brydone or Björnstähl—all of them firmly ensconced in the solitary confinement of their petrified pineal glands—cannot describe anything in the South Indies or Europe except that which each of them has figured out in his own head, in the complete absence of external impressions, spinning his yarn like a spiderweb from his own five daddy-long-leg spinnerets. So too Wuz evolved the journal of his travels entirely out of himself.

He wrote about everything. The learned world may marvel at the fact that five weeks after the publication of the Sorrows of Werther he took an old feather-duster, removed from it a good hard quill, and *stante pede* wrote them, the Sorrows that is—which all Germany subsequently took to imitating—but no one marvels less at the learned world than I, for how can it have seen and read Rousseau's Confessions as written by Wuz and still to be found only among his papers? Here J. J. Rousseau or Wuz—it makes no difference which—assures us (wording it a bit differently, to be sure) that he would scarcely be so stupid as to take up his quill and create the best of literary works if all he had to do was simply loosen the strings of his purse and purchase them. But, as he says, he had nothing in there but two black shirt studs and a dirty kreuzer. Consequently, if he wished to read anything intelligent, for example something on practical medicine and universal case histories, he would have to sit down by his dripping windowsill and contrive the stuff out of his own head. To whom was he supposed to turn if he wanted to pry into the background of Freemasonry and its secrets, to what ear of Dionysius, he asked himself, if not his own? He listened a great deal to the two of his, buttoned as they were to his own head, and by carefully perusing and trying to fathom the dialogues of Freemasonry which he wrote, he would finally notice all manner of remarkable things, generally causing him to smell a rat. Since he knew as much of chemistry and alchemy as Adam did after the Fall (when he had forgotten everything), it had come as a great boon to him to have forged the *annulus Platonis,* that silver ring around a leaden saturn, that Ring of Gyges that made so many different things invisible, metals and brains for example. For this book would doubtless make strikingly clear to him, if he could once attain a proper understanding of it, just who let the fox into the hen-house. And now let us return to his childhood.

In his tenth year he passed through the process of transformation into a mulatto-colored "alumnus" and upper fifth-form boy of the town of Scheerau. His examiner must bear me witness that I do not flatter my hero, if I venture to assert that he only wanted one more page in his primer to reach the fourth declension, and that he could rattle off like an alarum the whole list of exceptions beginning *thorax caudex pulexque*—it was only the rule he did not know. Of the small studies allotted to these seminarists, there was one as well scoured and arranged as the show-kitchen of a Nuremberg housewife, and that was Wuz's. Contented men are generally the most orderly. He bought out of his own purse a pennyworth of nails, and studded his cell with them, in order that he might have a special peg for each of his belongings. He adjusted his note-books until their backs lay as evenly on one another as the front rank of a Prussian regiment on parade. He got out of bed in the moonlight, and took the bearings of his shoes again and again, until they stood side by side exactly parallel. When everything was in mathematical order, he rubbed his hands, shrugged his shoulders above his ears, danced about, almost shook his head off, and laughed like a lunatic.

Before I go on to prove that Wuz was happy at school, I will first prove that this was no such easy matter, but indeed a very labor of Hercules. A hundred Egyptian plagues are reckoned as fleabites merely because they come upon us in youth when wounds and compound fractures of the spirit heal as quickly as bodily ones—green wood does not break so easily as dry. All the regulations show that a seminary, according to its original destination, is meant to be a Protestant boy's monastery, but people ought to be satisfied with that, and should not want to transform such a house of correction into a Sans-souci,—a "misanthropæum" into a "philanthropæum." Must not the happy prisoners in such a "Fürstenschule" take the three monastic vows? First of all that of obedience, since the guardian of the pupils and master of the novices continually pricks and goads his black novice with the spur of most repugnant commands and mortifications; and, secondly, that of poverty, as they have no scraps and fragments, but only hunger, to save and carry over from one day to the next; and Carminati might have cured entire sanatoria with the superfluous gastric juice of such seminaries and boarding-schools. The vow of chastity became a matter of course, when the subject of it has to run about and to fast the whole day, and is indulged with every variety of motion except the peristaltic. The citizen has to be jollied into important civic duties. But does that mean that only a Catholic novice is to be flagellated into being a monk, or a wretched shop boy in Bremen smoke-cured into a merchant's apprentice, or a degenerate South American given his finishing touches and sublimated into a cacique by either of those torments or by a number of others to be found in my volume of excerpts? Is not a Lutheran pastor just as important, and does not his future destiny in equal measure require such exercises of torment? Fortunately he has them at his disposal. Perhaps it was expressly for him that earlier generations laid the bricks of the great church schools like Schulpforta, the conclavists of which are without exception servants of servants, for this use of cross and the wheel are of insufficient interest to other faculties. Hence, too, the choirs, street songs and dirges of the boarding school boys, so often the object of adverse comment, are an excellent way of making them into Protestant cloister-folk—and even their black coats and the canonical Moor's skin of their capes bear some resemblance to a monk's cowl. And since after all the clerics there have to hang their wigs on their heads like dewlaps, one can see why the scholars of the Thomas School in Leipzig have sweet little buds of wiglets popping up all about their heads and looking like flying desk lids or the hardened fore-wings of an insect.

In the convents of former times, learning was a punishment. There, only culprits had to learn the Latin Psalms by heart, or to copy books. In well-kept schools of our time, this mode of punishment is not neglected, and a scanty measure of instruction is there always ordained as a harmless means of chastening and mortifying the poor scholar.

On our Dominie alone the discipline of this school of affliction had but little effect. All day long he was in a state of enjoyment, either present or prospective. "Before I get up," said he, "I rejoice in anticipation of breakfast; all the morning I look forward to dinner; at vesper time to my piece of vesperbread, and in the evening to the evening crust, and thus alumnus Wuz has always something to hope for." When he took a deep draught of water, he would say, "That was glorious, Wuz," and stroked his waistcoat. When he sneezed, he said, "God bless thee, Wuz." In biting November frost, he would comfort himself out of doors by picturing the warm stove, and thrusting each hand in turn under his cloak. If the day was extra wild and stormy—and there are such harrying days for us poor wretches, when the hunt is up of all the elements and we the quarry, when plagues are let loose on us on every side, as if waterworks were turned on by some wag in the sky to play on us and drench us to the skin,—our Dominie was, I say, so canny that on such a day he sat down in the rain, and did not care a straw. This was not resignation which submits to the inevitable, nor callousness which endures the unfelt, nor philosophy which dilutes the bitter potion, nor religion which finds compensation in the future; no, it was the thought of his warm bed. "Let them hunt and harry me all day as much as they please," he said to himself, "to-night, at all events, I shall lie under my warm feather-bed, and press my nose into the pillow, for eight long hours." And when he crept into his bed, at last, in the last hour of such a day of suffering, he cuddled himself up, with his knees touching his chin, and said to himself, "Look'ee, Wuz, it's over at last." I extract another paragraph from Wuz's "Art of Happiness," his second wrinkle, always to wake up merry. For this purpose he always put by for the following morning something nice from the previous day, either baked dumplings, or some most dangerous leaves of Robinson Crusoe—

whom he preferred to Homer—or sometimes young birds or plants, which he had to examine in the morning to see how much the feathers or leaves had grown over-night.

The third, and perhaps the most profound paragraph of his "Art of Happiness," he excogitated when he had reached the Fifth Form. He fell in love.

An elaborate delineation of Wuz falling in love would be just in my line; but as this is my first essay as a flower-painter of love, I had better break off here, to begin again tomorrow evening, at six, with a fire not quite so low as it is at present.

If Venice, Rome, Vienna, and all the other branches of the European Bank of Pleasure, were to club together to present me with a carnival to match that which we children celebrated in the parish-clerk's dark parlor at Joditz, where we danced from eight to eleven o'clock—this was the duration of our Saturnalia, in which we whetted our appetite for Lenten fare—those great capitals would be setting themselves a task absurd and impossible, but not so impossible as if they tried to give back to schoolboy Wuz that festival Shrove Tuesday morning when he actually, while away on leave, though only in the Lower Fifth, fell in love—time, ten a.m.; place, his father's school, converted for the nonce into a ballroom. *Such* a carnival treat, my good Dominie!—what are you thinking of? The fact is, he thought of nothing but his Justina, whom I shall seldom or never take the liberty of calling "Justel," as they did at Auenthal. As the seminarist during the dancing—few public schoolboys would have deigned to join in the dance, but Wuz was never proud, though ever vain—perceived in a moment, without reference even to himself, what there was in Justina, viz., that she was a sweet, lithesome thing, who could already write a letter, and had advanced to the Rule of Three and Fractions; that she was the godchild of the rector's wife, and fifteen years old, and that she was in the ballroom only as a guest; he, being likewise a guest, did in his turn, what is fit and proper in such cases—fell in love, as aforesaid. During the very first waltz he caught the infection; whilst they were waiting for the second, and he stood by her side, and felt the warm pressure of her hand, the fever increased alarmingly; and, before he knew where he was, he had danced right away into love, and was caught in its snare. And when she now loosened the red ribbons of her cap, and let them flutter in a debonair manner about her bare throat, he ceased to hear even the bass-viol; and when at last she fanned herself with a red handkerchief, and waved it about his head, he was gone past all recovery, nor would it have availed had all the four greater and the twelve minor prophets preached at him through the window. For to a handkerchief in a female hand he always surrendered without an attempt at resistance, as the lion to the creaking carriage-wheel, and the elephant to the mouse. Village coquettes use their handkerchiefs as culverins and war-engines, just as town coquettes use their fans; but the waving of a kerchief is more captivating than the rattling noise of the ladies' painted baton, the out-spread bubble-jock's tail.

At any rate, Wuz may allege in excuse that, according to his experience, places of public amusement open the heart to all those emotions that require a good deal of space—self-sacrifice, courage, and also love. Verily, in the stifling closeness of counting-houses and public offices, our hearts lie as on so many drying-floors and malt-kilns, and shrivel up.

Wuz carried back to school his heart-balloon inflated and uplifted with the gas of love, but he said not a word to anyone, least of all to the fair kerchief-banner-bearer herself—not, indeed, from bashfulness, but because he never desired more than the present moment; it was enough for him to be in love, and he thought of nothing beyond.

Why did Heaven ordain that the lustrum of love should fall in our youth? It may be because that is just the time when we sweat and groan in schoolrooms, offices, and other poison-factories; then love climbs, like some luxuriant creeper, about the windows of those prison-cells and tells with its shifting shadows of the great spring-tide without. For, look you, Mr. Præfectus, and you, too, worthy college servants, I will lay a wager with you,—you may force our joyous Wuz to put on a hair-shirt (the truth is, he always wears one); you may set him to move the wheel of Ixion, the philosopher's stone of Sisyphus, and your baby's perambulator; you may have him starved or whipped within an inch of his life; you may, to win your wretched wager (though I should not have thought this of you), show yourself to him an incarnate devil; Wuz will still be Wuz, and will still manage to smuggle his share of love's delight right into the dog days.

But his "canicular" holidays have, perhaps, been nowhere better described than in his "*Joys* of Werther," which his biographers need only copy. On Sunday, after evening service, he would walk home to Auenthal, pitying all the townfolk in the streets who were obliged to stay behind. In the fields, his breast expanded with the sky above him, and in the concert-hall of all the birds, intoxicated with joy, he listened in twofold blessedness, now to the feathered choristers, now to his own improvisations. Merely to give vent to his over-flowing spirits, he would often gallop along for half-a-mile with-out stopping. Having always, before and after sunset, felt a certain voluptuous dreamy yearning (for night, like a prolonged death, lifts man above the earth, and takes it from under him), he lingered on his way before his arrival in Auenthal, in the last cornfields before the village, until the westering sun, just then thridding the ears of corn, embroidered his blue coat, too, with threads of gold, and his shadow stalked like a giant along the side of the hill across the river. He reeled into the village whilst the vesper bells rang in his ear, as if from a far-distant past, and felt his heart warm to all mankind, including even his Head Master. Then he walked round his father's house, and saw in the dormer-window the reflection of the moon, and through a ground-floor window his Justina, who was having her Sunday lesson in correct letter-writing. Oh, if in this paradisaical quarter of an hour he could have conjured away parlor, letters, and village, and drawn around himself and the fair letter-writer, a lonely Vale of Tempe, bathed in dusky twilight—if in this valley, he with his ravished soul, which on the way threw its arms round all mankind, could have pressed to his heart *his* fairest of living beings; and if he and she, and Heaven and Earth, had sunk down and melted away in one intensest moment of fiery bliss! And so indeed he did, about eleven o'clock, in his bed; and even earlier he had no reason to complain. He told his father, but really Justina, about his course of studies, and his political influ-ence; he opposed the strictures which his father passed upon her letters with all the weight of authority that such an art-critic pos-sesses; and as he was just fresh from town, he had more than one good story to retail; in short, as he sank to sleep, he heard, in his dancing, reeling fancy, nothing but the music of the spheres.

Verily, thou, dear Wuz, mayest write the Joys of Werther, for thy outer and thy inner world are always soldered together like the two halves of a shell, and enclose thee as their oyster. But to us poor devils sitting here about the fire, the outer world is rarely indeed the counterpart and antistrophe of our inner joys—or at best, when all our vocal organs have fallen into decay, and we can only mumble and grumble; or, to use another metaphor, when we have a cold in the head, and a whole Eden of flowers might breathe upon us, and we scent it not.

At every visit, our Dominie presented his Joan Theresa Charlotte Mariana Clarissa Heloise Justel, with a piece of gingerbread and a "potentate." I will satisfy your curiosity about both. The potentates he edited in his own publishing-house. But whereas the Chancery of the Empire makes princes and counts with a little ink, parchment, and wax, he manufactured *his* potentates in a much grander style, with soot, grease, and twenty colors. At school, you must know, they used for lighting the fires the frames of a number of potentates, all of whom, Wuz, with the aforesaid materials, knew how to copy and to represent as well as if he had been their ambassador. He first smeared a sheet of paper all over with a candle-end, and then with soot; this sheet he placed black side down on another white sheet of paper; on top of the two sheets he placed one of the royal portraits. The he took a broken fork, and travelled with its point over the face and body of the royal personage. This process resulted in a duplication of the potentate, whose outline was thus transferred from the black sheet on to the white.

In this way he produced excellent copies of all the crowned heads of Europe; but I have never concealed the fact, that his grafting-fork scratched and hacked the late Empress of Russia, and a number of crown princes, so savagely that they were fit for nothing but to go the way of their frames. But his sooty quarto-sheet was only the hatching-house and etching-trough of glorious sovereigns, or, if you like, their breeding or spawning-pond. This stretching-board or finishing-machine of the potentates was his paint-box; with this he illuminated whole dynasties, and all the color-shells were put in requisition to dress a single grand duke, while the crown princesses obtained from the same shell their brilliant complexion, their blush of modesty, and their rouge. With these reigning beauties he presented his heart's queen, who did not know what in the world to do with the gallery of historical portraits.

But with the gingerbread she knew well enough what to do— she ate it. And it is not such an easy matter as you might think to

make one's ladylove a present of gingerbread, because it not un-
frequently happens that one eats it oneself before the presentation.
Had not Wuz already paid three kreutzers for the first? Had he
not already got the brown parallelogram in his pocket, and had he
not travelled with it within an hour of Auenthal and the term of
legal session? And did he not every quarter of an hour draw his
sweet votive tablet from his pocket, in order to see whether it was
still rectangular? But here was the mischief of it; for whilst conducting this *demonstratio ad oculos,* he always broke a few insignificant almonds out of the cake—it was a habit of his,—then, instead of the squaring of the circle, he set to work on the problem
how to restore the squared circle to its original form, and bit off
neatly the four right angles, thus constructing an octagon; then, by
continuing the process, a dodecagon, and so on; for a circle is
nothing more than a polygon with an infinite number of angles.
After these mathematical operations, to offer the polygon to a young
lady was out of the question. Whereupon Wuz jumped to a conclusion, and said, "Ah, well! I'll eat it myself!" and out came the
sigh, and in went the geometrical figure. There will be few Scotch
professors and members of the Cambridge Senate who will not be
glad to learn by what *Deus ex machina* Wuz got over the difficulty. It was by means of a second piece of gingerbread, which he
always put into his pocket to keep the first company. Whilst he
ate the one, the other reached its destination in safety, under the
escort of its twin brother. But he soon discovered that, in order
not to bring a mere torso or atom to Auenthal, he must from week
to week increase the escort, *i.e.,* the pieces of gingerbread.

He would have got his remove into the Head Form, had not his
father been removed from our planet into another or some satellite. It occurred to him, therefore, to imitate his father's promo-
tion, and slip from his seat on the Fifth Form into the schoolmaster's chair. The patron of his benefice, however, Herr von Ebern,
thrust himself between the two seats, supporting the claim of his
superannuated cook to an office for which his previous functions
had eminently fitted him. For here, too, there were young porkers
to be whipped* and dressed, if not to be eaten. I have before noticed, in a note to my "School Reform," that in every peasant boy

* Suckling pigs are, as everybody knows, much better eating when killed by whip-
ping.

there is hidden an undeveloped schoolmaster, who would naturally unfold himself in the space of a few ecclesiastical years; that
as ancient Rome took her world-consuls, so our modern villages
might take their school-consuls, from the plough and out of the
furrow; that a man might as well be *taught* by his peers, as he is
judged by them in England; that each of us most nearly resembles
the man to whom he owes the greater part of the knowledge, that
is, himself; that if a whole town (Norcia in the Appennines) could
be ruled by four unlettered magistrates (*i quatri illiterati),* it ought
to be possible for the children of a village to be ruled, and whipped,
by a single unlettered man; and that all legislators should take to
heart what I said above in the text. But as in this book the note is
itself the text, I simply hasten to say that I said that a village school
had an ample teaching staff. There is (1) the gymnasiarch, or pastor, who puts on his surplice once a year in order to visit and to
frighten the school; (2) the rector, conrector, and subrector are
present in the schoolroom, all three represented by the village
schoolmaster himself; (3) teachers of the lower forms are the
schoolmaster's wife, to whom, if to anyone, could be entrusted the
teaching of calisthenics in the girls' school; and her son as tertius
(third master) and schoolboy in the same person, whom his pupils
must bribe and flatter, to be excused from saying their lessons, and
who, when the master is not at home, oftentimes has on his shoulders the regency of a whole Protestant school-district; (4) lastly, a
whole caterpillar's nest of collaborateurs, themselves schoolboys,
because there, as in the famous orphanage at Halle, the pupils of
the higher forms are ready-made teachers of the lower classes. To
satisfy the clamor of educational reformers for "Practical Schools,"
communes and schoolmasters took up the cry, and gladly did all
they could. The communes selected for their professional chairs only
such pedagogic hams as had been installed on weavers', tailors',
and shoemakers' stools, and of whom, consequently, something
might be expected. And no doubt, by making in the presence of
the gaping institute, coats, boots, fishing baskets, &c., these men
easily change a theoretical into a practical school, where boys are
taught the knowledge of the processes of manufacture. But the village schoolmaster carries things further still, and meditates day and
night on practical school-keeping. There are few occupations of the
grown-up pater-familias, or of his servants, in which he does not

employ and exercise his village Stoa, and the whole morning you may see his practical seminary hurrying in and out, splitting wood, carrying water, &c., so that the practical lessons are pretty nearly the only ones he gives, and thus he earns his crust in the sweat of his—school-house. I am perfectly aware that some village schools are in a less satisfactory condition; we must be content if only the greater number possess all the advantages I have enumerated.

I will not say a word in defense of my digression, for that would have the effect of making my orbit still more eccentric than it is. Squire Ebern would have installed his cook as schoolmaster, if he could have found a proper successor to the cook, but he could not get one; and as the Squire thought it would perhaps be deemed too great an innovation to allow kitchen and school to be presided over by one and the same individual—although certainly the doubling of the servant class attendant upon its separation into school or manor house was a much greater and older innovation; in the ninth century even the pastor of the noble's chapel was also a serving man, responsible for waiting on his patron and saddling up for him, the master of his little church and state; and the two functions, like many others, were not separated until much later—so he retained the cook and appointed the seminarist, who had been prudent enough to remain in love.

In this part of my story I follow entirely the excellent testimonials which I have in my hands, and which Wuz obtained from the rector, after an examination which was, perhaps, one of the most severe and brilliant of modern times. Had he not to repeat the Lord's Prayer in Greek whilst the Board of Examiners was engaged in brushing, with a glass brush, its satin small clothes; and, afterwards, the Athanasian Creed in Latin? Did not the examinee enumerate correctly the books of the Bible from Genesis to Revelation, without stumbling over the painted flowers and cups on his examiner's breakfast tray? Had he not to catechise a little beggar boy, who kept his mind and his eye fixed on the penny he was to receive, and who did not by any means acquit himself so brilliantly as his examiner, but like an ox? Had he not to dip his fingers into five pots of warm water, in order to find which of them was the proper temperature for the head of the infant candidate for baptism? And had he not, finally, to pay three florins and thirty-six kreutzers?

On the 13th of May he walked out of his seminary as a school-boy, and into his house as a schoolmaster; and at the same time out of the chrysalis of a seminarist there burst forth the many-colored butterfly of an organist and choirmaster.

On the 9th of July, he stood before the altar and was married to his Justina. But, oh! the Elysian interval between that 13th of May and that 9th of July! For no mortal man will such a golden age of eight weeks again descend from Heaven; for our Dominie alone did heaven itself distil in dew on the starry fields of earth. Floating in ether, thou didst see, through the transparent earth, heaven and sun revolving round thee, a disembodied spirit. But to us, the alumni of nature, are never allotted eight such weeks as these,—not one week, nay, scarcely one entire day on which the heaven above and the heaven within us stains its pure blue with nought but the evening and morning red; on which we fly high away above this earthly life, transported, as in a happy dream; where the resistless torrent of life does not toss, and tumble, and rack us with its cataracts and whirlpools; but rocks us on spar-kling wavelets, and bears us gently along under overhanging flow-ers;—a day whose fellow we vainly seek among those that are past, and of which we sadly say, at the end of every following one, "We shall not see its like again."

It will do us all good to hear more in detail about these eight rapture weeks, or two rapture months. They were made up of days wonderfully like each other. Not a single cloud rose above the houses. The whole night long, the evening red hung about the ho-rizon, where the setting sun had faded like a rose. At one o'clock the larks had begun to sing, and nature played all night her night-ingale fantasias. The melodies of the outer world blended with his dreams, and in these he winged his way over blossoming trees, to which the real ones before his window lent their luscious fra-grance. The dream of dawn carried him, as gently as a crooning mother her child, from sleep to waking; and with senses all athirst he stepped forth into the busy world of a new-born day, where both sun and earth mingled in a surging ocean of brightness and rapture. Out of this morning flood-tide of life and joy he returned into his dark little room, and sought new strength in the lesser de-lights of existence. He rejoiced at everything—at every sunny and shadowed window; at the clean-swept room; at his breakfast, the cost of which was defrayed out of his official stipend; at the clock striking seven, because he had no longer to go to his class-room; at his mother, who rejoiced every morning that he had been made schoolmaster, and she had not been obliged to quit the dear old house.

Whilst he drank his coffee, he cut, at the same time as his roll, his pens for the "Messiah," which he quite completed at that time, with the exception of the last three cantos. He took the greatest pains to make his epic pens badly, either like sticks, or without a slit, or with a second extra slit, which spluttered; for as the whole work was to consist of hexameters, and of such as could not be understanded of the vulgar, the poet who toiled in vain to produce anything unintelligible, was obliged to have recourse to the expedient of *writing* his hexameters illegibly—which was not a bad idea. By this poetical license he obviated all risk of comprehension from the outset, and in quite a natural manner.

At eleven o'clock he spread the cloth, first for his birds, and then for his mother and himself. The table had four drawers, which contained more than was on it. He cut the bread, and gave the crust to his mother, although he did not care for the crumb himself. Oh, my friends, why cannot one dine as contentedly at the Hôtel de Bavière, or the Römer at Frankfort, as here at Wuz's table? Immediately after dinner he manufactured, not hexameters, but wooden table-spoons: my sister possesses a dozen of them still. Whilst his mother washed what he carved, their minds were not left starving; she told him all sorts of anecdotes about herself and his father, and what had happened while he was away at school; and he imparted to her his modest plans for his future housekeeping, for he was never tired of dwelling on his prospect of becoming the head of a family. "I shall make an excellent manager," he said. "I shall set up a suckling pig, to provide for the great feast days of the year; we have so much potato and turnip peelings that it will fatten of itself; and for the winter my father-in-law must get me a load of faggots; and the parlor door must be lined with felt, for you see, mother, we pedagogues have a lot of work in winter, and cannot stand the cold."

On the 29th of May there was a christening—his first. It was his first fee, and he had already at school prepared a large cash-book in anticipation. He examined and counted the few groschen twenty times, as if each time they were fresh ones. At the font he stood in full canonicals, and the spectators stood in the nave, and in the Squire's pew, in their work-a-day dress. "It is the sweat of my brow," he said, half an hour after the solemnity, as he consumed a portion of his fee in half a pint of beer—a most *intemperate* luxury for him. I expect a few psychological hints from a future biographer of Wuz, to tell me why he stitched for himself only a book for receipts, and none for expenses, and why in this book he had columns for louis d'or, groschen, and farthings, although he never had the first-named coin amongst his school-dues. The baptism over, and his beer digested, he brought out his table under the wild cherry tree in the garden, and sat down and scratched off a few more illegible hexameters for his "Messiah." Even whilst he was gnawing and polishing off his ham-bone for supper, he was still polishing a few more epic feet, and I know very well that, owing to the grease, several of the cantos present a somewhat oily appearance. As soon as he saw that the sunbeams had climbed from the road to the walls of the houses, he gave his mother the necessary funds for the housekeeping, and ran out-doors, in order quietly to sketch out for himself how he would live in the future—in autumn, in winter, on the three great Christian feast days—among the school children and his own.

And yet these are only week-days. Around the Sunday shines a glory brighter than any altar-piece. But, indeed, no souls of this century have so grand an idea of a Sunday as those that dwell in organists and schoolmasters; nor do I wonder if on such a gala-day they find it impossible to remain modest. Even our Wuz could not help feeling what it means to play the organ alone amidst a thousand people, to perform the functions of a real hereditary office, to hang the spiritual coronation-robe on the shoulders of the rector, and act as his *valet de fantaisie* and groom of the chamber; to exercise territorial sway over a whole sun-illumined choir, and from his organ-throne to rule over the poetry of a diocese even more absolutely than the vicar administers its prose; and leaning over the rail after the sermon to proclaim, or rather to promulgate *sans façon*, right royal edicts in a commanding voice. I really think that here, if anywhere, I am bound to admonish my Wuz: "Consider what you were only a few months ago! Consider that all men can't become organists, and use the fortunate inequalities of rank without abusing them, or thinking small beer of me and my audience here by the fire."

But, upon my honor, the kind-hearted Dominie never dreams of such a thing. I wish the peasants has been keen-sighted enough to look into your gall-less heart, full to over-flowing of the milk of human kindness—you foolish, beaming Dominie, tripping and rubbing your hands! what would they have there discovered? Joy in the two auricles of your heart, joy in both its ventricles. Up in your organ-loft, you good-natured, loveable creature, you were counting up your future schoolboys and schoolgirls in their pews, and grouping them in imagination round your diminutive nose in the schoolroom; and you were forming the resolution to take a pinch of snuff once every morning, and once every afternoon, merely in order that you might sneeze, and have the delight of seeing your whole institute jump up like mad, and hearing them cry, "God bless you, Mr. Organist!" And, furthermore, the peasants would have found in your heart the joy which you feel as a printer of folio figures as long as those on the dial of the church clock, seeing that every Sunday you publish in large type on the black board the number and page of the next hymn—(we authors appear in print with worse stuff than that)—and a further joy they would have discovered, viz., that of showing off your singing before your father-in-law and your *fiancée,* and finally your hope of drinking in solitude the dregs of the communion wine, with its sour taste. Some higher being must have been as affectionately attached to you as is your biographer, for he decreed that right in the midst of your eight-week lustrum in Eden your gracious patron should take communion, and he had sufficient insight to replace the communion wine, which was a reasonable imitation of what Christ drank on the Cross, with the Lachrima Christi from his own cellar. But what heavenly sensations flowed through all your limbs after the drinking of that to the dregs!

Truly, each trait of Wuz's character makes me go off into fresh raptures. But why, I ask, does this schoolmasterly happy heart afford so much joy to me, and perhaps to you also? Alas! it is perhaps because we ourselves never get such a full measure of it; because the thought of the vanity of earthly things lies heavy on us and oppresses our breath, because we have already seen the black churchyard mold underneath that flowery sward on which the little schoolmaster is frisking his life away.

The same communion wine was still bubbling in his veins that evening; and these last hours of his Sabbath remain for me to describe. Only on Sunday was he permitted to walk with his Justina. Before starting, he supped at his father-in-law's, though with small profit; even whilst grace was being said the edge of his appetite grew dull, and before the dessert it had disappeared altogether.

If I could decipher it, I could find the exact description of this evening in his "Messiah," into the sixth canto of which he has woven it, just as all great authors have immortalised in their *opera omnia* their wives, their children, their lands, and their cattle. He believed there was such an evening scene in the printed "Messiah." In his own is described, in true epic style, how the peasants sauntered along their corn-fields and scanned the growth of the green blades, and took off their hats to him from the other side of the water, as their duly ordained organist; how the children trumpeted on leaves, and performed on penny whistles; how every bush and flower, calix and blossom, formed a full-voiced orchestra, from which something sang, or hummed, or buzzed; and how, at last, the whole scene grew festal as if the earth itself kept Sunday, whilst hills and woods waved their censers around this magic circle, and the sun went down in the west through a golden arch of triumph, and the moon came forth in the east through a triumphal arch of silver. O, thou father of light, with how many colors and rays and balls of light dost thou invest thy pale earth!

And now the sun had dwindled to a single ruddy beam, which mingled with the reflection of the after-glow on the face of his beloved; and she, who felt but never put her feelings into words, told Wuz that in her childhood she had often longed to stand on the red mountains of sunset, and to descend with the sun into the beautiful rose-tinted lands which lay behind. Whilst his mother was ringing to evening prayers in the village church, he laid his hat on his knee and gazed, without folding his hands, at the red spot in the sky where the sun had last appeared, and down on the stream at his feet, moving in deep shadow, and he felt as if the vesper bell were ringing the world, and his dead father too, once more to his rest. For the first and last time in his life, his heart soared beyond this earthly scene, and a voice seemed to call to him from out of those evening chimes, that he was now to die of joy. . . . In ecstasy he clasped his beloved to his heart and cried, "How I love thee, love thee for ever!" From the river there came the sound of flutes and voices, which drew nearer. Beside himself with joy, he pressed her close and yet closer, longing to pass away in this embrace, and fancied that the heavenly ones would waft their two souls away from the earth, and distil them in shining dew-drops upon the fields of Eden. The voices sang—

> Fair, O God, is the earth thou madest!
> Well may gladness and love be there!
> So, my heart, till in death thou fadest,
> Love and be glad that the earth is fair!

It was a gondola, from the neighboring town, with a party of youths flute-playing and singing in chorus. He and Justina wandered, hand in hand, along the bank, keeping pace with the moving gondola, and Justina tried softly to chime in. Heaven within heaven lay about them. As the gondola was rounding a wooded bend in the river, Justina stopped him gently, in order that they might not keep alongside of it, and, when it was out of sight, threw her arms about his neck and gave him the first blushing kiss. "O never-to-be-forgotten first of June," he writes. They followed at a distance, and listened to the sailing music. Winged dreams flitted about them both. At last she said: "It is late; the evening light is fading, and all is quiet in the village." They walked home, he opened the windows of his moonlit room, and with a soft "goodnight!" he stole past his mother, who was already asleep.

Every morning there came to him, like a new dawn, the thought that he had slept himself one night nearer to his wedding day, the eighth of June; and during the day he carried about with him the joyful thought that he had not yet reached the end of the Elysian days which lay between him and his wedding. Thus, like the metaphysician's ass, he held his head between two bundles of hay, *i.e.,* the present and the future; but he was no ass or schoolman, but grazed and battened on both bundles at once. . . . Indeed, men should never be asses, whether of the adiaphorist, wooden, or Balaamitic order, and I have reasons for saying so. . . . I break off here, because I still have to consider whether I shall portray his wedding-day or not. Of pieces for a mosaic I have indeed enough, and to spare.

But the truth is, I have assisted neither at his nor at my own marriage festival, so I will describe it as well as I can; and to console myself make up a pleasure party for myself—the only one I am likely to get.

And, indeed, I do not know a more suitable place or page than the one on which I write to make the reader understand what I suffer. The magic landscapes of Switzerland, where I pitch my tent, the Venuses and Apollos on whose forms I feast my eyes, the glorious fatherland for which I sacrifice my life, the life it has ennobled, the bridal bed which receives me,—all these, alas! are pictures of my own or others' fancy, painted with ink or type; and if only thou, celestial beauty, who art true to me, and whose true knight I am, with whom I wander on Arcadian July nights, with whom I stand before the setting sun and before the rising moon, and for whose sake I love all thy sisters, if only thou wert real! But thou art an altar-piece, and I find thee not.

True, it was also the practice to offer up to the Nile, to Hercules and other gods (and to me as well) maidens who were only handcrafted imitations. But before that *they* got real ones.

Though it is only Saturday, we must take a peep into the school, and the bridal house, in order to explain the premises and clear the ground for the high argument of the wedding-day itself; on the Sunday we shall have no time for it. Thus, according to the older theologians, the world was created in six days, and not in a minute, that the angels might the better peruse the Book of Nature, as it was gradually unfolded. On the Saturday the bridegroom was conspicuous in his double capacity, running to and fro between the parsonage and the school-house in order to carry four chairs out of the former into the latter. These seats he borrowed of the rector for the accommodation of the self-same rector, as his prince bishop, the rector's wife as godmother of the bride, the subprefect of the seminary, and the bride herself.

I know as well as anyone how little can be said in defense of this borrowed luxury of the bridegroom. It is true the gigantic borrowed chairs (men and chairs have degenerated since then) wore their false cow-hair curl-papered in blue cloth, milky ways of yellow nails darted about on yellow tapes like forked lightnings, and it is certain that you sat as comfortably on the edge of these chairs as if nature had provided you with a double seat; still, as I said before, I have never held up as a model this *a posteriori* luxury either of the borrower or lender in the matter of seats. On the other hand, anyone who has glanced at the *Maire de Paris* must acknowledge that the extravagance of the Palais Royal and the Courts is manifestly greater. How can I reconcile rigid precisians of the Strict Observance to Wuz's old-fashioned easy-chair, its four wooden lions' claws which gripped the floor, its cross-bars which served as perches for gay finches and linnets, its chignon encased in a gorgeous covering of embroidered leather, and its two hairy arms of wood, which age had attenuated as it does human ones, extended to receive the occupant?. . . . This question mark will probably surprise some readers who may have forgotten the beginning of the paragraph.

Of the pewter dinner-service, which the bridegroom obtained also from his prince bishop, the public will be better judges than I, when they read their catalogue at the auctioneer's, if it is ever brought to the hammer. So much, however, the wedding-guests knew for certain, that the salad-bowl, the sauce-tureen, the cheese-dish, and the mustard-pot were represented by one and the same plate, which was, however, washed each time before it played a new part.

A whole Nile and Alpheus streamed over every board in the room from which there was actually garden mold to be washed off, and rose to the bed-posts and window-sills, leaving behind the usual deposit—to wit, sand. According to the established rules of romance, the hero should now array himself, and lie down in a meadow, beneath a waving coverlet of grass and flowers, and there sink deeper and deeper into dreams of love; but our hero was hard at work plucking ducks, chopping up fire-wood to roast the meat and coffee, and the meat itself for roasting, drinking a Saturday toast to Sunday, issuing and executing, in his mother's blue apron, fifty orders for the kitchen, frisking about here, there, and everywhere—his head adorned with horn-like curl-papers, and his hair trussed up behind like a squirrel's tail. "For," said he, "one doesn't get married every Sunday."

Nothing is more disagreeable than to see and hear a hundred running footmen and outriders assisting at some petty entertainment; but nothing is more delightful than to be one's self such a fugleman and outrider. The activity which we not only see, but share, makes the pleasure like a fruit planted, watered, and reared by ourselves; and, in addition, we are spared the impatience of waiting.

Heavens! it would take me a whole Saturday only to report this one. I can merely cast a passing glance into Wuz's kitchen. What death-quiverings! what stream of slaughter! Why are murder and marriage as near neighbors as the two commandments which refer to them? Why, as a royal marriage is not infrequently the signal for a St. Bartholomew's Eve for men, why, I say, is a plain middle-class wedding invariably the signal for a massacre of domestic fowls?

But no one passed these two days of joy more dolefully than two goldfinches and three bullfinches, which the bridegroom, a lover of cleanliness as well as of birds, succeeded in capturing, after a prolonged chase, with flapping of aprons and throwing of night-caps, and forced to leave their ball-room, and take up their quarters in two narrow Carthusian cells of cages, in which, suspended from the ceiling, they hopped about disconsolately.

Wuz narrates, both in his "Wuzian Genealogy," and in his "Child's Third Standard Reader," that by seven o'clock in the evening, when the tailor came to try on the hymeneal trousers, coat, and waistcoat, everything about the place was in apple-pie order, clean and burnished, except Wuz himself. An ineffable peace rests on each chair and table of a newly-tidied and brightly-polished room. In a disorderly one, we feel as if under notice to quit, and about to pack up at any moment.

This night, and the next, the sun and I pass over; and we meet him again on the Sunday morning, when, flushed and electrified with the thought of the heaven that is opening on him to-day, he trips down stairs into the brilliant wedding-room, which we all helped to decorate last night, with so much pains and ink, by the aid of toilet-water and beauty patches (dish-rags) powder-boxes (sand-boxes), and all the other apparatus of the toilet-table. He had woke up seven times in the course of the night, in order to rejoice seven times in anticipation of the day; and had risen two hours before his usual time, in order to feed on them minute by minute. I can see him opening the door; the minutes stand arrayed before him like so many honey-cells; he drains one after the other, and every succeeding minute is a fuller honey-cup. No, not if he had been offered a pension for life, could the organist have imagined a single house on the whole earth in which on that day there was not Sunday sunshine and joy! The second thing he opened, after the door, was an upper window, to let a fluttering butterfly—a floating silver spangle, a winged flower, a miniature Cupid—escape out of Hymen's chamber. Then he fed his bird choristers in their cages, in anticipation of the busy day; then he played at the open window, on his father's fiddle, the waltzes to whose music he had danced from Shrove Tuesday to his wedding-day. It is only five that's striking; we need not hurry, my friend. We shall have our pig-tail ribbon on without a crease, and our two yards of cravat (into which you are already dancing yourself, whilst your mother holds one end of it) adjusted two full hours before the church-bell rings. I would gladly give the family arm-chair in which I am sitting for the privilege of transforming myself and my audience into invisible sylphs, that our whole brotherhood might flit about the enraptured bridegroom without disturbing his quiet joy, and follow him out into the garden, where he is cutting natural flowers, not bejewelled artificial ones from Paris, for a female heart which is natural, and not made of diamonds or of French paste; where he shakes the glittering beetles and dewdrops from the flowers, and gladly waits for the bee whose proboscis sips the honey from the flower for the last time; where he thinks of the Sunday mornings of his boyhood, of the too short walk across the flower beds, and the chilly pulpit-desk on which the Rector used to place his nosegay. Go home, true son of thy father, and look not, on this eighth of June, towards the west, where the six feet of silent churchyard earth lie heavy on many a friend, but towards the east, where thou mayst see the sun, the parsonage door, and thy Justina just slipping in to be dressed and have her hair arranged by her godmother! I perceive that my audience would like to be turned once more into sylphs, in order to hover about the bride; but she would rather not.

At last, the sky-blue coat—the livery of millers and schoolmasters—the button-holes blackened, and every crease removed by his mother's careful hand, invested our Dominie; and he may now take up hat and prayer-book. I know all about pomp and ceremony, the princely splendors of princely weddings, cannonades, illuminations, parades, and hair-dressings; but all these are not to be compared with the glories of Wuz's wedding. Just look at the man, as he walks the way of the sun to his bride, and glances at the other road leading to the seminary, and thinks to himself, "Who would have dreamt of this four years ago?" Just look at him, I say. Doesn't the rector's maid-servant look, though she is carrying the water-bucket?—and doesn't she hang up in the clothes compartment of her memory that gorgeous full-dress, down to the last fringe. Is he not bepowdered from the tip of his nose to the tip of his shoe? Does he not stride through the red folding-doors of his father-in-law's house, which now stand wide open to receive him, while his betrothed slips through the back-door? And as she emerges out of her hairdresser's hands, are they not both so bepowdered and bedizened that they scarcely dare bid each other good morning? Have either of them, in all their lives, seen aught so grand and magnificent as themselves to-day? In this pardonable embarrassment, the skewer that her little brother has cut for her, and with which he now presents her, that she may wind and twine round it as a vine-pole the monstrous bunch of flowers for the organist's button-hole, proves a veritable godsend. Will envious ladies forgive me if I choose from my pallette the brightest colors, and paint to them the finery of the bride, the gold coins which tremble in her hair, the three gold medallions on her breast with miniatures of the German Emperors; and, lower down, the bars of silver cast into buttons?

But I could throw my brush at somebody's head if I imagined that my Wuz and his good bride would, when this is printed, be laughed at by coquettes and such-like creatures. Think you, forsooth, you fashionable, essenced, tattooed man-killers, who prize and love everything about a man, except his heart,—think you, that I, or the majority of my male readers, could remain indifferent in the presence of such a bride, or that we should not gladly resign your flushed cheeks and quivering lips, your rolling, wanton eyes, your arms ever ready to embrace, and all your sentimental eloquence, for a single scene, where the maiden blush reflects the dawn of rising love, and the transparent, innocent soul unrobes herself to every eye except her own, while her face reveals a hundred inward conflicts,—in a word, for the scene in which my pair of lovers were themselves the actors, when the old pantaloon, the bride's father, caught hold of the two frizzed and powdered heads, and artfully brought them together for a kiss? How rapturous thy blush, my dear Wuz—and how bashful thine, my dear Justina!

And who, shortly before his nuptials, could possibly reflect on these and similar matters with greater intensity and afterward stage them with more delicacy than the very author of the present biography?

The hubbub of the children, and the costermongers in the street, and of the reviewers in Leipzig, prevents me from describing the ceremony in detail—the elaborate flourishes and apoggiaturas with which the bridegroom embellished every line of the hymn he played on the organ; the wooden cherub's wings on which he hung up his hat in front of the choir; the name of Justina on the organ stops; his fun and delight when they joined hands before the service—the Golden Bull and Great Charter of the married estate—while, regardless of the proprieties, he tickled her clasping hand with his ring-finger; their entrance into the banqueting-hall, where perhaps the grandest and most distinguished personages and authorities of the village met—a parson and a parson's wife, a sub-prefect and a bride.

But I am sure my audience will not object, if I mend my pace, and pass over the whole wedding-banquet, and the afternoon, in order to hear what they are doing in the evening. The sub-prefect has led off a couple of dances. All the company are in a state of frantic excitement. Clouds of tobacco-smoke, and of steaming punch, roll around the three candles, and divide one guest from the other by banks of mist. The fiddler and the violoncellist are busier filling their own, than scraping their cat-guts. All Auenthal is peeping in at the window, struggling and squeezing like the gallery of a theatre; and the young people of the village are dancing on the green, about thirty yards from the orchestra, on the whole prettily enough. The old village La Bonne is screaming most important communications into the ear of the rector's wife, and the rector's wife is coughing and sneezing out hers, each dying to relieve herself of her burden of historical fact, and loath to see the other on the throne. The rector looks as if he were the bosom friend of the bosom disciple, St. John—who is represented by painters with a goblet in his hand—and his laugh is louder than his sermons. The sub-prefect darts about in the character of a fashionable exquisite, and is altogether unapproachable. Our Wuz dives and splashes about in all the four rivers of Paradise, and is tossed to and fro on the billows of an ocean of joy. Only the solitary bridesmaid—whose nature is too tender and sensitive for the trying duties of her position—hears the drums of joy, deadened as by an echo, or muffled with crape as at a royal burial, and her overwrought feelings find vent in a quiet sigh. Our Dominie—he may be allowed to appear twice in his own wedding performance—goes out with his better-half into the gateway of the house, whose *dessus de porte* is a round swallow's nest, and looks up to the silent starry heaven above, and fancies that every sun up there is looking down at him, and peering in at his window like the Auenthal natives. Sail merrily over thy summer sea, an evaporating drop in the ocean of time! thou mayest; we may not all; the solitary bridesmaid may not. Alas! had I, on a wedding morning, found, like thee, a fluttering captive butterfly—like thee, a lily-cradled bee—like thee, marked the church-clock that stopped at seven—like thee, beheld a silent Heaven above, and a noisy Heaven below,—I could not have banished the thought that not on this bustling globe, where rough winds shake the tender buds of May, and the rain dashes in our faces, not here is the resting-place to be found, where eyes are tearless, and no breath stirs the sleeping flowers. And had the dazzling goddess of joy revealed herself as visibly to me, I must yet have bent my eyes to those handfuls of ashes into which her fiery embrace (daughter of the sun is she, and not of our frigid zones) changes us poor mortals. And since even the description of such delight has left me thus sad, surely if thou, O Father, hadst stretched forth thy hand, that reaches from the infinite heights of Heaven to this low Earth, and brought me down such a delight, like a sungrown flower, I must needs have bedewed that fatherly hand with tears of joy, and turned away my swimming eyes from the gaze of men. But Wuz's wedding is now long past and over—his Justina is old, and he lies in the churchyard; the current of time has whelmed and buried him, and all these bright days, under a triple and quadruple layer of earth. And so around *us,* too, this churchyard-earth rises higher and higher. Three minutes more, and it has reached our hearts, and buries me and you.

Whilst I am in this solemn mood, let nobody ask me to communicate, out of his "Manual of Delights," the many joys of the schoolmaster, especially his Christmas-tide church fêtes, and school delights; possibly I may do it in a posthumous postscript, but not to-day. To-day it is better for us to see the happy Wuz for the last time, alive and dead, and then retire.

I should have known very little of the whole man, although I have passed his house-door fifty times, had not old Justina been standing at it last year, on the 12th of May, and, seeing me writing in my note-book as I walked, asked me whether I was not also a book-maker. "What else, dear Madam?" I replied, "I make one or more every year, and present them all to the public."

This being the case, would I take the trouble to come in for a moment to see her old man, who was also a book-maker, but now in a bad way?

An apoplectic stroke had paralysed the left side of our friend, perhaps because he had treated himself to a lupus growth on his neck the size of a dollar, or perhaps as a function of old age. He sat up in his bed, supported by cushions, and had a whole shopful of goods—which I shall specify directly—spread out before him on the counterpane. A sick man, like a traveller—and what else is he?— makes friends at once with every one. Standing on the border of a better world, we no longer stand on ceremony in this scurvy one. He complained to me that for the last three days he had told his old woman to look out for a book-writer, but she had not caught one until now. He must have one, he said, to take over, arrange, and catalogue his library, and to add to his biography, which was scattered up and down his works, a description of his last hours, if these were really his last; for his wife was no scholar, and as to his son, he had just sent him to the University of Heidelberg for three——weeks. Merry lights played about the pock-marks and wrinkles of his round little face, each of which seemed a smiling mouth; but it did not please me or my sense of semiotics to see the unnatural brightness of his eyes, the twitchings of his eye-brows and the corners of his mouth, and the trembling of his lips.

I will give you the inventory, according to my promise. On the counterpane there lay a child's cap of green taffeta, with one ribbon torn off; a child's whip, with some remains of tinsel gold here and there; a finger-ring of pewter, a box with dolls' books in 128mo, a house clock, a dirty copy-book, and a three-inch-long bird-trap.

These were the rubble and after-math of his played-out childhood. The art-gallery of these, his Grecian antiquities, had been from time immemorial under the staircase—for in a house which is, as it were, the flower-pot or hot-house of a single family tree, things may remain for half a century in one and the same place—and as, from his childhood upwards, it had ever been with him an inviolable law to preserve all his toys in chronological order, and as all the year round no one but himself ever looked under the staircase, he was able, even on the eve of preparation for death, to arrange about him these funeral urns of a life that was already sped, and to rejoice in looking *back*, since he could no longer rejoice in looking *forward*. Thou could'st not, indeed, dear Wuz, enter a temple of antiquities like that at Sans-souci or Dresden, in order to kneel down in adoration before the world-spirit of art; but thou could'st look into the tabernacle of thy childhood's antiquities, under the dark staircase, and the sunbeams of childhood's resurrection played upon the dark corners, as in the picture the manger is illumined by the light that streams from the Infant Christ. Oh, if greater souls than thine could suck as much sweetness and fragrance out of the entire flower-garden of nature as thou did'st out of the one prickly green leaf on which Fate had hung thee, they would feast on *gardens,* not on *leaves,* and these better and yet happier souls would no longer wonder at the existence of contented Dominies!

Wuz said, turning his eyes towards the bookshelves,—"When I have tired myself out with reading and correcting my serious works, I look for hours at these trivia; and I hope this is a pardonable indulgence for an author."

But, perhaps, the best service I can do my readers at this moment is to give them the "catalogue raisonné" of these artifacts and trivia, as the sick man explained them to me. The pewter ring the four-year-old daughter of the late pastor had put on his finger, when they were married in due form by a playfellow—the base metal soldered them more firmly together than the refined gold of refined gentle-folk, and they were faithful to their marriage vows for four-and-fifty minutes. He often thought of the ring, and of the good old times when, in later life—himself a sable seminarist—he saw her on the promenade, flaunting her nodding plumes, as she leaned on the arm of some smartly-dressed beau. But it is now time for me to confess what I have all along taken infinite but useless pains to conceal, that he fell in love with everything that had the semblance of a woman. All light-hearted people of his temperament do the same; and perhaps the reason is, that their love hovers between the two extremes of love—the Platonic and the Epicurean—and borrows of both.

When he assisted his father in winding up the church-clock (just as in former times the crown princes attended cabinet meetings together with their fathers) so small a matter as that was enough to give him a hint how to make holes in a little box of lacquered wood and to transform it into a house-clock—which, however, like a great many departments of State, never went. It has its long weights and its cog wheels, taken off the stand of some Nuremberg horses, and thus elevated to a higher use. The green child's-cap, with its fringe of lace—the only relic of the four-year-old boy—was the bust and plaster cast of the little Wuz, who had now grown a big man. The every-day dress brings the image of a dead friend much more vividly before us than his portrait. Thus Wuz examined the green cap with a yearning delight; he felt as though he saw from the winter of old age a spot of green,—of his childhood long buried in the snow. "I only wish I had my flannel petticoat too," he said, "which was always tied under my shoulders."

I know the first copy-book of the King of Prussia as well as that of schoolmaster Wuz. I have held both of them in my hand, and thus I am in a position to affirm that the king's handwriting grew worse, and the schoolmaster's better, with years. "Mother," he said to his wife, "just look how your husband wrote here (in the copy-book) and there (pointing to his calligraphic masterpiece—a deed of indenture, which he had nailed to the wall). I am still eaten up with self-conceit, mother!" He never used to boast, except in presence of his wife; and I set it down for what it is worth, as one of the privileges of married life, that the husband thereby secures an *alter ego*, before whom he may praise himself to his heart's content. I only wish the German public were such an *alter ego* for us authors!

The box was a library of Lilliputian tracts, which he had edited himself in his childhood, after this fashion: he copied a verse from the Bible, stitched the sheets together, and said, "Another excel-

lent Kober!" * Other authors can do as much, but not before they
are grown up. When he drew my attention to his juvenile com-
positions, he observed, "In childhood one is undoubtedly a fool,
but even in those early days the craving for authorship was manifest, though revealed in an immature and ridiculous form," and
he smiled contentedly at the later form of the same weakness. It
was the same story with his finch-snaring operation. For the fin-
ger-length finch stick, the lime-twig he spread beer on to catch flies
by their legs—wasn't that the ancestor of the arm's length finch
stick *behind* which he spent his loveliest moments of late autumn,
while *on* it the finches spent their ugliest? Bird-snaring must defi-
nitely have its own happy, quiet, inwardly contented kind of spir-
ituality.

You will easily understand how it was that his chief delight in
his illness was to look at an old almanac with its wretched plates,
representing the twelve months. Though he had not to take off his
hat to any curator, or sue for admission to a gallery, he found in
these plates more artistic pleasure than most Germans who undergo
these preliminaries. He made a pilgrimage through the eleven vi-
gnettes—that one in which he now was, he omitted—and filled up
the woodcuts to suit his own needs and theirs. It pleased him, on
his sick-bed, no less than in his days of health, to swarm up the
bare black trunk of a tree in the January vignette and to stand (in
imagination) beneath that lowering sky, that hung like a canopy
over meadows and fields bound in their winter sleep. The whole
month of June, with its long days and long grasses, passed before
him when he sat brooding over the June landscape of the wood-
cut, in which small crosses representing birds flew about the grey
paper, and skeleton leaves did duty for the full foliage of the leafy
month. But imagination makes of every shred and shaving a miraculous relic, a fountain out of every jaw-bone of an ass; the five
senses do nothing but present to the imagination the cartoons—
only the outlines of pleasure or sorrow.

The sick man skipped the month of May, for May itself was all
around him. The cherry-blossoms with which the lovers' month
entwines her green hair, and the lilies which she wears in her bosom,

---

* Kober's *Family Preacher*, a work that shows more wit, though it is often senseless
wit, than twenty of our modern washy collections of sermons.

he did not smell—his smell was gone; but he saw them, and had some in a glass by his bedside.

I have compassed my object, which was to draw myself and my audience for five or six pages away from that sad minute in which, in the sight of us all, Death steps up to the bed of our sick friend, and slowly, with his ice-cold hand, feels his warm breast, and paralyses, arrests, and stops for ever the heart that beat so merrily. Come it slow or fast, that minute and its attendant must come.

I stayed there all day, and in the evening I said I would sit with him through the night. His excited brain and twitching features had firmly convinced me that the apoplectic stroke would return during the night; but it did not, much to my own relief, and to that of the Dominie. For he had told me—and you may read it in his last little tract—that nothing was more beautiful and more easy than to die on a bright day, because the soul sees the sun up above through the closed eyes, and flies out of the withered body into the wide blue ocean of light without. But to leave the warm body in a dark tempestuous night, to make in utter loneliness that long leap into the grave, when all Nature herself sits there a-dying with closed eyes—that is a hard death indeed!

About half-past eleven the two dear friends of Wuz's youth appeared once more at his bedside, Sleep and Dream, in order to take leave of him for ever. Or do ye not rather tarry? Are ye not rather those friends of mankind who take the murdered man out of the bloody hands of Death, and bear him, cradled in your motherly arms, through cold subterranean caves, up into the bright land where a new morning sun and new morning flowers breathe upon him in a waking life?

I was alone in the room. I heard nothing but the breathing of the patient and the ticking of my watch, which measured his ebbing life. The yellow full moon hung large and low in the south, and shed a deadly pallor on the lilies of the valley that were the man's and the stopped clock and the green cap of the child. The snowy cherry-tree before the window cast its quivering shade upon the moon-lit floor. In the quiet heavens a shooting star fell from time to time, and passed away like a soul. It occurred to me that the next morning, the 13th of May, would be the forty-third anniversary of the day on which the dying man began his Elysian eight-weeks, and took up his residence in this very room, now the darkened ante-chamber of the grave. I saw that he, on whom this cherry-tree was shedding fragrance and dreams, lay himself, scentless and sightless, in a heavy dream, and was flitting, perhaps even to-day, and that everything was over and would never return; and in this minute Wuz seemed to catch at something with the arm that was not paralysed, as if he wished to seize a falling heaven— and in this trembling minute the month-index of my watch clicked, and, as it was twelve o'clock, moved forward from the 12th to the 13th of May. Death seemed to set my watch; I heard him grind to powder man and his joys, and World and Time seemed to crumble and crash into the abyss in a ruining avalanche!

Whenever the month-index of my watch gives a leap at midnight, I think of that moment; but may it never come back to me in the moments I have yet to live!

The dying man—he will not bear this name much longer—opened two flashing eyes, and looked at me for a long time, trying to recognize me. He had dreamed that he was a child again, and rocking to and fro on a bed of lilies, which had risen like a wave under him; this had melted away into a rose-colored cloud, which was sailing along with him toward the rosy dawn, over odorous fields of flowers; the sun smiled at him and shone upon him with a white girl's face, and then taking the shape of a girl, with a halo round her head, dropt into the cloud; and he was vexed because he could not reach her and embrace her with his withered arm. And this woke him out of his last dream, or rather his last dream but one; for the short motley dreams of the night are like fancy flowers painted and embroidered on the long dream of life.

The stream of life flowed faster to his brain; once more he dreamed he was young again; the moon he took for the overclouded sun; he fancied himself a winged altar angel, hanging from a rainbow by a chain of buttercups, swaying up and down in a vast arch, swung across abysses nearer and nearer up to the sun by the child bride who gave him the pewter ring. Towards four o'clock in the morning he could see us no longer, although the dawn was already in the room; his eyes stared with a stony look; one convulsive twitch followed the other; the lips parted with a happier and happier smile; spring fancies, which neither this life will know nor the next possess, played with his sinking soul. At last the Angel of Death threw the pale shroud over his face, and, up-rooting the soul flower, transplanted it from its tenement of clay.

Death is sublime! Hidden behind black curtains, he works his silent miracle, and labors for the other world; and we mortals stand, with moist, but dull eyes, gazing at the marvellous scene!

"Daddy," said his widow, "if anyone had told you forty-three years ago, that they would carry you out of the house on the 13th of May—the day on which your eight weeks began!" "His eight weeks," I said, "begin again; but they will last longer this time."

When I left the house, at eleven, the earth was, as it were, sacred to me, and dead men seemed to walk by my side. I looked up to heaven as if, in the infinite expanse, I could seek only in *that* direction for him who had died. And when I had reached the top of the hill which commands a view of Auenthal, and looked out once more for the scene of sorrow; when, among the many houses with smoking chimneys, I saw the house of mourning alone standing there without its little cloud of smoke, whilst higher up in the churchyard the sexton was digging the grave; when I heard the toll of the church bell, and thought that it was the widow herself who was ringing it, with streaming eyes, down there in the silent belfry, then I felt the nothingness of us all, and swore to despise, to deserve, and to enjoy this petty life.

Happy art thou, dear Wuz!—when I go to Auenthal, and seek out the grass-grown grave; and the thought troubles me that the chrysalis is buried there from which the night moth creeps forth and flies; that thy grave is a play-ground for burrowing worms, crawling snails, teeming ants, and gnawing caterpillars, whilst thou liest there in the midst of them, thy head motionless on thy shavings of wood, and no caressing sunbeam to pierce thy coffin-boards and thy bandaged eyes,—happy art thou, that I can still say of thee, "While he had life he enjoyed it more merrily than we all!"

Enough, friends, it is midnight, the month-index has leapt forward to a new day, and reminded us of our twofold sleep—the sleep of the short and of the long night.

Translated by F. and R. Storrs

Army-chaplain Schmelzle's Journey to Flätz

With a Running Commentary of Notes by

Jean Paul

PREFACE

This, I conceive, may be managed in two words.

The *first* word must relate to the Circular Letter of Army-chaplain Schmelzle, wherein he describes to his friends his Journey to the metropolitan city of Flätz; after having, in an introduction, premised some proofs and assurances of his valor. Properly speaking, the *Journey* itself has been written purely with a view that his courageousness, impugned by rumor, may be fully evinced and demonstrated by the plain facts which he therein records. Whether, in the mean time, there shall not be found certain quick-scented readers, who may infer, directly contrariwise, that his breast is not everywhere bomb-proof, especially in the left side: on this point I keep my judgment suspended.

For the rest, I beg the judges of literature, as well as their satellites, the critics of literature, to regard this *Journey,* for whose literary contents I, as Editor, am answerable, solely in the light of a Portrait (in the French sense), a little Sketch of Character. It is a voluntary or involuntary comedy-piece, at which I have laughed so often that I purpose in time coming to paint some similar Pictures of Character myself. And, for the present, when could such a little comic toy be more fitly imparted and set forth to the world, than in these very days, when the sound both of heavy money and of light laughter has died away from among us; when, like the Turks, we count and pay merely with sealed *purses,* and the coin within them has vanished?

Despicable would it seem to me if any clownish squire of the goose-quill should publicly and censoriously demand of me, in what way this self-cabinet-piece of Schmelzle's has come into my hands? I know it well, and do not disclose it. This comedy-piece, for which I, at all events, as my Bookseller will testify, draw the profit myself, I got hold of so unblamably, that I await with unspeakable composure what the Army-chaplain shall please to say against the publication of it, in case he say anything at all. My conscience bears me witness that I acquired this article at least by more honorable methods than are those of the learned persons who steal with their ears, who, in the character of spiritual auditory-thieves, and classroom cutpurses and pirates, are in the habit of disloading their plundered Lectures, and vending them up and down the country as productions of their own. Hitherto, in my whole life, I have stolen little, except now and then in youth some—glances.

The *second* word must explain or apologise for the singular form of this little Work, standing as it does on a substratum of Notes. I myself am not contented with it. Let the World open and look and determine, in like manner. But the truth is, this line of demarcation, stretching through the whole book, originated in the following accident: certain thoughts (or digressions) of my own, with which it was not permitted me to disturb those of the Army-chaplain, and which could only be allowed to fight behind the lines, in the shape of Notes, I, with a view to conveniency and order, had written down in a separate paper; at the same time, as will be observed, regularly providing every Note with its Number, and thus referring it to the proper page of the main Manuscript. But, in the copying of the latter, I had forgotten to insert the corresponding numbers in the Text itself. Therefore, let no man, any more than I do, cast a stone at my worthy Printer, inasmuch as he (perhaps in the thought that it was my way, that I had some purpose in it) took these Notes, just as they stood, pell-mell, without arrangement of Numbers, and clapped them under the Text; at the same time, by a praiseworthy artful computation, taking care at least that at the bottom of every page in the Text there should some portion of this glittering Note-precipitate make its appearance. Well, the thing at any rate is done, nay, perpetuated, namely printed. After all, I might almost partly rejoice at it. For, in good truth, had I meditated for years (as I have done for the last twenty) how to provide for my digression-comets new orbits, if not focal suns, for my episodes new epopees,—I could scarce possibly have hit upon a better or more spacious Limbo for such Vanities than Chance and Printer here accidentally offer me ready-made. I have only to regret that the thing has been printed before I could turn it to account. Heavens! what remotest allusions (had I known it before printing) might not have been privily introduced in every Text-page and Note-number; and what apparent incongruity in the real congruity between this upper and under side of the cards! How vehemently and devilishly might one not have cut aloft, and to the right and left, from these impregnable casemates and covered ways; and what *læsio ultra dimidium* (injury beyond the half of the Text) might not, with these satirical injuries, have been effected and completed!*

But Fate meant not so kindly with me: of this golden harvest-field of satire I was not to be informed till three days before the Preface.

Perhaps, however, the writing world, by the little blue flame of this accident, may be guided to a weightier acquisition, to a larger subterranean treasure than I, alas, have dug up! For, to the writer, there is now a way pointed out of producing in one marbled volume a group of altogether different works; of writing in one leaf, for both sexes at the same time, without confounding them, nay, for the five faculties all at once, without disturbing their limitations; since now, instead of boiling up a vile fermenting shove-together, fit for nobody, he has nothing to do but draw his note-lines or partition-lines; and so on his five-story leaf give board and lodging to the most discordant heads. Perhaps one might then read many a book for the fourth time, simply because every time one had read but a fourth part of it.

On the whole, this Work has at least the property of being a short one; so that the reader, I hope, may almost run through it and read it at the bookseller's counter, without, as in the case of thicker volumes, first needing to buy it. And why, indeed, in this

---

* Carlyle compounded the Printer's liberty by not translating quite all the footnotes. In deference to the integrity both of his text, a historic one, and of his distinctive style, we have undertaken no restoration. (In general we have limited ourselves to correcting Carlyle's rare slips of interpretation.) [Editor's note]

world of Matter should anything whatever be great, except only what belongs not to it, the world of Spirit?

JEAN PAUL FR. RICHTER.

Bayreuth, in the Hay and Peace Month, 1807

Schmelzle's Journey to Flätz

Circular Letter of the proposed Catechetical Professor ATTILA SCHMELZLE *to his Friends; containing some Account of a Holiday's Journey to Flätz, with an Introduction, touching his Flight, and his Courage as former Army-chaplain.*

Nothing can be more ludicrous, my esteemed Friends, than to hear people stigmatising a man as cowardly and hare-hearted, who perhaps is struggling all the while with precisely the opposite faults, those of a lion; though indeed the African lion himself, since the time of Sparrmann's Travels, passes among us for a poltroon. Yet this case is mine, worthy Friends; and I purpose to say a few words thereupon before describing my Journey.

You in truth are all aware that, directly in the teeth of this calumny, it is courage, it is desperadoes (provided they be not braggarts and tumultuous persons), whom I chiefly venerate; for example, my brother-in-law, the Dragoon, who never in his life bastinadoed one man, but always a whole social circle at the same time. How truculent was my fancy, even in childhood, when I, as the parson was toning away to the silent congregation, used to take it into my head: "How now, if thou shouldst start up from the pew, and shout aloud; I am here too, Mr. Parson!" and to paint out this thought in such glowing colors that for very dread I have often been obliged to leave the church! Anything like Rugendas' battle-pieces; horrid murder-tumults, sea-fights or Stormings of Toulon, exploding fleets; and, in my childhood, Battles of Prague on the harpsichord; nay, in short, every map of any remarkable scene of war: these are perhaps too much my favorite objects; and I read—and purchase nothing sooner; and doubtless they might lead me into many errors, were it not that my circumstances restrain

103. Good princes easily obtain good subjects; not so easily good subjects good princes: thus Adam, in the state of innocence, ruled over animals all tame and gentle, till simply through his means they fell and grew savage.

me. Now, if it be objected that true courage is something higher than mere thinking and willing, then you, my worthy Friends, will be the first to recognise mine when it shall break forth into, not barren and empty, but active and effective words, while I strengthen my future Catechetical Pupils, as well as can be done in a course of College Lectures, and steel them into Christian heroes.

It is well known that, out of care for the preservation of my life, I never walk within at least ten fields of any shore full of bathers or swimmers; merely because I foresee to a certainty that in case one of them were drowning I should that moment (for the heart overbalances the head) plunge after the fool to save him, into some bottomless depth or other, where we should both perish. And if dreaming is the reflex of waking, let me ask you, true Hearts, if you have forgotten my relating to you dreams of mine which no Cæsar, no Alexander or Luther, need have felt ashamed of? Have I not, to mention a few instances, taken Rome by storm; and done battle with the Pope, and the whole Elephant Order of the Cardinal College, at one and the same time? Did I not once on horseback, while simply looking at a review of military, dash headlong into a *bataillon quarré;* and then capture, in Aix-la-Chapelle, the Peruke of Charlemagne, for which the town pays yearly ten reichsthalers of barber-money; and carrying it off to Halberstadt and Herr Gleim's, there in like manner seize the Great Frederick's Hat; put both Peruke and Hat on my head, and yet return home, after I had stormed their batteries and turned the cannon against the cannoneers themselves? Did I not once submit to be made a Jew of, and then be regaled with hams; though they were ape-hams on the Orinoco (see Humboldt)? And a thousand such things; for I have thrown the Consistorial President of Flätz out of the Palace window; those alarm-fulminators, sold by Heinrich Backofen in Gotha, at six groschen the dozen, and each going off like a cannon, I have listened to so calmly that the fulminators did not even awaken me; and more of the like sort.

But enough! It is now time briefly to touch that farther slander of my chaplainship, which unhappily has likewise gained some cir-

---

5. For a good Physician saves, if not always from the disease, at least from a bad Physician.

100. In books lie the Phoenix-ashes of a past Millennium and Paradise; but War blows, and much ashes are scattered away.

culation in Flätz, but which, as Cæsar did Alexander, I shall now by my touch dissipate into dust. Be what truth in it there can, it is still little or nothing. Your great Minister and General in Flätz (perhaps the very greatest in the world, for there are not many Schabackers) may indeed, like any other great man, be turned against me, but not with the Artillery of Truth; for this Artillery I here set before you, my good Hearts, and do you but fire it off for my advantage! The matter is this: Certain foolish rumors are afloat in the Flätz country that I, on occasion of some important battles, took leg-bail (such is their plebeian phrase) and that afterwards, on the chaplain's being called for to preach a Thanksgiving sermon for the victory, no chaplain whatever was to be found. The ridiculousness of this story will best appear when I tell you that I never was in any action; but have always been accustomed, several hours prior to such an event, to withdraw so many miles to the rear that our men, so soon as they were beaten, would be sure to find me. A good retreat is reckoned the masterpiece in the art of war; and at no time can a retreat be executed with such order, force and security as just before the battle, when you are not yet beaten.

It is true, I might perhaps, as expectant Professor of Catechetics, sit still and smile at such nugatory speculations on my courage; for if by Socratic questioning I can hammer my future Catechist Pupils into the habit of asking questions in their turn, I shall thereby have tempered *them* into heroes, seeing they have nothing to fight with but children—(Catechists at all events, though dreading fire, have no reason to dread light, since in our days, as in London illuminations, it is only the *unlighted* windows that are battered in; whereas in other ages it was with nations and light as it is with dogs and water; if you give them none for a long time they at last get a horror at it);—and on the whole, for Catechists, any park looks kindlier and smiles more sweetly than a sulphurous park of artillery; and the Warlike Foot, which the age is placed on, is to them the true Devil's cloven-foot of human nature.

But for my part I think not so: almost as if the hereditary influence of my Christian name, Attila, had passed into me more strongly than was proper, I feel myself impelled still farther to prove my

102. Dear Political or Religious Inquisitor! art thou aware that Turin tapers never rightly begin shining till thou breakest them, and then they take fire?

courageousness; which, dearest Friends! I shall here in a few lines again do. This proof I could manage by mere inferences and learned citations. For example, if Galen remarks that animals with large hindquarters are timid, I have nothing to do but turn round and show the enemy my back, and what is under it, in order to convince him that I am not deficient in valor but in flesh. Again, if by well-known experiences it has been found that flesh-eating produces courage, I can evince that in this particular I yield to no officer of the service; though it is the habit of these gentlemen not only to run up long scores of roast-meat with their landlords but also to leave them unpaid, that so at every hour they may have an open document in the hands of the enemy himself (the landlord), testifying that they have eaten their own share (with some of other people's too), and so put common butcher's-meat on a war-footing, living not like others *by* bravery, but *for* bravery. As little have I ever, in my character of chaplain, shrunk from comparison with any officer in the regiment, who may be a true lion, and so snatch every sort of plunder, but yet, like this King of the Beasts, is afraid of *fire;* or who—like King James of England, that scampered off at sight of drawn swords, yet so much the more gallantly, before all Europe, went out against the storming Luther with book and pen—does, from a similar idiosyncrasy, attack all warlike armaments, both by word and writing. And here I recollect with satisfaction a brave sub-lieutenant, whose confessor I was (he still owes me the confession-money and what's more his landladies their hushmoney) and who, in respect of stout-heartedness, had in him perhaps something of that Indian dog which Alexander had presented to him, as a sort of Dog-Alexander. By way of trying this crack dog, the Macedonian made various heroic or heraldic beasts be let loose against him: first a stag; but the dog lay still: then a sow; he lay still: then a bear; he lay still. Alexander was on the point of condemning him, when a lion was let forth: the dog rose, and tore the lion in pieces. So likewise the sub-lieutenant. A challenger, a foreign enemy, a Frenchman, are to him only stag, and sow, and bear, and he lies still in his place; but let his oldest enemy, his

86. Very true! In youth we love and enjoy the most ill-assorted friends, perhaps more than, in old age, the best-assorted.
128. In Love there are Summer Holidays; but in Marriage also there are Winter Holidays, I hope.

creditor, come and knock at his gate, and demand of him actual smart-money for long bygone pleasures, thus presuming to rob him both of past and present; the sub-lieutenant rises and throws his creditor down-stairs. I, alas, am still standing by the sow; and thus, naturally enough, misunderstood.

Quo, says Livy, xii. 5, and with great justice, *quo timoris minus est, eo minus ferme periculi est,* The less fear you have, the less danger you are likely to be in. With equal justice I invert the maxim, and say: The less the danger, the smaller the fear; nay, there may be situations in which one has absolutely no knowledge of fear; and among these mine is to be reckoned. The more hateful, therefore, must that calumny about hare-heartedness appear to me.

To my Holidays' Journey I shall prefix a few facts, which prove how easily foresight—that is to say, when a person would not resemble the stupid marmot, that will even attack a man on horseback—may pass for cowardice. For the rest, I wish only that I could with equal ease wipe away a quite different reproach, that of being a foolhardy desperado; though I trust in the sequel I shall be able to advance some facts which invalidate it.

What boots the heroic arm without a hero's eye? The former readily grows stronger and more sinewy; but the latter is not so soon ground sharper, like glasses. Nevertheless, the merits of foresight obtain from the mass of men less admiration (nay, I should say, more ridicule) than those of courage. Whoso, for instance, shall see me walking under quite cloudless skies, with a wax-cloth umbrella over me, to him I shall probably appear ridiculous, so long as he is not aware that I carry this umbrella as a thunder-screen, to keep off any bolt out of the blue heaven (whereof there are several examples in the history of the Middle Ages) from striking me to death. My thunder-screen, in fact, is exactly that of Reimarus: on a long walking-stick I carry the wax-cloth roof, from the peak of which depends a string of gold-lace as a conductor; and this, by means of a key fastened to it, which it trails along the ground, will lead off every possible bolt and easily distribute it over the whole superficies of the Earth. With this *Paratonnerre Portatif* in my hand,

143. Women have weekly at least one active and passive day of glory, the holy day, the Sunday. The higher ranks alone have more Sundays than workdays; as in great towns, you can celebrate your Sunday on Friday with the Turks, on Saturday with the Jews, and on Sunday with yourself.

I can walk about for weeks, under the clear sky, without the smallest danger. This Diving-bell, moreover, protects me against something else; against shot. For who, in the latter end of Harvest, will give me black on white that no lurking ninny of a sportsman somewhere, when I am out enjoying Nature, shall so fire off his piece, at an angle of 45°, that in falling down again the shot needs only light directly on my crown, and so come to the same as if I had been shot through the brain from a side?

It is bad enough, at any rate, that we have nothing to guard us from the Moon; which at present is bombarding us with stones like a very Turk: for this paltry little Earth's trainbearer and errand-maid and *valet de fantasie* thinks, in these rebellious times, that she too must begin, forsooth, to sling somewhat out of Shepherd David's pouch against her Sovereign Mother! In good truth, as matters stand, any young Catechist of feeling may go out o' nights, with whole limbs, into the moonshine, a-meditating; and ere long (in the midst of his meditation the villainous Satellite hits him) come home a pounded jelly. By heaven! new sword-proofs of courage are required of us on every hand! No sooner have we, with great effort, melted down thunderbolts and cropped the tails of comets than the enemy opens new batteries in the Moon, or somewhere else in the Blue!

Suffice one other story to manifest how ludicrous the most serious foresight, with all imaginable inward courage, often externally appears in the eyes of the many. Equestrians are well acquainted with the dangers of a horse that runs away. My evil star would have it that I should once in Vienna get upon a hack-horse; a pretty enough honey-colored nag, but old and hard-mouthed as Satan; so that the beast, in the next street, went off with me; and this unfortunately—only at a *walk*. No pulling, no tugging took effect; I, at last, on the back of this Self-riding-horse, made signals of distress and cried: "Stop him, good people, for God's sake stop him, my horse is running away!" But these simple persons, seeing the beast move along as slowly as a Reichshofrath law-suit, or the Daily Postwagen, could not in the least understand the matter, till I cried as if possessed: "Stop him then, ye blockheads and jolt-

---

21. Schiller and Klopstock are Poetic Mirrors held up to the Sun-god: the Mirrors reflect the Sun with such dazzling brightness, that you cannot find the Picture of the World imaged forth in them.

heads; don't you see that I cannot hold the nag?" But now, to these noodles, the sight of a hard-mouthed horse going off with its rider step by step seemed ridiculous rather than otherwise; half Vienna gathered itself like a comet-tail behind my beast and me. Prince Kaunitz, the best horseman of the century (the last), pulled up to follow me. I myself sat and swam like a perpendicular piece of drift-ice on my honey-colored nag, which stalked on, on, step by step: a many-cornered, red-coated letter-carrier was delivering his let-ters, to the right and left, in the various stories, and he still crossed over before me again, with satirical features, because the nag went along too slowly. The Schwanzschleuderer, or Train-dasher (the person, as you know, who drives along the streets with a huge barrel of water, and besplashes them with a leathern pipe of three ells long from an iron trough), came across the haunches of my horse, and, in the course of his duty, wetted both these and myself in a very cooling manner, though, for my part, I had too much cold sweat on me already to need any fresh refrigeration. On my infer-nal Trojan Horse (only I myself was Troy, not beridden but riding to destruction), I arrived at Matzleinsdorf (a suburb of Vienna), or perhaps, so confused were my senses, it might be quite another range of streets. At last, late in the dusk, I had to turn into the Prater; and here, long after the Evening Gun, to my horror, and quite against the police-rules, keep riding to and fro on my honey-colored nag; and possibly I might even have passed the night on him, had not my brother-in-law, the Dragoon, observed my plight, and so found me still sitting firm as a rock on my runaway steed. He made no ceremonies; caught the brute; and put the pleasant question: Why I had not vaulted, and come off by ground-and-lofty tumbling; though he knew full well that for this a wooden-horse, which stands still, is requisite. However, he took me down; and so, after all this riding, horse and man got home with whole skins and unbroken bones.

But now at last to my Journey!

Journey to Flätz
You are aware, my friends, that this Journey to Flätz was nec-essarily to take place in Vacation time; not only because the Cat-

---

34. Women are like precious carved works of ivory; nothing is whiter and smoother, and nothing sooner grows *yellow*.

tle-market, and consequently the Minister and General von Schabacker, was there then; but more especially, because the latter (as
I had it positively from a private hand) did annually, on the 23rd
of July, the market-eve, about five o'clock, become so full of gaudium and graciousness, that in many cases he did not so much snarl
on people, as listen to them, and grant their prayers. The cause of
this gaudium I had rather not trust to paper. In short, my Petition,
praying that he would be pleased to indemnify and reward me, as
an unjustly deposed Army-chaplain, by a Catechetical Professorship, could plainly be presented to him at no better season, than
exactly about five o'clock in the evening of the first dog-day. In
less than a week, I had finished writing my Petition. As I spared
neither summaries nor copies of it, I had soon got so far as to see
the relatively best lying completed before me; when, to my terror,
I observed, that, in this paper, I had introduced above thirty *dashes,*
or breaks, in the middle of my sentences! Nowadays, alas, these
stings shoot forth involuntarily from learned pens, as from the tails
of wasps. I debated long within myself whether a private scholar
could justly be entitled to approach a minister with dashes,—greatly
as this level interlineation of thoughts, these horizontal note-marks
of poetical *music*-pieces, and these rope-ladders or Achilles' ten-
dons of philosophical *see*-pieces, are at present fashionable and indispensable: but, at last, I was obliged (as erasures may offend
people of quality) to write my best proof-petition over again; and
then to afflict myself for another quarter of an hour over the name
Attila Schmelzle, seeing it is always my principle that this and the
address of the letter, the two cardinal points of the whole, can never
be written legibly enough.

First Stage; from Neusattel to Vierstädten.

The 22nd of July, or Wednesday, about five in the afternoon,
was now, by the way-bill of the regular Post-coach, irrevocably fixed
for my departure. I had still half a day to order my house; from
which, for two nights and two days and a half, my breast, its
breastwork and palisado, was now, along with my Self, to be

72. The Half-learned is adored by the Quarter-learned; the latter by the Sixteenth-
part-learned; and so on; but not the Whole-learned by the Half-learned.
35. *Bien écouter c'est presque répondre,* says Marivaux justly of social circles: but
I extend it to round Councillor-tables and Cabinet-tables, where reports are made,
and the Prince listens.

withdrawn. Besides this, my good wife Bergelchen, as I call my Teutoberga, was immediately to travel after me, on Friday the 24th, in order to see and to make purchases at the yearly Fair; nay, she was ready to have gone along with me, the faithful spouse. I therefore assembled my little knot of domestics, and promulgated to them the Household Law and Valedictory Rescript, which, after my departure, in the first place *before* the outset of my wife, and in the second place *after* this outset, they had rigorously to obey; explaining to them especially whatever, in case of conflagrations, housebreakings, thunder-storms, or transits of troops, it would behove them to do. To my wife I delivered an inventory of the best goods in our little Registership; which goods she, in case the house took fire, had, in the first place, to secure. I ordered her, in stormy nights (the peculiar thief-weather), to put our Eolian harp in the window, that so any villainous prowler might imagine I was fantasying on my instrument, and therefore awake: for like reasons, also, to take the house-dog within doors by day, that he might sleep then, and so be livelier at night. I farther counselled her to have an eye on the focus of every knot in the panes of the stable-window, nay, on every glass of water she might set down in the house; as I had already often recounted to her examples of such accidental burning-glasses having set whole buildings in flames. I then appointed her the hour when she was to set out on Friday morning to follow me; and recapitulated more emphatically the household precepts, which, prior to her departure, she must afresh inculcate on her domestics. My dear, heart-sound, blooming Berga answered her faithful lord, as it seemed very seriously: "Go thy ways, little old one; it shall all be done as smooth as velvet. Wert thou but away! There is no end of thee!" Her brother, my brother-in-law the Dragoon, for whom, out of complaisance, I had paid the coach-fare, in order to have in the vehicle along with me a stout swordsman and hector, as spiritual relative and bully-rock, so to speak; the Dragoon, I say, on hearing these my regulations, puckered up (which I easily forgave the wild soldier and bachelor) his sunburnt face considerably into ridicule, and said: "Were I in thy

17. The Bed of Honor, since so frequently whole regiments lie on it, and receive their last unction, and last honor but one, really ought from time to time to be new-filled, beaten and sunned.

120. Many a one becomes a free-spoken Diogenes, not when he dwells in a Cask, but when the Cask dwells in him.

place, sister, I should do what I liked, and then afterwards take a peep into these regulation-papers of his."

"O!" answered I, "misfortune may conceal itself like a scorpion in any corner: I might say, we are like children, who, looking at their gaily-painted toy-box, soon pull off the lid, and, pop! out springs a mouse, who has young ones."

"Mouse, mouse, leave your house!" said he, stepping up and down. "But, good brother, it is five o'clock; and you will find, when you return, that all looks exactly as it does today; the dog like the dog, and my sister like a pretty woman: *allons donc!*" It was purely his blame that I, fearing his misconceptions, had not previously made a sort of testament.

I now packed-in two different sorts of medicines, heating as well as cooling, against two different possibilities; also my old splints for arm or leg breakages, in case the coach overset; and (out of foresight) two times the money I was likely to need. Only here I could have wished, so uncertain is the stowage of such things, that I had been an Ape with cheek-pouches, or some sort of Opossum with a natural bag, that so I might have reposited these necessaries of existence in pockets which were sensitive. Shaving is a task I always go through before setting out on journeys; having a rational mistrust against strange and bloodthirsty barbers: but, on this occasion, I retained my beard; since, however close shaved, it would have grown again by the road to such a length that I could have fronted no Minister and General with it.

With a vehement emotion, I threw myself on the pith-heart of my Berga, and, with a still more vehement one, tore myself away: in her, however, this our first marriage-separation seemed to produce less lamentation than triumph, less consternation than rejoicing; simply because she turned her eye not half so much on the parting, as on the meeting, and the journey after me, and the wonders of the Fair. Yet she threw and hung herself on my somewhat long and thin neck and body, almost painfully, being indeed a too fleshy and weighty load, and said to me: "Whisk thee off quick, my charming Attel (Attila), and trouble thy head with no cares by

3. Culture makes whole lands, for instance Germany, Gaul, and others, physically warmer, but spiritually colder.
1. The more Weakness the more Lying: Force goes straight; any cannon-ball with holes or cavities in it goes crooked.

the way, thou singular man! A whiff or two of ill-luck we can stand, by God's help, so long as my father is no beggar. And for thee, Franz," continued she, turning with some heat to her brother, "I leave my Attel on thy soul: thou well knowest, thou wild fly, what I will do, if thou play the fool, and leave him anywhere in the lurch." Her meaning here was good, and I could not take it ill; to you also, my Friends, her wealth and her open-heartedness are nothing new.

Melted into sensibility, I said: "Now Berga, if there be a reunion appointed for us, surely it is either in Heaven or in Flätz; and I hope in God, the latter." With these words, we whirled stoutly away. I looked round through the back-window of the coach at my good little village of Neusattel, and it seemed to me, in my melting mood, as if its steeples were rising aloft like an epitaphium over my life, or over my body, perhaps to return a lifeless corpse. "How will it all be," thought I, "when thou at last, after two or three days, comest back?" And now I noticed my Bergelchen looking after us from the garret-window. I leaned far out from the coach-door, and her falcon eye instantly distinguished my head; kiss on kiss she threw with both hands after the carriage, as it rolled down into the valley. "Thou true-hearted wife," thought I, "how is thy lowly birth, by thy spiritual new-birth, made forgettable, nay, remarkable!"

I must confess, the assemblage and conversational picnic of the stage-coach was much less to my taste: the whole of them suspicious, unknown rabble, whom (as markets usually do) the Flätz cattle-market was alluring by its scent. I dislike becoming acquainted with strangers: not so my brother-in-law, the Dragoon; who now, as he always does, had in a few minutes elbowed himself into close quarters with the whole ragamuffin posse of them. Beside me sat a person who, in all human probability, was a Harlot; on her breast, a Dwarf intending to exhibit himself at the Fair; on the other side was a Ratcatcher gazing at me; and a Blind Passenger,* in a red mantle, had joined us down in the valley. No one of them, except my brother-in-law, pleased me. That the Harlot would not misuse my acquaintance for the purpose of sworn testimony, that rascals among these people would not study me and

* "Live Passenger," "Nip"; a passenger taken up only by Jarvie's authority, and for Jarvie's profit.—[Carlyle's note]

my properties and accidents, to entangle me in their snares, no man could be my surety. In strange places, I even, out of prudence, avoid looking long up at any jail-window; because some lozel, sitting behind the bars, may in a moment call down out of mere malice: "How goes it, comrade Schmelzle?" or farther, because any lurking catchpole may fancy I am planning a rescue for some confederate above. From another sort of prudence, little different from this, I also make a point of never turning round when any booby calls, Thief! behind me.

As to the Dwarf himself, I had no objection to his travelling with me whithersoever he pleased; but he thought to raise a particular delectation in our minds, by promising that his Pollux and Brother in Trade, an extraordinary Giant, who was also making for the Fair to exhibit himself, would by midnight, with his elephantine pace, infallibly overtake the coach, and plant himself among us, or behind on the outside. Both these noodles, it appeared, are in the habit of going in company to fairs, as reciprocal exaggerators of opposite magnitudes: the Dwarf is the convex magnifying-glass of the Giant, the Giant the concave diminishing-glass of the Dwarf. Nobody expressed much joy at the prospective arrival of this Antidwarf, except my brother-in-law, who (if I may venture on a play of words) seems made, like a clock, solely for the purpose of *striking,* and once actually said to me: "That if in the Upper world he could not get a soul to curry and towzle by a time, he would rather go to the Under, where most probably there would be plenty of cuffing and to spare." The Ratcatcher, besides the circumstance that no man can prepossess us much in his favor, who lives solely by poisoning, like this Destroying Angel of rats, this mouse-Atropos; and also, which is still worse, that such a fellow bids fair to become an increaser of the vermin kingdom, the moment he may cease to be a lessener of it; besides all this, I say, the present Ratcatcher had many baneful features about him: first, his stabbing look, piercing you like a stiletto; then the lean sharp bony visage, conjoined with his enumeration of his considerable stock of poisons; then (for I hated him more and more) his sly stillness, his sly smile,

2. In his Prince, a soldier reverences and obeys at once his Prince and his Generalissimo; a Citizen only his Prince.
45. Our present writers shrug their shoulders most at those on whose shoulders they stand; and exalt those most who crawl up along them.

as if in some corner he noticed a mouse, as he would notice a man! To me, I declare, though usually I take not the slightest exception against people's looks, it seemed at last as if his throat were a Dog-grotto, a *Grotta del cane,* his cheek-bones cliffs and breakers, his hot breath the wind of a calcining furnace, and his black hairy breast a kiln for parching and roasting.

Nor was I far wrong, I believe; for soon after this, he began quite coolly to inform the company, in which were a dwarf and a female, that, in his time, he had, not without enjoyment, run ten men through the body; had with great convenience hewed off a dozen men's arms; slowly split four heads, torn out two hearts, and more of the like sort; while none of them, otherwise persons of spirit, had in the least resisted: "but why?" added he, with a poisonous smile, and taking the hat from his odious bald pate; "I am invulnerable. Let any one of the company that chooses lay as much fire on my bare crown as he likes, I shall not mind it."

My brother-in-law, the Dragoon, directly kindled his tinder-box, and put a heap of the burning matter on the Ratcatcher's poll; but the fellow stood it, as if it had been a mere picture of fire, and the two looked expectingly at one another; and the former smiled very foolishly, saying: "It was simply pleasant to him, like a good warming-plaster; for this was always the wintry region of his body."

Here the Dragoon groped a little on the naked skull, and cried with amazement, that "it was as cold as a knee-pan."

But now the fellow, to our horror, after some preparations, actually lifted off the quarter-skull and held it out to us, saying: "He had sawed it off a murderer, his own having accidentally been broken"; and withal explained, that the stabbing and arm-cutting he had talked of was to be understood as a jest, seeing he had merely done it in the character of Famulus at an Anatomical Theatre. However, the jester seemed to rise little in favor with any of us; and for my part, as he put his brain-lid and sham-skull on again, I thought to myself: "This dungbed-bell has changed its place indeed, but not the hemlock it was made to cover."

38. Epictetus advises us to travel, because our old acquaintances, by the influence of shame, impede our transition to higher virtues; as a bashful man will rather lay aside his provincial accent in some foreign quarter, and then return wholly purified to his own countrymen: in our days, people of rank and virtue follow this advice, but inversely; and travel because their old acquaintances, by the influence of shame, would too much deter them from new sins.

Farther, I could not but reckon it a suspicious circumstance, that he as well as all the company (the Blind Passenger too) were making for this very Flätz, to which I myself was bound: much good I could not expect of this; and, in truth, turning home again would have been as pleasant to me as going on, had I not rather felt a pleasure in defying the future.

I come now to the red-mantled Blind Passenger; most probably an *Emigré* or *Réfugié;* for he speaks German not worse than he does French; and his name, I think, was *Jean Pierre* or *Jean Paul,* or some such thing, if indeed he had any name. His red cloak, notwithstanding this his identity of color with the Hangman, would in itself have remained heartily indifferent to me, had it not been for this singular circumstance, that he had already five times, contrary to all expectation, come upon me in five different towns (in great Berlin, in little Hof, in Coburg, Meiningen, and Bayreuth), and each of these times had looked at me significantly enough, and then gone his ways. Whether this *Jean Pierre* is dogging me with hostile intent or not, I cannot say; but to our fancy, at any rate, no object can be gratifying that thus, with corps of observation, or out of loopholes, holds and aims at us with muskets, which for year after year it shall move to this side and that, without our knowing in which year it is to fire. Still more offensive did Redcloak become to me, when he began to talk about his soft mildness of soul; a thing which seemed either to betoken pumping you or undermining you.

I replied: "Sir, I am just come, with my brother-in-law here, from the field of battle (the last affair was at Pimpelstadt), and so perhaps am too much of a humor for fire, pluck and war-fury; and to many a one, who happens to have a roaring waterspout of a heart, it may be well if his clerical character (which is mine) rather

32. Our Age (by some called the Paper Age, as if it were made from the rags of some better-dressed one) is improving in so far, as it now tears its rags rather into Bandages than into Papers; although, or because, the Rag-hacker (the Devil as they call it) will not altogether be at rest. Meanwhile, if Learned Heads transform themselves into Books, Crowned Heads transform and coin themselves into Government-paper: in Norway, according to the *Universal Indicator,* the people have even paper-houses; and in many good German States, the Exchequer Collegium (to say nothing of the Justice Collegium) keeps its own paper-mills, to furnish wrappage enough for the meal of its wind-mills. I could wish, however, that our Collegiums would take pattern from that Glass Manufactory at Madrid, in which (according to Baumgärtner) there were indeed nineteen clerks stationed, but also eleven workmen.

enjoins on him mildness than wildness. However, all mildness has its iron limit. If any thoughtless dog chance to anger me, in the first heat of rage I kick my foot through him; and after me, my good brother here will perhaps drive matters twice as far, for he is the man to do it. Perhaps it may be singular; but I confess I regret to this day, that once when a boy I received three blows from another, without briskly returning them; and I often feel as if I must still pay them to his descendants. In sooth, if I but chance to see a child running off like a dastard from the weak attack of a child like himself, I cannot for my life understand his running, and can scarcely keep from interfering to save him by a decisive knock."

The Passenger meanwhile was smiling, not in the best fashion. He gave himself out for a Legations-Rath, and seemed fox enough for such a post; but a mad fox will, in the long-run, bite me as rabidly as a mad wolf will. For the rest, I calmly went on with my eulogy on courage; only that, instead of ludicrous gasconading, which directly betrays the coward, I purposely expressed myself in words at once cool, clear and firm.

"I am altogether for Montaigne's advice," said I: "Fear nothing but fear."

"I again," replied the Legations-man, with useless wire-drawing, "I should fear again that I did not sufficiently fear fear, but continued too dastardly."

"To this fear also," replied I coldly, "I set limits. A man, for instance, may not in the least believe in, or be afraid of ghosts; and yet by night may bathe himself in cold sweat, and this purely out of terror at the dreadful fright he should be in (especially with what whiffs of apoplexies, falling-sickness and so forth, he might be visited), in case simply his own too vivid fancy should create any wild fever-image, and hang it up in the air before him."

"One should not, therefore," added my brother-in-law the Dragoon, contrary to his custom, moralising a little, "one should not bamboozle the poor sheep of a man, with any ghost-tricks; the hen-heart may die on the spot."

A loud storm of thunder, overtaking the stage-coach, altered the

103. The Great perhaps take as good charge of their posterity as the Ants: the eggs once laid, the male and female Ants fly about their business, and confide them to the trusty *working-Ants*.

discourse. You, my Friends, knowing me as a man not quite destitute of some tincture of Natural Philosophy, will easily guess my precautions against thunder. I place myself on a chair in the middle of the room (often, when suspicious clouds are out, I stay whole nights on it), and by careful removal of all conductors, rings, buckles, and so forth, I here sit thunder-proof, and listen with a cool spirit to this elemental music of the cloud-kettledrum. These precautions have never harmed me, for I am still alive at this date; and to the present hour I congratulate myself on once hurrying out of church, though I had confessed but the day previous; and running, without more ceremony, and before I had received the sacrament, into the charnel-house, because a heavy thunder-cloud (which did, in fact, strike the churchyard linden-tree) was hovering over it. So soon as the cloud had disloaded itself, I returned from the charnel-house into the church, and was happy enough to come in after the Hangman (usually the last), and so still participate in the Feast of Love.

Such, for my own part, is my manner of proceeding: but in the full stage-coach I met with men to whom Natural Philosophy was no philosophy at all. For when the clouds gathered dreadfully together over our coach-canopy, and sparking, began to play through the air like so many fireflies, and I at last could not but request that the sweating coach-conclave would at least bring out their watches, rings, money and suchlike, and put them all into one of the carriage-pockets, that none of us might have a conductor on his body; not only would no one of them do it, but my own brother-in-law the Dragoon even sprang out, with naked drawn sword, to the coach-box, and swore that he would conduct the thunder all away himself. Nor do I know whether this desperate mortal was not acting prudently; for our position within was frightful, and any one of us might every moment be a dead man. At last, to crown all, I got into a half altercation with two of the rude members of our leathern household, the Poisoner and the Harlot; seeing, by their questions, they almost gave me to understand that in my pro-

10. And does Life offer us, in regard to our ideal hopes and purposes, anything but a prosaic, unrhymed, unmetrical Translation?
78. Our German frame of Government, cased in its harness, had much difficulty in moving, for the same reason why Beetles cannot fly, when their *wings* have *wing-shells,* of very sufficient strength, and—grown together.

posed deposition of metallic valuables I had perhaps not had the most honest intentions. Such an imputation wounds your honor to the quick; and in my breast there was a thunder louder than that above us: however, I was obliged to carry on the needful exchange of sharp words as quietly and slowly as possible; and I quarrelled softly, and in a low tone, lest in the end a whole coachful of people, set in arms against each other, might get into heat and perspiration; and so, by vapor steaming through the coach-roof, conduct the too-near thunderbolt down into the midst of us. At last, I laid before the company the whole theory of Electricity, in clear words, but low and slow (striving to avoid all emission of vapor); and especially endeavored to frighten them away from fear. For indeed, through fear, the stroke—nay, two strokes, the electric or the apopletic—might hit any one of us; since in Erxleben and Reimarus, it is sufficiently proved, that violent fear, by the transpiration it causes, may attract the lightning. I accordingly, in some fear of my own and other people's fear, represented to the passengers that now, in a coach so hot and crowded, with a drawn sword on the coach-box piercing the very lightning, with the thunder-cloud hanging over us, and even with so many transpirations from incipient fear; in short, with such visible danger on every hand, they must absolutely fear nothing, if they would not, all and sundry, be smitten to death in a few minutes.

"O Heaven!" cried I, "Courage! only courage! No fear, not even fear of fear! Would you have Providence to shoot you here sitting, like so many hares hunted into a pinfold? Fear, if you like, when you are out of the coach; fear to your heart's content in other places, where there is less to be afraid of; only not here, not here!"

I can not determine—since among millions scarcely one man dies by thunder-clouds, but millions perhaps by snow-clouds, and rain-clouds, and thin mist—whether my Coach-sermon could have made any claim to a prize for man-saving; however, at last, all uninjured, and driving towards a rainbow, we entered the town of Vierstädten, where dwelt a Postmaster, in the only street which the place had.

8. Constitutions of Government are like highways: on a new and quite untrodden one, where every carriage helps in the process of bruising and smoothing, you are as much jolted and pitched as on an old worn-out one, full of holes. What is to be done then? Travel on.

Second Stage; from Vierstädten to Niederschöna

The Postmaster was a churl and a striker; a class of mortals whom I inexpressibly detest, as my fancy always whispers to me, in their presence, that by accident or dislike I might happen to put on a scornful or impertinent look, and hound these mastiffs on my own throat; and then I already feel my features twitching. Happily, in this case (supposing I even had made a wrong face), I could have shielded myself with the Dragoon; for whose giant force such matters are a tidbit. This brother-in-law of mine, for example, cannot pass any tavern where he hears a sound of battle, without entering, and, as he crosses the threshold, shouting, "Peace, dogs!"— and therewith, under show of a peace-deputation, he directly snatches up the first chair-leg in his hand, as if it were an American peace-calumet, and cuts to the right and left among the belligerent powers, or he gnashes the hard heads of the parties together (he himself takes no side), catching each by the hind-lock; in such cases the rogue is in Heaven!

I, for my part, rather avoid discrepant circles than seek them; as I likewise avoid all dead or killed people: the prudent man easily foresees what is to be got by them; either vexations and injurious witnessing, or often even (when circumstances conspire) painful investigation, and suspicions of your being an accomplice.

In Vierstädten, nothing of importance presented itself, except— to my horror—a dog without tail, which came running along the town or street. In the first fire of passion at this sight, I pointed it out to the passengers, and then put the question, Whether they could reckon a system of Medical Police well arranged, which, like this of Vierstädten, allowed dogs openly to scour about, when their tails were wanting? "What am I to do," said I, "when this member is cut away, and such beast comes running towards me, and I cannot, either by the tail being cocked up or being drawn in, since the whole is snipt off, come to any conclusion whether the vermin is mad or not? In this way, the most prudent man may be bit, and become rabid, and so make shipwreck purely for want of a tail-compass."

---

3. In Criminal Courts, murdered children are often represented as still-born; in Anticritiques, still-born as murdered.
101. Not only were the Rhodians, from their Colossus, called Colossians; but also innumerable Germans are, from their Luther, called Lutherans.

The Blind Passenger (he now got himself inscribed as a Seeing one, God knows for what objects) had heard my observation; which he now spun out in my presence almost into ridicule, and at last awakened in me the suspicion, that by an overdone flattery in imitating my style of speech, he meant to banter me. "The Dog-tail," said he, "is, in truth, an alarm-beacon, and finger-post for us, that we come not even into the outmost precincts of madness: cut away from Comets their tails, from Bashaws theirs, from Crabs theirs (outstretched it denotes that they are burst); and in the most dangerous predicaments of life we are left without clew, without indicator, without hand *in margine;* and we perish, not so much as knowing how."

For the rest, this stage passed over without quarrelling or peril. About ten o'clock, the whole party, including even the Postillion, myself excepted, fell asleep. I indeed pretended to be sleeping, that I might observe whether some one, for his own good reasons, might not also be pretending it; but all continued snoring; the moon threw its brightening beams on nothing but down-pressed eye-lids.

I had now a glorious opportunity of following Lavater's counsel, to apply the physiognomical ellwand specially to sleepers, since sleep, like death, expresses the genuine form in coarser lines. Other sleepers not in stage-coaches I think it less advisable to mete with this ellwand; having always an apprehension lest some fellow, but pretending to be asleep, may, the instant I am near enough, start up as in a dream, and deceitfully plant such a knock on the physiognomical mensurator's own facial structure, as to exclude it forever from appearing in any Physiognomical Fragments (itself being reduced to one), either in the stippled or line style. Nay, might not the most honest sleeper in the world, just while you are in hand with his physiognomical dissection, lay about him, spurred on by honor in some cudgelling-scene he may be dreaming; and in a few instants of clapper-clawing, and kicking, and trampling, lull you into a much more lasting sleep than that out of which he was awakened?

88. Hitherto I have always regarded the Polemical writings of our present philosophic and aesthetic Idealist Logic-buffers,—in which, certainly, a few contumelies, and misconceptions, and misconclusions do make their appearance,—rather on the fair side; observing in it merely an imitation of classical Antiquity, in particular of the ancient Athletes, who (according to Schöttgen) besmeared their bodies with *mud*, that they might not be laid hold of; and filled their hands with *sand*, that they might lay hold of their antagonists.

In my *Adumbrating Magic-lantern,* as I have named the Work, the whole physiognomical contents of this same sleeping stage-coach will be given to the world: there I shall explain to you at large how the Poisoner, with the murder-cupola, appeared to me devil-like; the Dwarf old-childlike; the Harlot languidly shameless; my Brother-in-law peacefully satisfied, with revenge or food; and the Legations-Rath, *Jean Pierre,* Heaven only knows why, like a half angel,—though, perhaps, it might be because only the fair body, not the other half, the soul, which had passed away in sleep, was affecting me.

I had almost forgotten to mention, that in a little village, while my Brother-in-law and the Postillion were sitting at their liquor, I happily fronted a small terror, Destiny having twice been on my side. Not far from a Hunting Box, beside a pretty clump of trees, I noticed a white tablet, with a black inscription on it. This gave me hopes that perhaps some little monumental piece, some pillar of honor, some battle memento, might here be awaiting me. Over an untrodden flowery tangle, I reach the black on white; and to my horror and amazement, I decipher in the moonshine: *Beware of Spring-guns!* Thus was I standing perhaps half a toe-nail's breadth from the trigger, with which, if I but stirred my heel, I should shoot myself off like a forgotten ramrod, into the other world, beyond the verge of Time! The first thing I did was to cramp-down my toe-nails, to bite, and, as it were, eat myself into the ground with them; since I might at least continue in warm life so long as I pegged my body firmly in beside the Atropos-scissors and hangman's block, which lay beside me; then I endeavored to recollect by what steps the fiend had led me hither unshot, but in my agony I had per-spired the whole of it, and could remember nothing. In the Devil's village close at hand, there was no dog to be seen and called to, who might have plucked me from the water; and my Brother-in-law and the Postillion were both carousing with full can. How-ever, I summoned my courage and determination; wrote down on a leaf of my pocket-book my last will, the accidental manner of my death, and my dying remembrance of Berga; and then, with full sails, flew helter-skelter through the midst of it the shortest way;

103. Or are all Mosques, Episcopal-churches, Pagodas, Chapels-of-Ease, Taber-nacles and Pantheons, anything else than the Ethnic Forecourt of the Invisible Temple and its Holy of Holies?

expecting at every step to awaken the murderous engine, and thus to clap over my still long candle of life the *bonsoir,* or extinguisher, with my own hand. However, I got off without shot. In the tavern, indeed, there was more than one fool to laugh at me; because, forsooth, what none but a fool could know, this Notice had stood there for the last ten years, without any gun, as guns often do without any notice. But so it is, my Friends, with our game-police, which warns against all things, only not against warnings.

For the rest, throughout the whole stage, I had a constant source of altercation with the coachman, because he grudged stopping perhaps once in the quarter of an hour, when I chose to come out for a natural purpose. Unhappily, in truth, one has little reason to expect urine prophets among the postillion class, since Physicians themselves have so seldom learned from Haller's large *Physiology,* that a postponement of the above operation, will precipitate devilish stoneware, and at last precipitate the proprietor himself; this stone-manufactory being generally concluded, not by the Lithotomist, but by Death. Had postillions read that Tycho Brahe died like a bombshell by bursting, they would rather pull up for a moment; with such unlooked-for knowledge, they would see it to be reasonable that a man, though expecting some time to carry his death-stone *on* him, should not incline, for the time being, to carry it *in* him. Nay, have I not often, at Weimar, in the longest concluding scenes of Schiller, run out with tears in my eyes; purely that, while his Minerva was melting me on the whole, I might not by the Gorgon's head on her breast be partially turned to stone? And did I not return to the weeping playhouse, and fall into the general emotion so much the more briskly, as now I had nothing to give vent to but my heart?

Deep in the dark we arrived at Niederschöna.

Third Stage; from Niederschöna to Flätz

While I am standing at the Posthouse musing, with my eye fixed on my portmanteau, comes a beast of a watchman, and bellows and brays in his night-tube so close by my ear, that I start back in

40. The common man is copious only in narration, not in reasoning; the cultivated man is brief only in the former, not in the latter: because the common man's reasons are a sort of sensations, which, as well as things visible, he merely *looks at;* by the cultivated man, again, both reasons and things visible are rather *thought* than looked at.

trepidation, I whom even a too hasty accosting will vex. Is there no medical police, then, against such efflated hour-fulminators and alarm-cannon, by which notwithstanding no powder cannon are saved? In my opinion, nobody should be invested with the watch-man-horn but some reasonable man, who had already blown himself into an asthma, and who would consequently be in case to sing out his hour-verse so low, that you could not hear it.

What I had long expected, and the Dwarf predicted, now took place: deeply stooping, through the high Posthouse door, issued the Giant, and raised, in the open air, a most unreasonably high figure, heightened by the ell-long bonnet and feather on his huge jobber-nowl. My Brother-in-law, beside him, looked but like his son of fourteen years; the Dwarf like his lap-dog waiting for him on its two hind legs. "Good friend," said my bantering Brother-in-law, leading him towards me and the stage-coach, "just step softly in, we shall all be happy to make room for you. Fold yourself neatly together, lay your head on your knee, and it will do." The unseasonable banterer would willingly have seen the almost stupid Giant (of whom he had soon observed that his brain was no active substance, but in the inverse ratio of his trunk) squeezed in among us in the post-chest, and lying kneaded together like a sandbag before him. "Won't do! Won't do!" said the Giant, looking in. "The gentleman perhaps does not know," said the Dwarf, "how big the Giant is; and so he thinks that because I go in—But that is another story; I will creep into any hole, do but tell me where."

In short, there was no resource for the Postmaster and the Giant, but that the latter should plant himself behind, in the character of luggage, and there lie bending down like a weeping willow over the whole vehicle. To me such a back-wall and rear-guard could not be particularly gratifying: and I may refer it, I hope, to any

9. In any national calamity, the ancient Egyptians took revenge on the god Typhon, whom they blamed for it, by hurling his favorites, the Asses, down over rocks. In similar wise have countries of a different religion now and then taken their revenge.

70. Let Poetry veil itself in Philosophy, but only as the latter does in the former. Philosophy in poetised Prose resembles those tavern drinking-glasses, encircled with parti-colored wreaths of figures, which disturb your enjoyment both of the drink, and (often awkwardly eclipsing and covering each other) of the carving also.

158. Governments should not too often change the penny-trumps and child's-drums of the Poets for the regimental trumpet and fire-drum: on the other hand, good subjects should regard many a princely drum-tendency simply as a disease, in which the patient, by air insinuating under the skin, has got dreadfully swollen.

one of you, ye Friends, if with such ware at your back, you would not, as clearly and earnestly as I, have considered what manifold murderous projects a knave of a Giant behind you, a *pursuer* in all senses, might not maliciously attempt; say, that he broke in and assailed you by the back-window, or with Titanian strength laid hold of the coach-roof and demolished the whole party in a lump. However, this Elephant (who indeed seemed to owe the similarity more to his overpowering mass than to his quick light of inward faculty), crossing his arms over the top of the vehicle, soon began to sleep and snore above us; an Elephant, of whom, as I more and more joyfully observed, my Brother-in-law the Dragoon could easily be the tamer and bridle-holder, nay, had already been so.

As more than one person now felt inclined to sleep, but I, on the contrary, as was proper, to wake, I freely offered my seat of honor, the front place in the coach (meaning thereby to abolish many little flaws of envy in my fellow-passengers), to such persons as wished to take a nap thereon. The Legations-man accepted the offer and the pillow with eagerness, and soon fell asleep there sitting, under the Titan.* To me this sort of coach-sleeping of a diplomatic *chargé d'affaires* remained a thing incomprehensible. A man that, in the middle of a stranger and often barbarously-minded company, permits himself to slumber, may easily, supposing him to talk in his sleep and coach (think of the Saxon minister before the Seven-Years War!), blab out a thousand secrets, and crimes, some of which, perhaps, he has not committed. Should not every minister, ambassador, or other man of honor and rank, really shudder at the thought of insanity or violent fevers; seeing no mortal can be his surety that he shall not in such cases publish the greatest scandals, of which, it may be, the half are lies?

At last, after the long July night, we passengers, together with Aurora, arrived in the precincts of Flätz. I looked with a sharp yet moistened eye at the steeples: I believe, every man who has anything decisive to seek in a town, and to whom it is either to be a judgment-seat of his hopes, or their anchoring-station, either a battle-field or a sugar-field, first and longest directs his eye on the steeples of the town, as upon the indexes and balance-tongues of his future destiny; these artificial peaks, which, like natural ones,

---

* *Titan* is also the title of this Legations-Rath Jean Pierre or Jean Paul (Friedrich Richter)'s chief novel.—[Carlyle's note]

are the thrones of our Future. As I happened to express myself on this point perhaps too poetically to *Jean Pierre,* he answered, with sufficient want of taste: "The steeples of such towns are indeed the Swiss Alpine peaks, on which we milk and manufacture the Swiss cheese of our Future." Did the Legations-Peter mean with this style to make me ridiculous, or only himself? Determine!

"Here is the place, the town," said I in secret, "where today much and for many years is to be determined; where thou, this evening, about five o'clock, art to present thy petition and thyself: May it prosper! May it be successful! Let Flätz, this arena of thy little efforts become a building-space for fair castles and air-castles to two hearts, thy own and thy Berga's!"

At the Tiger Inn I alighted.

First Day in Flätz

No mortal, in my situation at this Tiger-Hotel, would have triumphed much in his more immediate prospects. I, as the only man known to me, especially in the way of love (of the runaway Dragoon anon!), looked out from the windows of the overflowing Inn, and down on the rushing sea of marketers, and very soon began to reflect, that except Heaven and the rascals and murderers, none knew how many of the latter two classes were floating among the tide; purposing perhaps to lay hold of the most innocent strangers, and in part cut their purses, in part their throats. My situation had a special circumstance against it. My Brother-in-law, who still comes plump out with everything, had mentioned that I was to put up at the Tiger: O Heaven, when will such people learn to be secret, and to cover even the meanest pettiness of life under mantles and veils, were it only that a silly mouse may as often give birth to a mountain, as a mountain to a mouse! The whole rabble of the stage-coach stopped at the Tiger; the Harlot, the Rat-catcher, *Jean Pierre,* the Giant, who had dismounted at the Gate of the town, and carrying the huge blockhead of the Dwarf on his

89. In great towns, a stranger, for the first day or two after his arrival, lives purely at his own expense in an inn; afterwards, if you arrive at the Earth, as, for instance, I have done, you are courteously maintained, precisely for the first few years, free of charges; but in the next and longer series—for you often stay sixty—you are actually obliged (I have the documents in my hands) to pay for every drop and morsel, as if you were in the great Earth Inn, which indeed you are.

shoulders as his own (cloaking over the deception by his cloak), had thus, like a ninny, exhibited himself gratis by half a dwarf more gigantic than he could be seen for money.

And now for each of the Passengers who dismounted the question was, how he could make the Tiger, the heraldic emblem of the Inn, his prototype; and so, what lamb he might suck the blood of, and tear in pieces, and devour. My Brother-in-law too left me, having gone in quest of some horse-dealer; but he retained the chamber next mine for his sister: this, it appeared, was to denote attention on his part. I remained solitary, left to my own intrepidity and force of purpose.

Yet among so many villains, encompassing if not even beleaguering me, I thought warmly of one far distant, faithful soul, of my Berga in Neusattel; a true heart of pith, which perhaps with many a weak marriage-partner might have given protection rather than sought it.

"Appear, then, quickly tomorrow at noon, Berga," said my heart; "and if possible before noon, that I may lengthen thy market paradise so many hours as thou arrivest earlier!"

A clergyman, amid the tempests of the world, readily makes for a free harbor, for the church: the church-wall is his casemate-wall and fortification; and behind are to be found more peaceful and more accordant souls than on the market-place: in short, I went into the High Church. However, in the course of the psalm, I was somewhat disturbed by a Heiduk, who came up to a well-dressed young gentleman sitting opposite me, and tore the double opera-glass from his nose, it being against rule in Flätz, as it is in Dresden, to look at the Court with glasses which diminish and approximate. I myself had on a pair of spectacles, but they were magnifiers. It was impossible for me to resolve on taking them off; and here again, I am afraid, I shall pass for a foolhardy person and a

---

107. Germany is a long lofty mountain—under the sea.
144. The Reviewer does not in reality employ his pen for writing; but he burns it, to awaken weak people from their swoons, with the smell; he tickles with it the throat of the plagiary, to make him render back; and he picks with it his own teeth. He is the only individual in the whole learned lexicon that can never exhaust himself, never write himself out, let him sit before the ink-glass for centuries or tens of centuries. For while the Scholar, the Philosopher, and the Poet, produce their new book solely from new materials and growth, the Reviewer merely lays his old gage of taste and knowledge on a thousand new works; and his light, in the ever-passing, ever-differently-cut glass-world which he *elucidates,* is still refracted into new colors.

desperado; so much only I reckoned fit, to look invariably into my psalm-book; not once lifting my eyes while the Court was rustling and entering, thereby to denote that my glasses were ground convex. For the rest, the sermon was good, if not always finely conceived for a Court-church; it admonished the hearers against innumerable vices, to whose counterparts, the virtues, another preacher might so readily have exhorted us. During the whole service, I made it my business to exhibit true deep reverence, not only towards God, but also towards my illustrious Prince. For the latter reverence I had my private reason: I wished to stamp this sentiment strongly and openly as with raised letters on my countenance, and so give the lie to any malicious imp about Court, by whom my contravention of Linguet's *Panegyric on Nero,* and my free German satire on this real tyrant himself, which I had inserted in the *Flätz Weekly Journal,* might have been perverted into a secret character portrait of my own Sovereign. We live in such times at present, that scarcely can we compose a pasquinade on the Devil in Hell, but some human Devil on Earth will apply it to an angel.

When the Court at last issued from church, and were getting into their carriages, I kept at such a distance that my face could not possibly be noticed, in case I had happened to assume no reverent look, but an indifferent or even proud one. God knows, who has kneaded into me those mad desperate fancies and crotchets, which perhaps would sit better on a Hero Schabacker than on an Army-chaplain under him. I cannot here forbear recording to you, my Friends, one of the maddest among them, though at first it may throw too glaring a light on me. It was at my ordination to be Army-chaplain, while about to participate in the Sacrament, on the first-day of Easter. Now, here while I was standing, moved into softness, before the balustrade of the altar, in the middle of the whole male congregation,—nay, I perhaps more deeply moved than

71. The Youth is singular from caprice, and takes pleasure in it; the Man is so from constraint, unintentionally, and feels pain in it.
198. The Populace and Cattle grow giddy on the edge of no abyss; with the Man it is otherwise.
11. The Golden Calf of Self-love soon waxes to be a burning Phalaris' Bull, which reduces its father and adorer to ashes.
103. The male Beau-crop which surrounds the female Roses and Lilies, must (if I rightly comprehend its flatteries) most probably presuppose in the fair the manners of the Spaniards and Italians, who offer any valuable, by way of present, to the man who praises it excessively.

any among them, since, as a person going to war, I might consider myself a half-dead man, that was now partaking in the last Feast of Souls, as it were like a person to be hanged on the morrow,—here then, amid the pathetic effects of the organ and singing, there rose something—were it the first Easter-day which awoke in me what primitive Christians called their Easter-laughter, or merely the contrast between the most devilish predicaments and the most holy,—in short there rose something in me (for which reason, I have ever since taken the part of every simple person, who might ascribe such things to the Devil), and this something started the question: "Now, could there be aught more diabolical than if thou, just in receiving the Holy Supper, wert madly and blasphemously to begin laughing?" Instantly I took to wrestling with this hell-dog of a thought; neglected the most precious feelings, merely to keep the dog in my eye, and scare him away; yet was forced to draw back from him, exhausted and unsuccessful, and arrived at the step of the altar with the mournful certainty that in a little while I should, without more ado, begin laughing, let me weep and moan inwardly as I liked. Accordingly, while I and a very worthy old Bürgermeister were bowing down together before the long parson, and the latter (perhaps kneeling on the low cushion, I fancied him too long) put the wafer in my clenched mouth, I felt all the muscles of laughter already beginning sardonically to contract; and these had not long acted on the guiltless integument, till an actual smile appeared there; and as we bowed the second time, I was grinning like an ape. My companion the Bürgermeister justly expostulated with me, in a low voice, as we walked round behind the altar: "In Heaven's name, are you an ordained Preacher of the Gospel, or a Merry-Andrew? Is it Satan that is laughing out of you?"

"Ah, Heaven! who else?" said I; and this being over, I finished my devotions in a more becoming fashion.

From the church (I now return to the Flätz one), I proceeded to the Tiger Inn, and dined at the *table-d'hôte,* being at no time shy of encountering men. Previous to the second course, a waiter handed me an empty plate, on which, to my astonishment, I noticed a French verse scratched-in with a fork, containing nothing less than

199. But not many existing Governments, I believe, do behead under pretext of trepanning; or sew (in a more choice allegory) the people's lips together, under pretence of sewing the harelips in them.

a lampoon on the Commandant of Flätz. Without ceremony, I held out the plate to the company; saying, I had just, as they saw, got this lampooning cover presented to me, and must request them to bear witness that I had nothing to do with the matter. An officer directly changed plates with me. During the fifth course, I could not but admire the chemico-medical ignorance of the company; for a hare, out of which a gentleman extracted and exhibited several grains of shot, that is to say, therefore, of lead alloyed with arsenic, and then cleaned by hot vinegar, did, nevertheless, by the spectators (I excepted) continue to be pleasantly eaten.

In the course of our table-talk, one topic seized me keenly by my weak side, I mean by my honor. The law custom of the city happened to be mentioned, as it affects natural children; and I learned that here a loose girl may convert any man she pleases to select into the father of her brat, simply by her oath. "Horrible!" said I, and my hair stood on end. "In this way may any head of a family, with a wife and children, or clergyman lodging in the Tiger, be stript of honor and innocence, by any wicked chambermaid whom he may have seen, or who may have seen him, in the course of her employment!"

An elderly officer observed: "But will the girl swear herself to the Devil so readily?"

What logic! "Or suppose," continued I, without answer, "a man happened to be travelling with that Vienna Locksmith, who afterwards became a mother, and was brought to bed of a baby son; or with any disguised Chevalier d'Eon, who often passes the night in his company, whereby the Locksmith or the Chevalier can swear to their intimacies: no delicate man of honor will in the end risk travelling with another; seeing he knows not how soon the latter may pull off his boots, and pull on his women's-pumps, and swear his companion into fatherhood, and himself to the Devil!"

Some of the company, however, misunderstood my oratorical fire so much, that they, sheep-wise, gave some insinuations as if I my-

67. Hospitable Entertainer, wouldst thou search into thy guest? Accompany him to another Entertainer, and listen to him. Just so: Wouldst thou become better acquainted with Mistress in an hour, than by living with her for a month? Accompany her among her female friends and female enemies (if that is no pleonasm), and look at her!

80. In the summer of life, men keep digging and filling ice-pits as well as circumstances will admit; that so, in their Winter, they may have something in store to give them coolness.

self were not strict in this point, but lax. By Heaven! I no longer knew what I was eating or speaking. Happily, on the opposite side of the table, some lying story of a French defeat was started: now, as I had read on the street-corners that French and German Proclamation, calling before the Court Martial any one who had heard war-rumors (disadvantageous, namely), without giving notice of them,—I, as a man not willing ever to forget himself, had nothing more prudent to do in this case, than to withdraw with empty ears, telling none but the landlord why.

It was no improper time; for I had previously determined to have my beard shaven about half-past four, that so, towards five, I might present myself with a chin just polished by the razor smoothing-iron, and sleek as wove-paper, without the smallest root-stump of a hair left on it. By way of preparation, like Pitt before Parliamentary debates, I poured a devilish deal of Pontac into my stomach, with true disgust, and contrary to all sanitary rules; not so much for fronting the mere stranger of a Barber, as the Minister and General von Schabacker, with whom I had it in view to exchange perhaps more than one fiery statement.

The common Hotel Barber was ushered in to me; but at first view you noticed in his polygonal zigzag visage, more of a man that would finally go mad, than of one growing wiser. Now madmen are a class of persons whom I hate incredibly; and nothing can take me to see any madhouse, simply because the first maniac among them may clutch me in his giant fists if he like; and because, owing to contagion, I cannot be sure that I shall ever get out again with the sense which I brought in. In a general way, I sit (when once I am lathered) in such a posture on my chair as to keep both my hands (the eyes I fix intently on the barbering countenance) lying clenched along my sides, and pointed directly at the midriff of the barber; that so, on the smallest ambiguity of movement, I may dash in upon him, and overset him in a twinkling.

I scarce know rightly how it happened; but here, while I am anxiously studying the foolish twisted visage of the shaver, and he

28. It is impossible for me, amid the tendril-forest of allusions (even this again is a tendril-twig), to state and declare on the spot whether all the Courts or Heights, the (Bougouer) *Snowline* of Europe, have ever been mentioned in my Writings or not; but I could wish for information on the subject, that if not, I may try to do it still.

just then chanced to lay his long-whetted weapon a little too abruptly against my bare throat, I gave him such a sudden bounce on the abdominal viscera, that as he fell the silly varlet had well-nigh suicidally slit his own windpipe. For me, truly, nothing remained but to indemnify the man; and then, contrary to my usual principles, to tie round a broad stuff cravat, by way of cloak to what remained unshorn.

And now at last I sallied forth to the General, drinking out the remnant of the Pontac, as I crossed the threshold. I hope there were plans lying ready within me for answering rightly, nay, for asking. The Petition I carried in my pocket, and in my right hand. In the left I had a duplicate of it. My fire of spirit easily helped over the living fence of ministerial obstructions; and soon I unexpectedly found myself in the ante-chamber, among his most distinguished lackeys; persons, so far as I could see, not inclined to change flour for bran with any one. Selecting the most respectable individual of the number, I delivered him my paper request, accompanied with the verbal one that he would hand it in. He took it, but ungraciously: I waited in vain till far in the sixth hour, at which season alone the gay General can safely be applied to. At last I pitch upon another lackey, and repeat my request: he runs about seeking his runaway brother, or my Petition; to no purpose, neither of them could be found. How happy was it that in the midst of my Pontac, before shaving, I had written out the duplicate of this paper; and therefore—simply on the principle that you should always keep a second wooden leg packed into your knapsack when you have the first on your body—and out of fear that if the original petition chanced to drop from me in the way between the Tiger and Schabacker's, my whole journey and hope would melt into water—and therefore, I say, having stuck the repeating work of that original paper into my pocket, I had, in any case, something to hand in, and that something truly a Ditto. I handed it in.

36. And so I should like, in all cases, to be the First, especially in Begging. The first prisoner-of-war, the first cripple, the first man ruined by burning (like him who brings the first fire-engine), gains the head-subscription and the heart; the next-comer finds nothing but Duty to address; and at last, in this melodious *mancando* of sympathy, matters sink so far, that the last (if the last but one may at least have retired laden with a rich "God help you!") obtains from the benignant hand nothing more than its fist. And as in Begging the first, so in Giving I should like to be the last: one obliterates the other, especially the last the first. So, however, is the world ordered.

Unhappily six o'clock was already past. The lackey, however, did not keep me long waiting; but returned with—I may say, the text of this whole Circular—the almost rude answer (which you, my Friends, out of regard for me and Schabacker, will not divulge) that: "In case I were the Attila Schmelzle of Schabacker's Regiment, I might lift my pigeonliver flag again, and fly to the Devil, as I did at Pimpelstadt." Another man would have dropt dead on the spot: I, however, walked quite stoutly off, answering the fellow: "With great pleasure indeed, I fly to the Devil; and so Devil a fly I care." On the road home I examined myself whether it had not been the Pontac that spoke out of me (though the very examination contradicted this, for Pontac never examines); but I found that nothing but I, my heart, my courage perhaps, had spoken: and why, after all, any whimpering? Does not the patrimony of my good wife endow me better than ten Catechetical Professorships? And has she not furnished all the corners of my book of Life with so many golden clasps, that I can open it forever without wearing it out? Pregnant women in sudden fright may grasp their behinds in order to transfer thither the birthmark due to such an inadvertency; I in my courage grasped my heart and said: "Dash boldly through it, come what may!" I felt myself excited and exalted; I fancied Republics to which I might return a hero; I longed to be in that noble Grecian time, when one hero readily put up with bastinadoes from another, and said: "Strike, but hear!" and out of this ignoble one, where men will scarcely put up with hard words, to say nothing of more. I painted out to my mind how I should feel, if, in happier circumstances, I were uprooting hollow Thrones, and before whole nations mounting on mighty deeds as on the Temple-steps of Immortality; and in gigantic ages, finding quite other men to outman and outstrip, than the mite-populace about me, or, at the best, here and there a Vulcanello. I thought and thought, and grew wilder and wilder, and intoxicated myself (no

136. If you mount too high above your time, your ears (on the side of Fame) are little better off than if you sink too deep below it: in truth, Charles up in his Balloon, and Halley down in his Diving-bell, felt equally the same strange pain in their ears.

25. In youth, like a blind man just couched (and what is birth but a couching of the sight?), you take the Distant for the Near, the starry heaven for tangible room-furniture, pictures for objects; and, to the young man, the whole world is sitting on his very nose, till repeated bandaging and unbandaging have at last taught him, like the blind patient, to estimate *Distance* and *Appearance*.

Pontac intoxication therefore, which, you know, increases more by continuance than cessation of drinking), and gesticulated openly, as I put the question to myself: "Wilt thou be a mere state-lap-dog? A dog's-dog, a *pium desiderium* of an *impium desiderium*, an Ex-Ex, a Nothing's-Nothing?—Fire and Fury!" With this, how-ever, I dashed down my hat into the mud of the market. On lifting and cleaning this old servant, I could not but perceive how worn and faded it was; and I therefore determined instantly to purchase a new one, and carry the same home in my hand.

I accomplished this; I bought one of the finest cut. Strangely enough, by this hat, as if it had been a graduation-hat, was my head tried and examined, in the Ziegengasse or Goat-gate of Flätz. For as General Schabacker came driving along that street in his carriage, and I (it need not be said) was determined to avenge my-self, not by vulgar clownishness, but by courtesy, I had here got one of the most ticklish problems imaginable to solve on the spur of the instant. You observe, if I swung only the fine hat which I carried in my hand, and kept the faded one on my head,—I might have the appearance of a perfect clown, who does not doff at all: if, on the other hand, I pulled the old hat from my head, and therewith did my reverence, then two hats, both in play at once (let me swing the other at the same time or not), brought my sa-lute within the verge of ridicule. Now do you, my Friends, before reading farther, bethink you how a man was to extricate himself from such a plight, without losing head! I think, perhaps, by this means: by merely losing hat. In one word, then, I simply dropped the new hat from my hand into the mud, to put myself in a con-dition for taking off the old hat by itself, and swaying it in needful courtesy, without any shade of ridicule.

Arrived at the Tiger,—to avoid misconstructions, I first had the glossy, fine and superfine hat cleaned, and some time afterwards the mud-hat or rubbish-hat.

And now, weighing my momentous Past in the adjusting bal-ance within me, I walked in fiery mood to and fro. The Pontac must—I know that there is no unadulterated liquor here below—

125. In the long-run, out of mere fear and necessity, we shall become the warmest cosmopolites I know of; so rapidly do ships shoot to and fro, and, like shuttles, weave Islands and Quarters of the World together. For, let but the political weath-erglass fall today in South America, tomorrow we in Europe have storm and thun-der.

have been more than usually adulterated; so keenly did it chase my fancy out of one fire into the other. I now looked forth into a wide glittering life, in which I lived without post, merely on money; and which I beheld, as it were, sowed with the Delphic caves, and Zenonic walks, and Muse-hills of all the Sciences, which I might now cultivate at my ease. In particular, I should have it in my power to apply more diligently to writing Prize-essays for Academies; of which (that is to say, of the Prize-essays) no author need ever be ashamed, since, in all cases, there is a whole crowning Academy to stand and blush for the crownee. And even if the Prize-marksman does not hit the crown, he still continues more unknown and more anonymous (his Device not being unsealed) than any other author, who indeed can publish some nameless Long-ear of a book, but not hinder it from being, by a Literary Ass-burial *(sepultura asinina)*, publicly interred, in a short time, before half the world.

Only one thing grieved me by anticipation; the sorrow of my Berga, for whom, dear tired wayfarer, I on the morrow must overcloud her arrival, and her shortened market-spectacle, by my negatory intelligence. She would so gladly (and who can take it ill of a rich farmer's daughter?) have made herself somebody in Neusattel, and overshone many a female dignitary! Every mortal longs for his parade-place, and some earlier living honor than the last honors. Especially so good a lowly-born housewife as my Berga, conscious perhaps rather of her metallic than of her spiritual treasure, would still wish at banquets to be mistress of some seat or other, and so in place to overtop this or that plucked goose of the neighborhood.

It is in this point of view that husbands are so indispensable. I therefore resolved to purchase for myself, and consequently for her, one of the best of those titles, which our Courts in Germany (as in a Leipzig sale-room) stand offering to buyers, in all sizes and sorts, from Noble and Half-noble down to Rath or Councillor; and once invested therewith, to reflect from my own Quarter-nobility such an Eighth-part-nobility on this true soul, that many a Neusattelitess (I hope) shall half burst with envy, and say and cry:

---

19. It is easier, they say, to climb a hill when you ascend back foremost. This, perhaps, might admit of application to political eminences; if you still turned towards them that part of the body on which you sit, and kept your face directed down to the people; all the while, however, removing and mounting.

"Pooh, the stupid farmer thing! See how it wabbles and bridles! It has forgot how matters stood when it had no money-bag, and no Hofrath!" For to the Hofrathship I shall before this have attained.

But in the cold solitude of my room, and the fire of my remembrances, I longed unspeakably for my Bergelchen: I and my heart were wearied with the foreign busy day; no one here said a kind word to me, which he did not hope to put in the bill. Friends! I languished for my friend, whose heart would pour out its blood as a balsam for a second heart; I cursed my over-prudent regulations, and wished that, to have the good Berga at my side, I had given up the stupid houseware to all thieves and fires whatsoever: as I walked to and fro, it seemed to me easier and easier to become all things, an Exchequer-Rath, an Excise-Rath, any Rath in the world, and whatever she required when she came.

"See thou take thy pleasure in the town!" Bergelchen had kept saying the whole week through. But how, without her, can I take any? Our tears of sorrow friends dry up, and accompany with their own; but our tears of joy we find most readily repeated in the eyes of our wives. Pardon me, good Friends, these libations of my sensibility; I am but showing you my heart and my Berga. If I need an Absolution-merchant, the Pontac-merchant is the man.

First Night in Flätz

Yet the wine did not take from me the good sense to look under the bed, before going into it, and examine whether any one was lurking there; for example, the Harlot or the Dwarf, or the Legations-Rath; also to shove the key under the latch (which I reckon the best bolting arrangement of all), and then, by way of farther assurance, to bore my night-screws into the door, and pile all the chairs in a heap behind it; and, lastly, to keep on my breeches and shoes, wishing absolutely to have no care upon my mind.

26. Few German writers are not original, if we may ascribe originality (as is at least the conversational practice of all people) to a man, who merely dishes out his own thoughts without foreign admixture. For as, between their Memory, where their reading or foreign matter dwells, and their Imagination or Productive Power, where their writing or own peculiar matter originates, a sufficient space intervenes, and the boundary-stones are fixed-in so conscientiously and firmly that nothing foreign may pass over into their own, or inversely, so that they may really read a hundred works without losing their own primitive flavor, or even altering it,—their individuality may, I believe, be considered as secured; and their spiritual nourishment, their pancakes, loaves, fritters, caviar, and meat-balls, are not assimilated to their system, but given back pure and unaltered. Often in my own mind I figure

But I had still other precautions to take in regard to sleep-walking. To me it has always been incomprehensible how so many men can go to bed, and lie down at their ease there, without reflecting that perhaps, in the first sleep, they may get up again as Somnambulists, and crawl over the tops of roofs and the like; awakening in some spot where they may fall in a moment and break their necks and everything else. Indeed, it would be danger enough for me if I, a man of unsullied reputation, an Army Chaplain, were to go to sleep in my own bed and then wake up on silken pillows in the bed-chamber of the most distinguished lady of the town, perhaps expecting from her my bliss. While at home, there is little risk in my sleep: because, my right toe being fastened every night with three ells of tape (I call it in jest our marriage-tie) to my wife's left hand, I feel a certainty that, in case I should start up from this bed-arrest, I must with the tether infallibly awaken her, and so by my Berga, as by my living bridle, be again led back to bed. But here in the Inn, I had nothing for it but to knot myself once or twice to the bed-foot, that I might not wander; though in this way, an irruption of villains would have brought double peril with it.— Alas! so dangerous is sleep at all times, that every man, who is not lying on his back a corpse, must be on his guard lest with the general system some limb or other also fall asleep; in which case the sleeping limb (there are not wanting examples of it in Medical History) may next morning be lying ripe for amputation. For this reason, I have myself frequently awakened, that no part of me fall asleep.

Having properly tied myself to the bed-posts, and at length got under the coverlid, I now began to be dubious about my Pontac Fire-bath, and apprehensive of the valorous and tumultuous dreams too likely to ensue; which, alas, did actually prove to be nothing better than heroic and monarchic feats, castle-stormings, rock-throwings, and the like. This point also I am sorry to see so little attended to in medicine. Medical gentlemen, as well as their cus-

---

such writers as living but thousandfold more artificial Ducklings from Vaucanson's Artificial Duck of Wood. For in fact they are not less cunningly put together than this timber Duck, which will gobble meat, and apparently void it again, under show of having digested it, and derived from it blood and juices; though the secret of the business is, the artist has merely introduced an ingenious compound ejective matter behind, with which concoction and nourishment have nothing to do, but which the Duck illusorily gives forth and publishes to the world.

tomers, all stretch themselves quietly in their beds, without one among them considering whether a furious rage (supposing him also directly after to drink cold water in his dream), or a heart-devouring grief, all which he may undergo in vision, does harm to life or not. I'll admit that if I were a woman and of a woman's fearful disposition, especially if I were expecting, I would in such case be in despair about the fruit of my womb if I were sleeping and then in my dreams beheld all the monsters, wild beasts, abortions and so on forbidden by the Medical Police, *one* of which would be sufficient (if the confirmed doctrine of inadvertent fright remains true) to bring me to bed with a malformed child that looked exactly like a hare and was hare-lipped besides or one that had a lion's mane on its bottom or devil's claws on its hands or any of those abominable things abortions have. Perhaps a number of monstrosities have been begotten from such inadvertent visions in dreams.

Shortly before midnight, I awoke from a heavy dream, to encounter a ghost-trick much too ghostly for my fancy. My Brother-in-law, who manufactured it, deserves for such vapid cookery to be named before you without reserve, as the malt-master of this washy brewage. Had suspicion been more compatible with intrepidity, I might perhaps, by his moral maxim about this matter, on the road, as well as by his taking up the side-room, at the middle door of which stood my couch, have easily divined the whole. But now, on awakening, I felt myself blown upon by a cold ghost-breath, which I could nowise deduce from the distant bolted window; a point I had rightly decided, for the Dragoon was producing the phenomenon, through the keyhole, by a pair of bellows. Every sort of coldness, in the night-season, reminds you of clay-coldness and spectre-coldness. I summoned my resolution, however, and abode the issue: but now the very coverlid began to get in motion; I pulled it towards me; it would not stay; sharply I sit upright in my bed, and cry: "What is that?" No answer; everywhere silence in the Inn; the whole room full of moonshine. And now my drawing-plaster, my coverlid, actually rose up, and let in the air; at which I felt like a wounded man whose cataplasm you suddenly pull off. In this crisis, I made a bold leap from this Devil's-torus, and, leaping,

15. After the manner of the fine polished English folding-knives, there are now also folding-war-swords, or in other words—Treaties of Peace.

snapped asunder my somnambulist tether. "Where is the silly human fool," cried I, "that dares to ape the unseen sublime world of Spirits, which may, in the instant, open before him?" But on, above, under the bed, there was nothing to be heard or seen. I looked out of the window: everywhere spectral moonlight and street stillness; nothing moving except (probably from the wind), on the distant Gallows-hill, a person lately hanged.

Any man would have have taken it for self-deception as well as I: therefore I again wrapped myself in my passive *lit de justice* and air-bed, and waited with calmness to see whether I should freeze in terror or not.

In a few minutes, the coverlid, the infernal Faust's-mantle, again began flying and towing (I alone was the condemned man); also, by way of change, the invisible bed-maker again lifted me up. Accursed hour!—I should beg to know whether, in the whole of cultivated Europe, there is one cultivated or uncultivated man, who, in a case of this kind, would not have lighted on ghost-devilry? I lighted on it, under my piece of (self) movable property, my coverlid: and thought Berga had died suddenly, and was now, in spirit, laying hold of my bed. However, I could not speak to her, nor as little to the Devil, who might well be supposed to have a hand in the game; but I turned myself solely to Heaven, and prayed aloud: "To thee I commit myself; thou alone heretofore hast cared for thy weak servant; and I swear that I will turn a new leaf,"—a promise which shall be kept nevertheless, though the whole was but stupid treachery and trick.

My prayer had no effect with the unchristian Dragoon, who now, once for all, had got me prisoner in the dragnet of a coverlid; and heeded little whether a guest's bed were, by his means, made a state-

13. *Omnibus una* Salus *Sanctis, sed* Gloria *dispar:* that is to say (as Divines once taught) according to Saint Paul, we have all the same Beatitude in Heaven, but different degrees of Honor. Here, on Earth, we find a shadow of this in the writing world; for the Beatitude of authors once beatified by Criticism, whether they be genial, good, mediocre, or poor, is the same throughout; they all obtain the same pecuniary Felicity, the same slender profit. But, Heavens! in regard to the degrees of Fame, again, how far (in spite of the same emolument and sale) will a Dunce, even in his lifetime, be put below a Genius! Is not a shallow writer frequently forgotten in a single Fair, while a deep writer, or even a writer of genius, will blossom through fifty Fairs, and so may celebrate his Twenty-five Years' Jubilee, before, late forgotten, he is lowered into the German Temple of Fame; a Temple imitating the peculiarity of the *Padri Lucchesi* churches in Naples, which (according to Volkmann) permit *burials* under their roofs, but no *tombstone.*

bed and death-bed or not. He span out my nerves, like gold-wire through smaller and smaller holes, to utter inanition and evanition; for the bed-clothes at last literally marched off to the door of the room.

Now was the moment to rise into the sublime; and to trouble myself no longer about aught here below, but softly to devote myself to death. "Snatch me away," cried I, and, without thinking, cut three crosses; "quick, despatch me, ye ghosts: I die more innocent than thousands of tyrants and blasphemers, to whom ye yet appear not, but to unpolluted me." Here I heard a sort of laugh, either on the street or in the side-room: at this warm human tone, I suddenly bloomed up again, as at the coming of a new Spring, in every twig and leaf. Wholly despising the winged coverlid, which was not now to be picked from the door, I laid myself down uncovered, but warm and perspiring from other causes, and soon fell asleep. For the rest, I am not the least ashamed, in the face of all refined capital cities,—though they were standing here at my hand,—that by this Devil-belief and Devil-address I have attained some likeness to our great German Lion, to Luther.

Second Day in Flätz

Early in the morning, I felt myself awakened by the well-known coverlid; it had laid itself on me like a nightmare: I gaped up; quiet, in a corner of the room, sat a red, round, blooming, decorated girl, like a full-blown tulip in the freshness of life, and gently rustling with gay ribbons as with leaves.

"Who's there—how came you in?" cried I, half-blind.

"I covered thee softly, and thought to let thee sleep," said Bergelchen; "I have walked all night to be here early; do but look!"

She showed me her boots, the only remnant of her travelling-gear (the Achilles' heel), which, in the moulting process of the toilette, she had not stript at the gate of Flätz.

"Is there," said I, alarmed at her coming six hours sooner, and the more, as I had been alarmed all night, and was still so, at her mysterious entrance,—"is there some fresh woe come over us, fire, murder, robbery?"

79. Weak and wrong heads are the hardest to change; and their inward man acquires a scanty covering: thus capons never moult.

She answered: "The old Rat thou hast chased so long died yesterday; farther, there was nothing of importance."

"And all has been managed rightly, and according to my Letter of Instructions, at home?" inquired I.

"Yes, truly," answered she; "Only I did not see the Letter; it is lost; thou hast packed it among thy clothes."

Well, I could not but forgive the blooming brave pedestrian all omissions. Her eye, then her heart, was bringing fresh cool morning air and morning red into my sultry hours. And yet, for this kind soul, looking into life with such love and hope, I must in a little while overcloud the merited Heaven of today, with tidings of my failure in the Catechetical Professorship! I dallied and postponed to the utmost. I asked how she had got in, as the whole *chevaux-de-frise* barricado of chairs was still standing fast at the door. She laughed heartily, curtseying in village fashion, and said she had planned it with her brother the day before yesterday, knowing my precautions in locking, that he should admit her into my room, that so she might cunningly awaken me. And now bolted the Dragoon with loud laughter into the apartment, and cried: "Slept well, brother?"

In this wise truly the whole ghost-story was now solved and expounded, as if by the pen of a Biester or a Hennings; I instantly saw through the entire ghost-scheme, which our Dragoon had executed. With some bitterness I told him my conjecture, and his sister my story. But he lied and laughed; nay, attempted shamelessly enough to palm spectre-notions on me a second time, in open day. I answered coldly, that in me he had found the wrong man, granting even that I had some similarity with Luther, with Hobbes, with Brutus, all of whom had seen and dreaded ghosts. He replied, tearing the facts away from their originating causes: "All he could say was, that last night he had heard some poor sinner creaking and lamenting dolefully enough; and from this he had inferred, it must be an unhappy brother set upon by goblins."

In the end, his sister's eyes also were opened to the low character which he had tried to act with me: she sharply flew at him,

89. In times of misfortune, the Ancients supported themselves with Philosophy or Christianity; the moderns again (for example, in the reign of Terror), take to Pleasure; as the wounded Buffalo, for bandage and salve, rolls himself in the mire.

pushed him with both hands out of his and my door, and called after him: "Wait, thou villain, I'll remember this!"

Then hastily turning round, she fell on my neck, and (at the wrong place) into laughter, and said: "The wild fool! But I could not keep my laugh another minute, and he was not to see it. Forgive the ninny, thou a learned man, his ass pranks."

I inquired whether she, in her nocturnal travelling, had not met with any spectral persons; though I knew that to her, a wild beast, a river, a half-abyss, are nothing. No, she had not; but the gay-dressed town's-people, she said, had scared her in the morning. O! how I do love these soft Harmonica-quiverings of female fright!

At last, however, I was forced to bite or cut the coloquinta-apple, and give her the half of it; I mean the news of my rejected petition for the Catechetical Professorship. Wishing to spare this joyful heart the rudeness of the whole truth, and to subtract something from a heavy burden, more fit for the shoulders of a man, I began: "Bergelchen, the Professorship affair is taking another, though still a good enough course: the General, whom may the Devil and his Grandmother teach sense, will not be taken except by storm; and storm he shall have, as certainly as I have on my nightcap."

"Then, thou art nothing yet?" inquired she.

"For the moment, indeed, not!" answered I.

"But before Saturday night?" said she.

"Not quite," said I.

"Then am I sore stricken, and could leap out of the window," said she, and turned away her rosy face, to hide its wet eyes, and was silent very long. Then, with painfully quivering voice, she began: "Good Christ stand by me at Neusattel on Sunday, when these high-prancing prideful dames look at me in church, and I grow scarlet for shame!"

Here in sympathetic woe I sprang out of bed to the dear soul, over whose brightly blooming cheeks warm tears were rolling, and

181. God be thanked that we live nowhere forever except in Hell or Heaven; on Earth otherwise we should grow to be the veriest rascals, and the World a House of Incurables, for want of the dog-doctor (the Hangman), and the issue-cord (on the Gallows), and the sulphur and chalybeate medicines (on Battlefields). So that we too find our gigantic moral force dependent on the *Debt of Nature* which we have to pay, exactly as your politicians (for example, the author of the *New Leviathan*) demonstrate that the English have their *National Debt* to thank for their superiority.

cried: "Thou true heart, do not tear me in pieces so! May I die, if yet in these dog-days I become not all and everything that thou wishest! Speak, wilt thou be Mining-räthin, Building-räthin, Court-räthin, War-räthin, Chamber-räthin, Commerce-räthin, Legations-räthin, or Devil and his Dam's räthin: I am here and will buy it, and be it. Tomorrow I send riding posts to Saxony and Hessia, to Prussia and Russia, to Freisland and Katzenellenbogen, and demand patents. Nay, I will carry matters farther than another, and be all things at once, Flachsenfingen Court-rath, Scheerau Excise-rath, Haarhaar Building-rath, Pestitz Chamber-rath (for we have the cash); and thus, alone and single-handed, represent with one *podex* and *corpus* a whole Rath-session of select Raths; and stand, a complete Legion of Honor, on one single pair of legs: the like no man ever did."

"O! now thou art angel-good!" said she, and gladder tears rolled down; "thou shalt counsel me thyself which are the finest Raths, and these we will be."

"No," continued I, in the fire of the moment, "neither shall this serve us: to me it is not enough that to Mrs. Chaplin thou canst announce thyself as Building-räthin, to Mrs. Town-parson as Legations-räthin, to Mrs. Bürgermeister as Court-räthin, to Mrs. Road-and-toll-surveyor as Commerce-räthin, or how and where thou pleasest——"

"Ah! my own too good Attelchen!" said she.

"—But," continued I, "I shall likewise become corresponding member of the several Learned Societies in the several best capital cities (among which I have only to choose); and truly no common regular member, but a whole honorary member; then thee, as another honorary member, growing out of my honorary membership, I shall uplift and exalt."

Pardon me, my Friends, this warm cataplasm, or deception-balsam for a wounded breast, whose blood is so pure and precious, that one may be permitted to endeavor, with all possible stanching-lints and spider-webs, to drive it back into the fair heart, its home.

---

63. To apprehend danger from the Education of the People, is like fearing lest the thunderbolt strike into the house because it has *windows;* whereas the lightning never comes through these, but through their *lead* framing, or down by the *smoke* of the chimney.

But now came bright and brightest hours. I had conquered Time, I had conquered myself and Berga: seldom does a conqueror, as I did, bless both the victorious and the vanquished party. Berga called back her former Heaven, and pulled off her dusty boots, and on her flowery shoes. Precious morning beverage, intoxicating to a heart that loves! I felt (if the low figure may be permitted) a double-beer of courage in me, now that I had one being more to protect. In general it is my nature—which the honorable General seems not to be fully aware of—to grow bolder not among the bold, but fastest among poltroons, the bad example acting on me by the rule of contraries. Little touches may in this case shadow forth man and wife, without casting them into the shade: When the trim waiter with his green silk apron brought up cracknels for breakfast, and I told him: "Johann, for two!" Berga said: "He would oblige her very much," and called him Herr Johann.

Bergelchen, more familiar with rural burghs than capital cities, felt a good deal amazed and alarmed at the coffee-trays, dressing-tables, paper-hangings, sconces, alabaster ink-holders, with Egyptian emblems, as well as at the gilt bell-handle, lying ready for any one to pull out or to push in. Accordingly, she had not courage to walk through the hall, with its lustres, purely because a whistling, whiffling Cap-and-feather was posturing up and down in it. Nay, her poor heart was like to fail when she peeped out of the window at so many gay promenading town's-people (I was briskly whistling a Gascon air down over them); and thought that in a little while, at my side, she must break into the middle of this dazzling courtly throng. In a case like this, reasons are of less avail than examples. I tried to elevate my Bergelchen, by reciting some of my nocturnal dream-feats; for example, how, riding on a whale's back, with a three-pronged fork, I had pierced and eaten three eagles; and by more of the like sort: but I produced no effect; perhaps, because to the timid female heart the battle-field was presented rather than the conqueror, the abyss rather than the over-leaper of it.

76. Your economical, preaching Poetry apparently supposes that a surgical Stone-cutter is an Artistical one; and a Pulpit or a Sinai a Hill of the Muses.

115. According to Smith, the universal measure of economical value is *Labor*. This fact, at least in regard to spiritual and poetical value, we Germans had discovered before Smith; and to my knowledge we have always preferred the learned poet to the poet of genius, and the heavy book full of labor to the light one full of sport.

At this time a sheaf of newspapers was brought me, full of gallant decisive victories. And though these happen only on one side, and on the other are just so many defeats, yet the former somehow assimilate more with my blood than the latter, and inspire me (as Schiller's *Robbers* used to do) with a strange inclination to lay hold of some one, and thrash and curry him on the spot. Unluckily for the waiter, he had chanced, even now, like a military host, to stand a triple bell-order for march, before he would leave his ground and come up. "Sir," began I, my head full of battle-fields, and my arm of inclination to baste him; and Berga feared the very worst, as I gave her the well-known anger and alarm signal, namely, shoved up my cap to my hindhead—"Sir, is this your way of treating guests? Why don't you come promptly? Don't come so again; and now be going, friend!" Although his retreat was my victory, I still kept briskly cannonading on the field of action, and fired the louder (to let him hear it), the more steps he descended in his flight. Bergelchen,—who felt quite horrorstruck at my fury, particularly in a quite strange house, and at a quality waiter with silk apron,—mustered all her soft words against the wild ones of a man-of-war, and spoke of dangers that might follow. "Dangers," answered I, "are just what I seek; but for a man there are none; in all cases he will either conquer or evade them, either show them front or back."

I could scarcely lay aside this indignant mood, so sweet was it to me, and so much did I feel refreshed by the fire of rage, and quickened in my breast as by a benignant stimulant. It belongs certainly to the class of Unrecognised Mercies (on which, in ancient times, special sermons were preached), that one is never more completely in his Heaven and *Monplaisir* (a pleasure-palace) than while in the midst of right hearty storming and indignation. Heavens! what might not a man of weight accomplish in this new walk of charity! The gall-bladder is for us the chief swimming-bladder and Montgolfier; and the filling of it costs us nothing but a contumelious word or two from some bystander. And does not the whirlwind Luther, with whom I nowise compare myself, confess,

4. The Hypocrite does not imitate the old practice, of cutting fruit by a knife poisoned only on the one side, and giving the poisoned side to the victim, the cutter eating the sound side himself; on the contrary, he so disinterestedly inverts this practice, that to others he shows and gives the sound moral half, or side, and retains for himself the poisoned one. Heavens! compared with such a man, how wicked does the Devil seem!

in his *Table-Talk,* that he never preached, sung, or prayed so well, as while in a rage? Truly he was a man sufficient of himself to rouse many others into rage.

The whole morning till noon now passed in viewing sights, and trafficking for wares; and indeed, for the greatest part, in the broad street of our Hotel. Berga needed but to press along with me into the market throng; needed but to look, and see that she was decorated more according to the fashion than hundreds like her. But soon, in her care for household (to use her words) gear, she forgot that of dress, and in the potter-market the toilette-table faded from her thoughts.

I, for my share, full of true tedium, while gliding after her through her various marts, with their long cheapenings and chafferings, merely acted the Philosopher hid within me: I weighed this empty Life, and the heavy value which is put upon it, and the daily anxiety of man lest it, this lightest down-feather of the Earth, fly off, and feather him, and take him with it. These thoughts, perhaps, I owe to the street-fry of boys, who were turning their market-freedom to account, by throwing stones at one another all round me: for, in the midst of this tumult, I vividly imagined in my mind a man who had never seen war; and who, therefore, never having experienced, that often of a thousand bullets not one will hit, feels apprehensive of these few silly stones lest they beat-in his nose and eyes. O! it is the battle-field alone that sows, manures and nourishes true courage, courage even for daily, domestic and smallest perils. For not till he comes from the battle-field can a man both sing and cannonade; like the canary-bird, which, though so melodious, so timid, so small, so tender, so solitary, so soft-feathered, can yet be trained to fire off cannon, though cannon of smaller calibre.

After dinner (in our room), we issued from the Purgatory of the market-tumult,—where Berga, at every booth, had something to order, and load her attendant maid with,—into Heaven, into the Dog Inn, as the best Flätz public and pleasure-house without the gates is named, where, in market-time, hundreds turn in, and see

67. Individual Minds, nay, Political Bodies, are like organic bodies; extract the *interior* air from them, the atmosphere crushes them together; pump off under the bell the *exterior* resisting air, the interior inflates and bursts them. Therefore, let every State keep up its internal and its external resistance both at once.

thousands going by. On the way thither, my little wife, my elbow-tendril, as it were, had extracted from me such a measure of courage, that, while going through the Gate (where I, aware of the military order that you must not pass *near* the sentry, threw myself over to the other side), she quietly glided on, close by the very guns and fixed bayonets of the City Guard. Outside the wall, I could direct her with my finger, to the bechained, begrated, gigantic Schabacker-Palace, mounting up even externally on stairs, where I last night had called and (it may be) stormed: "I had rather take a peep at the Giant," said she, "and the Dwarf: why else are we under one roof with them?"

In the pleasure-house itself we found sufficient pleasure; encircled, as we were, with blooming faces and meadows. In my secret heart, I all along kept looking down, with success, on Schabacker's refusal; and till midnight made myself a happy day of it: I had deserved it, Berga still more. Nevertheless, about one in the morning, I was destined to find a windmill to tilt with; a windmill, which truly lays about it with somewhat longer, stronger and more numerous arms than a giant, for which Don Quixote might readily enough have taken it. On the market-place, for reasons more easily fancied than specified in words, I let Berga go along some twenty paces before me; and I myself, for these foresaid reasons, retire without malice behind a covered booth, the tent most probably of some rude trader; and linger there a moment according to circumstances: lo! steering hither with dart and spear, comes the Booth-watcher, and coins and stamps me, on the spot, into a filcher and housebreaker of his Booth-street; though the simpleton sees nothing but that I am standing in the corner, and doing anything but—taking. A sense of honor without callosity is never blunted for such attacks. But how in the dead of night was a man of this kind, who had nothing in his head—at the utmost beer, instead of brains—to be enlightened on the truth of the matter?

I shall not conceal my perilous resource: I seized the fox by the tail, as we say; in other words, I made as if I had been muddled, and knew not rightly, in my liquor, what I was about: I therefore mimicked everything I was master of in this department; staggered

8. In great Saloons, the real stove is masked into a pretty ornamented sham stove; so likewise, it is fit and pretty that a virgin *Love* should always hide itself in an interesting virgin *Friendship*.

hither and thither; splayed out my feet like a dancing-master; got into zigzag in spite of all efforts at the straight line; nay, I knocked my good head (perhaps one of the clearest and emptiest of the night), like a full one, against real posts.

However, the Booth-bailiff, who probably had been oftener drunk than I, and knew the symptoms better, or even felt them in himself at this moment, looked upon the whole exhibition as mere craft, and shouted dreadfully: "Stop, rascal; thou art no more drunk than I! I know thee of old. Stand, I say, till I speak to thee! Wouldst have thy long finger in the market, too? Stand, dog, or I'll make thee!"

You see the whole *nodus* of the matter: I whisked away zigzag among the booths as fast as possible, from the claws of this rude Tosspot; yet he still hobbled after me. But my Teutoberga, who had heard somewhat of it, came running back; clutched the tipsy market-warder by the collar, and said (shrieking, it is true, in village-wise) "Stupid sot, go sleep the drink out of thy head, or I'll teach thee! Dost know, then, whom thou art speaking to? My husband, Army-chaplain Schmelzle under General and Minister von Schabacker at Pimpelstadt, thou blockhead!—Fye! Take shame, fellow!" The watchman mumbled: "Meant no harm," and reeled about his business. "O thou Lioness!" said I, in the transport of love, "why hast thou never been in any deadly peril, that I might show thee the Lion in thy husband?"

Thus lovingly we both reached home; and perhaps in the sequel of this Fair day might still have enjoyed a glorious after-midnight, had not the Devil led my eye to the ninth volume of Lichtenberg's Works, and the 206th page, where this passage occurs: "It is not impossible that at a future period, our Chemists may light on some means of suddenly decomposing the Atmosphere by a sort of Ferment. In this way the world may be destroyed." Ah! true indeed! Since the Earth-ball is lapped up in the larger Atmospheric ball, let but any chemical scoundrel, in the remotest scoundrel-island, say in New Holland, devise some decomposing substance for the Atmosphere, like what a spark of fire would be for a powder-wagon: in a few seconds, the monstrous devouring world-storm

12. Nations—unlike rivers, which precipitate their impurities in level places and when at rest—drop their baseness just whilst in the most violent motion; and become the dirtier the farther they flow along through lazy flats.

catches me and you in Flätz by the throat; my breathing, and the like, in this choke-air is over, and the whole game ended! The Earth becomes a boundless gallows, where the very cattle are hanged: worm-powder, and bug-liquor, Bradley ant-ploughs, and rat-poison, and wolf-traps are, in this universal world-trap and world-poison, no longer specially needful; and the Devil takes the whole, in the Bartholomew-night, when this cursed "Ferment" is by chance invented.

From the true soul, however, I concealed these deadly Night Thoughts; seeing she would either painfully have sympathised in them, or else mirthfully laughed at them. I merely gave orders that next morning (Saturday) she was to be standing booted and ready, at the outset of the returning coach; if so were she would have me speedily fulfil her wishes in regard to that stock of Rathships which lay so near her heart. She rejoiced in my purpose, gladly surrendering the market for such prospects. I too slept sound, my great toe tied to her finger, the whole night through.

The Dragoon, next morning, twitched me by the ear, and secretly whispered into it that he had a pleasant fairing to give his sister; and so would ride off somewhat early, on the nag he had yesterday purchased of the horse-dealer. I thanked him beforehand.

At the appointed hour, all gaily slipped down the ways, I excepted; for I still retained, even in the fairest daylight, that nocturnal Devil's-Ferment and Decomposition (of my cerebral globe as well as of the Earth-globe) fermenting in my head; a proof that the night had not affected me, or exaggerated my fear. The Blind Passenger, whom I liked so ill, also mounted along with us, and looked at me as usual, but without effect; for on this occasion, when the destruction not of myself only, but of worlds, was occupying my thoughts, the Passenger was nothing to me but a joke and a show: as a man, while his leg is being sawed off, does not feel the throbbing of his heart; or amid the humming of cannon, does not guard

28. When Nature takes the huge old Earth-round, the Earth-loaf, and kneads it up again, for the purpose of introducing under this pie-crust new stuffing and Dwarfs,— she then, for most part, as a mother when baking will do to her daughters, gives in jest a little fraction of the dough (two or three thousand square leagues of such dough are enough for a child) to some Poetical or Philosophical, or Legislative polisher, that so the little elf may have something to be shaping and manufacturing beside its mother. And when the other young ones get a taste of sisterkin's baking, they all clap hands, and cry: "Aha, Mother! canst bake like *Suky* here?"

himself from that of wasps; so to me any Passenger, with all the fire-brands he might throw into my near or distant Future, could appear but ludicrous, at a time when I was reflecting that the "Ferment" might, even in my journey between Flätz and Neusattel, be, by some American or European man of science, quite guiltlessly experimenting and decomposing, hit upon by accident and let loose. The question, nay, prize-question now, however, were this: "In how far, since Lichtenberg's threatening, it may not appear world-murderous and self-murderous, if enlightened Potentates of chemical nations do not enjoin it on their chemical subjects, who in their decompositions and separations may so easily separate the soul from their body, and unite Heaven with Earth,— not in future to make any other chemical experiments than those already made, which hitherto have profited the State rather than harmed it?"

Unfortunately, I continued sunk in this Doomsday of the Ferment with all my thoughts and meditations, without in the whole course of our return from Flätz to Neusattel, suffering or observing anything, except that I actually arrived there, and at the same time saw the Blind Passenger once more go his ways.

My Bergelchen alone had I constantly looked at by the road, partly that I might see her, so long as life and eyes endured; partly that, even at the smallest danger to her, be it a great, or even all-over-sweeping Deluge and World's-doom, I might die, if not *for* her, at least *by* her, and so united with that staunch true heart, cast away a plagued and plaguing life, in which, at any rate, not half of my wishes for her have been fulfilled.

So then were my Journey over,—crowned with some *Historiolae;* and in time coming, perhaps, still more rewarded through you, ye Friends about Flätz, if in these pages you shall find any well-ground pruning-knives, whereby you may more readily out-root the weedy tangle of Lies, which for the present excludes me from the gallant Schabacker:—Only, this cursed Ferment still sits in my head. Farewell then, so long as there are Atmospheres left us to breathe. I wish I had that Ferment out of my head.

Yours always, ATTILA SCHMELZLE.

P.S.—My Brother-in-law has kept his promise well, and Berga is dancing. Particulars in my next!

Translated by Thomas Carlyle

ACKNOWLEDGMENTS

Every reasonable effort has been made to locate the parties who hold rights to previously published translations reprinted here. We gratefully acknowledge permission to reprint the following:

"The Marquise of O——" from *The Marquise of O—— and Other Stories* by Heinrich von Kleist, translated and with an introduction by David Luke and Nigel Reeves. Copyright © David Luke and Nigel Reeves, 1978. Reprinted by permission of Penguin Books Ltd.

"Michael Kohlhaas: From an Old Chronicle," slightly adapted from the story of the same name in *The Marquise of O—— and Other Stories* by Heinrich von Kleist, translated by Martin Greenberg (Criterion). Introduction and English translation of the stories copyright © 1960 by Martin Greenberg. Reprinted by permission of Harper & Row, Publishers, Inc.

"The Earthquake in Chile" by Heinrich von Kleist, translated by, and reprinted by permission of, Michael Hamburger.

THE GERMAN LIBRARY
in 100 Volumes

Volume 30
German Literary Fairy Tales
Edited by Frank G. Ryder and Robert M. Browning
Introduction by Gordon Birrell
Foreword by John Gardiner

Volume 32
Heinrich Heine
Poetry and Prose
Edited by Jost Hermand and Robert C. Holub
Foreword by Alfred Kazin

Volume 39
German Poetry from 1750 to 1900
Edited by Robert M. Browning
Foreword by Michael Hamburger

Volume 44
Gottfried Keller
Stories
Edited by Frank G. Ryder
Foreword by Max Frisch

Volume 45
Wilhelm Raabe
Novels
Edited by Volkmar Sander
Foreword by Joel Agee

Volume 46
Theodore Fontane
Short Novels and Other Writings
Edited by Peter Demetz
Foreword by Peter Gay

Volume 50
Wilhelm Busch and Others
German Satirical Writings
Edited by Dieter P. Lotze and Volkmar Sander
Foreword by John Simon